I0901091

IMAGES
of America

LANGLADE COUNTY

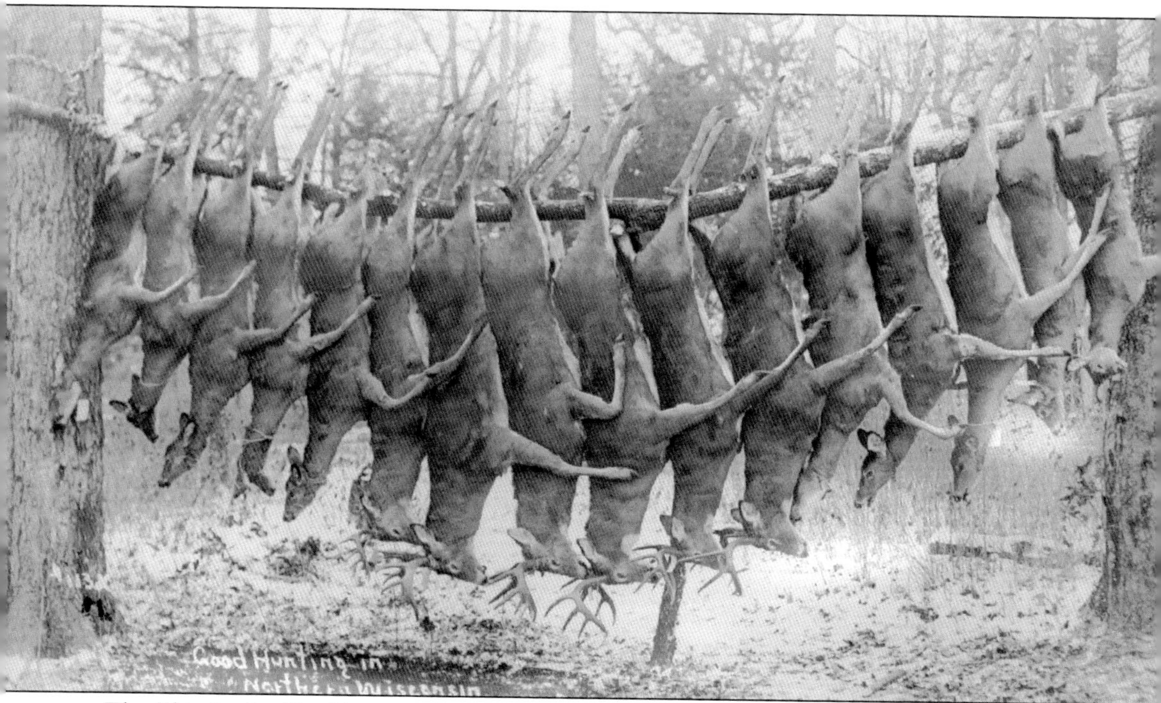

The *Rhinelander Herald* reported on November 6, 1909, "Next Thursday, Nov. 11th, is the first of the open season for deer. Notwithstanding the so-called protection, this fleet-footed animal, typical of the wild life of the great forests of the north, is rapidly thinning out and in another generation will have passed into history along with the pines." (Courtesy of Prestor Pictures.)

On the Cover: This wigwam was a relatively permanent, typical Ojibwe home. These dwellings were easily constructed. A framework of saplings would be covered by panels of birch bark and/or animal hides, depending on the season. A cattail mat would be unrolled around the circumference of the wigwam. The units of the wigwam could easily be disassembled and packed up when the tribe moved. (Courtesy of the Langlade County Historical Society.)

IMAGES
of America

LANGLADE COUNTY

Richard Klatte Prestor and Joseph Hermolin

ARCADIA
PUBLISHING

ISBN 978-0-7385-8863-6

Published by Arcadia Publishing
Charleston, South Carolina

Printed in the United States of America

Library of Congress Control Number: 2012932365

For all general information, please contact Arcadia Publishing:
Telephone 843-853-2070
Fax 843-853-0044
E-mail sales@arcadiapublishing.com
For customer service and orders:
Toll-Free 1-888-313-2665

Visit us on the Internet at www.arcadiapublishing.com

To all photographers who record life beyond
their placidly darkened studio walls

CONTENTS

ACKNOWLEDGMENTS

The authors wish to thank Mary Kay Wolf, curator of the Langlade County Historical Society Museum, and the late Ed Morrissey, former president of the Langlade County Historical Society, for their work in maintaining the photographic collection and offering assistance. Ross Fischer and Jeff Robinson assisted in scanning photographs. Special thanks to Monique Tyndall of the College of the Menominee Nation in Kesheena, Wisconsin, and Teresa Mitchell of the George W. Brown Ojibwe Museum and Cultural Center in Lac du Flambeau, Wisconsin, for help in identifying and gaining insight to the Indian photographs.

We would also like to thank these kind people who, in 1996, were most helpful in providing and gathering information regarding photographer A.J. Kingsbury: Patricia Kolz, William Grosnick, and the staff of the Antigo Public Library, who tracked down and listed dozens of Kingsbury newspaper articles for our reference. In fact, the *Antigo Daily Journal*'s long history of reporting Antigo's daily life provided an essential base of historical information.

We gratefully thank our editor, Jeff Ruetsche, for his patience and for always having the right answers for our questions. We appreciate the last-minute editorial assistance from Owen Klatte, and we say thank you to Jennifer Rauser for allowing flexible work at critical times.

Finally, unless otherwise noted, all photographs appearing in this book are courtesy of the Langlade County Historical Society.

Introduction

In 1967, thousands of people, both native and non-native, were obliterated as decades-old negatives and glass-plate images were incinerated by roaring flames. A tragic fire had gutted the 60-year-old photography studio of A.J. Kingsbury. Presumably the greatest early photographic record ever created of northeastern Wisconsin, nearly all was lost in the time it would have taken Kingsbury to shoot and print a few glass-plate images.

This book celebrates the people, times, and transitions of early northern Wisconsin by presenting the highlights of this photographer's lifetime labors. What remains of Kingsbury's work is perhaps 600 images and negatives preserved in the Langlade County Historical Society and an untold number of century-old Kingsbury real-photo postcards scattered nationally in postcard collections or forgotten in dusty old attic boxes.

Beginning in May 1906, A.J. Kingsbury sought to earn his living by photographing Langlade County and beyond. From his photography studio in Antigo, Wisconsin, he traveled frequently through northern towns, forests, and fledgling tourist areas, capturing images that he could sell and resell to the growing numbers of tourists seeking escape from the modern pressures of city life in the lower counties.

The more long-lasting effects of Kingsbury's numerous rustic automobile excursions, however, were not only that he created a wonderfully documented history of several counties' growth, but that his personal efforts actually helped develop the tourism trade. Thousands of people purchased his real-photo postcards and mailed them to distant friends and relatives. The cards generated and multiplied the public's interest in personally visiting those wonderfully rustic scenes of lakeside cabins, old forests, wildlife, and Indians.

All of that, and indeed this very book, is possible only because of the development of photography. As with many other inventions, fixed-image photographs were not simply created one day in a laboratory. Many individuals, spanning hundreds of years, experimented with ways of reflecting or capturing light images on different surfaces. The year 1839 is generally considered to be the beginning of photography as we know it. As the science of photography advanced over the decades, photographs were developed on such surfaces as copper, paper, iron, glass, and leather.

In 1884, George Eastman invented the first photographic film in a continuous roll form to be used in the Kodak camera he was inventing. This combination afforded middle-class families the possibility of making their own photographs at home.

What would become A.J. Kingsbury's favorite medium, the real-photo postcard, was not far behind. By 1901, someone had printed a real photograph onto a penny postcard. Non-photograph postcards were already quite popular in America by 1900, and the photography industry soon recognized a good thing. By the time Kingsbury opened his Antigo shop, many citizens had become aware that for a fairly cheap price, real-photo postcards could easily immortalize their pets or a prize bull, the day's glistening Musky catch, smiling friends, or the whole family carefully posed in front of their new home. It was a brand-new form of visual communication for the masses, and apparently, Kingsbury recognized the developing possibilities of the postcard market.

Let us briefly look back to Kingsbury's own beginning. Arthur J. "A.J." Kingsbury was born to John Jerome and Alice (nee Paige) Kingsbury on September 23, 1876. A.J. was one of eight siblings, three of whom did not survive to adulthood. His father operated lumberyards and sawmills in various small towns, moving to Antigo around 1889, where A.J. stayed long enough to finish his secondary education. After attending an agricultural college in Michigan, Kingsbury returned home and married Antigo's Myrtle Cunningham in 1897. But settling down in one place was not in their plans. The young family wandered for nearly seven years, as Kingsbury tried farming and assorted oil-field jobs from Michigan to Oklahoma, finally returning to Antigo about 1904. A couple of years later, on May 19, 1906, their seven-year-old son Wayne died quite suddenly.

Only two weeks before that sorrowful day, Kingsbury had opened the Kingsbury Kodak Store in downtown Antigo. There is a possibility that he may have previously worked in another Antigo photography studio. Once he started his own business, though, the fact that the town already had two operating photography studios may have influenced his drive to find business farther afield.

Most likely, Kingsbury understood that the personal portraits business was already well covered by other photographers. We have found no proof that he attempted any studio portrait work in the early years. A reasonable guess is that it was his conscious decision to specialize in postcard-format photography. This was the modern, flexible medium of the era, and the public was beginning to accept it with a delightful fascination. Postcard photographs could be taken of any subject, at any location, and at very modest prices. A photographer might logically reconsider the concept of taking a family portrait that would normally sell only one or two copies, when a single Indian papoose photograph could be resold continuously over 10 or 15 years.

Still, another business incentive for Kingsbury may have been a personal reluctance to settle in one place. His early family life had revolved around his father's multi-town job changes, and Kingsbury's early married years were marked by frequent relocations over several states. Perhaps he saw postcard photography as an opportunity to keep moving while maintaining a secure home base. For many years after opening his first store, Kingsbury spent large amounts of time exploring the roads north of Antigo. Apparently, it was not unusual for him to be gone days at a time.

The early 20th century was a time of expansive growth in northern Wisconsin. The railroad system had its steel tendrils reaching into wide areas of land, connecting lumbering interests to small towns. The vast natural beauty of the forests and lakes, combined with southern Wisconsinites' growing awareness of still abundant hunting and fishing resources, gradually beckoned curious tourists.

Railroads allowed more travelers access, more tourist camps and resorts began appearing, and northern populations increasingly recognized the monetary advantages of welcoming new summer sightseers. Although much of northern Wisconsin's charm was the rustic quality of it all, the increasing intrusions by seasonal visitors naturally changed the old order of life. Anglo business owners spruced up their shops, towns improved their streets, and some Native Americans changed ancient ways in pursuit of tourist dollars. Kingsbury was there to record those transitions.

Kingsbury's favorite photography subjects appear to have been railroads, logging, tourism, and Indians, primarily members of the Menominee and Ojibwe tribes.

This book displays a sparkling selection of Kingsbury's best photography. His pictures clearly portrayed his close-up and personal vision of Wisconsin as it existed in his daily life. Happily for us, his extensive efforts warmly immortalized Wisconsin's past as the state evolved into its own future.

One

ANTIGO, WISCONSIN

Antigo sits on a rich agricultural plain created by retreating ice-age glaciers over 12,000 years ago. Lands long occupied by Ojibwe and Menominee Indians featured dense forests of hardwood and pine, which attracted the first white settlers after the Civil War. Francis Deleglise was a timber cruiser who later speculated in real estate and platted the city. He originally called the settlement Springbrook, but it was changed to Antigo after the Ojibwe phrase *Nequi-Antigo-Seebeh*, which means, "Where the stream runs past evergreen balsam."

Deleglise's cabin, Antigo's first building, was constructed in 1879, the same year that New County (later renamed Langlade County) was created from part of Marathon County. Census data from 1880 indicate an official county population of 685. Most political power in the area was in the lumber towns along the Wolf River, but a special county election in 1881 named Antigo the county seat. By 1886, Antigo had grown from a population of a few dozen to over 2,500, and by 1893, it had 5,000 year-round inhabitants.

A major reason for the rapid growth was that Francis Deleglise foresaw the importance of the railroad, and he convinced the expanding Milwaukee, Lake Shore, and Western Railway (MLS&W) to run through Antigo. The first train pulled into the Antigo depot in 1881. The MLS&W was taken over by the Chicago & North Western Railway (C&NW) in 1892. In 1907, Antigo became headquarters of the Ashland division of the C&NW. For the next 50 years, Antigo was a major rail hub for passengers and freight. It is estimated that in the 1940s, about 40 percent of the workforce in Antigo was somehow connected to the railroad.

Other major industries in Antigo's early years included several lumber and feed mills, many situated along the shores of Kellogg's Pond, now Lake Antigo. These industries were made possible by the railroad and the many lumber camp spur lines that brought a steady supply of logs into Antigo. In 1922, the Kraft Cheese Company, looking to expand beyond northern Illinois, chose Antigo as the site of a plant. It, too, became a major employer in Antigo.

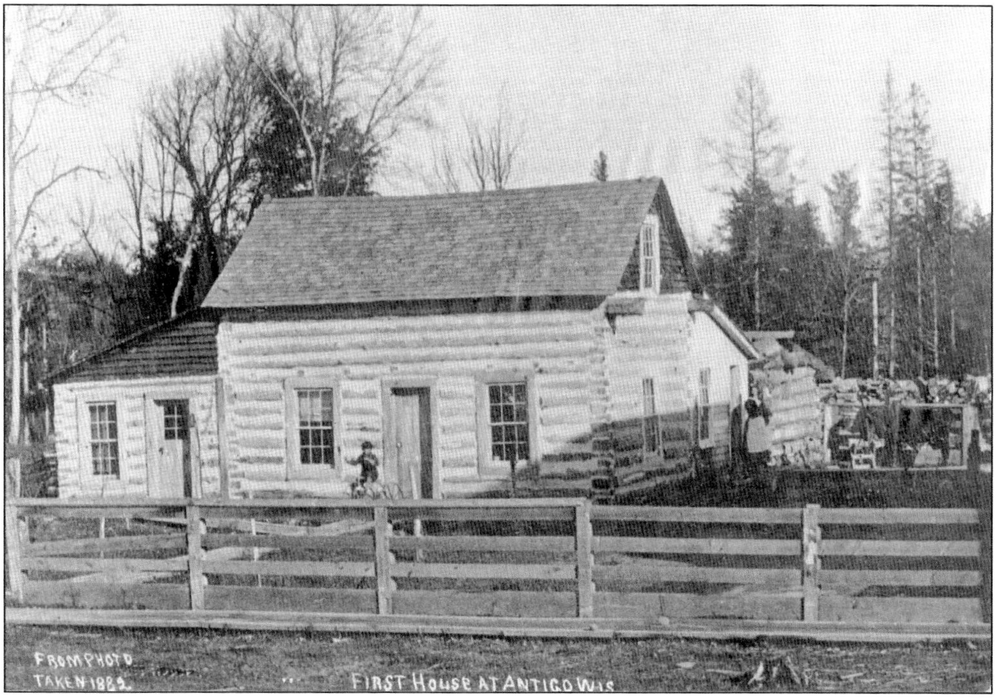

Francis Deleglise emigrated from Switzerland as a boy with his family. He saw potential in what later became Langlade County and built this as his home in 1879. A kitchen and dining area in the back and an office on the left were added soon afterward. Kingsbury sold this image on postcards but likely did not photograph it.

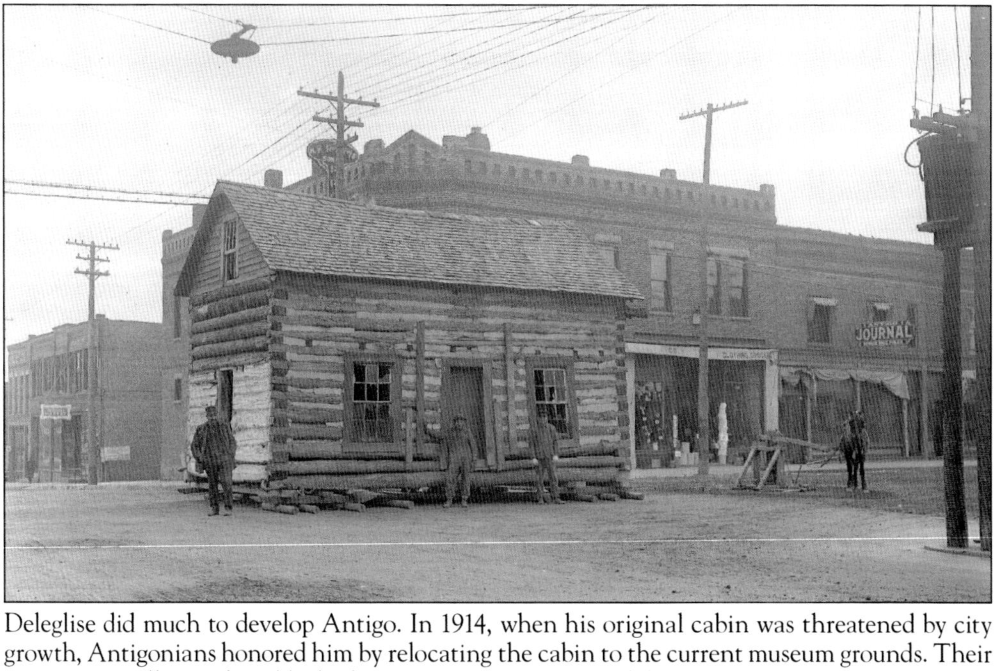

Deleglise did much to develop Antigo. In 1914, when his original cabin was threatened by city growth, Antigonians honored him by relocating the cabin to the current museum grounds. Their exertions in rolling it three blocks down Superior Street turned this event into a very early example of a Wisconsin community making an effort to preserve its historic structures.

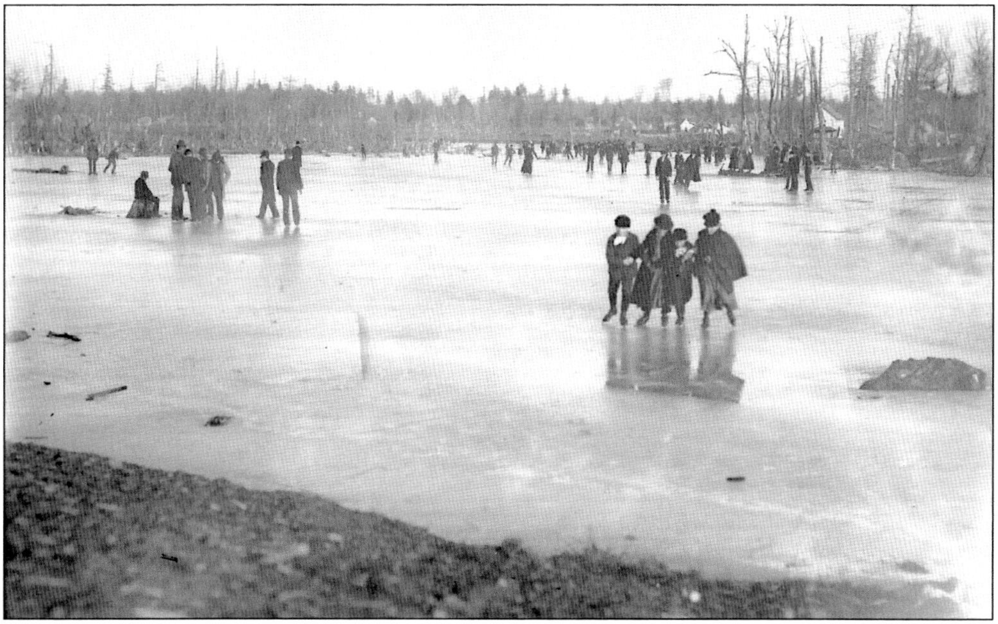

The Novotny brothers came to Antigo in 1879 to operate a sawmill. They erected a dam across Spring Brook, thus creating a pond for storing lumber. In 1883, T.D. Kellogg purchased the mill, and the pond became Kellogg's Pond. After all the industry left in 1934, land surrounding the lake was designated a recreational park open to the public. It remains a centerpiece of downtown Antigo.

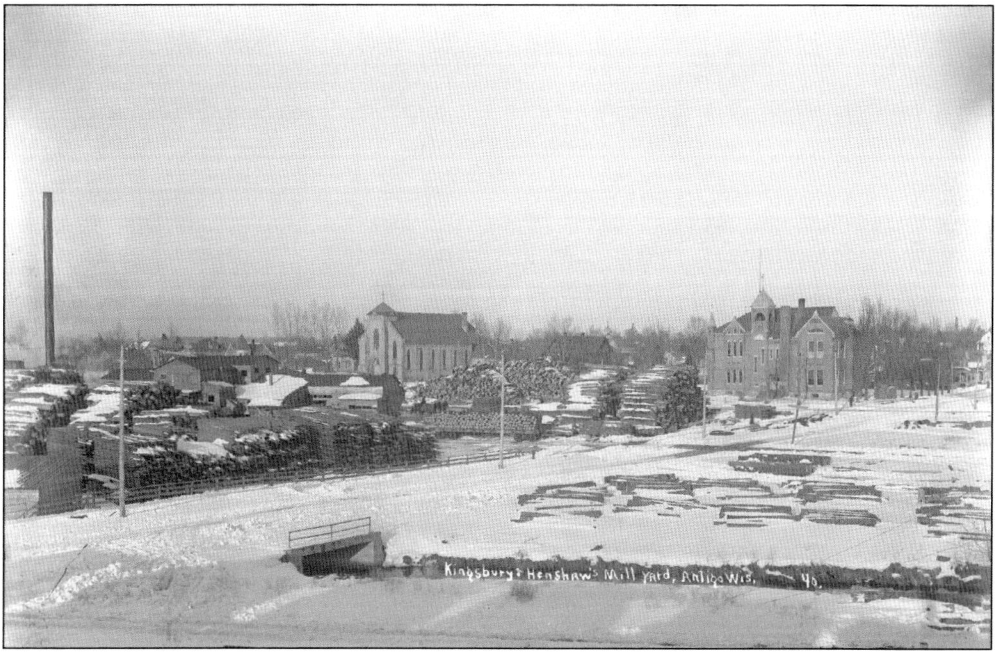

At least four sawmills and factories surrounded Kellogg's Pond in the 20th century's early decades, including Kingsbury and Henshaw's Mill. Business partner Jerome Kingsbury was A.J. Kingsbury's father. In the background is St. John's Catholic Church, an Antigo landmark. This is the second of the three church structures at this site.

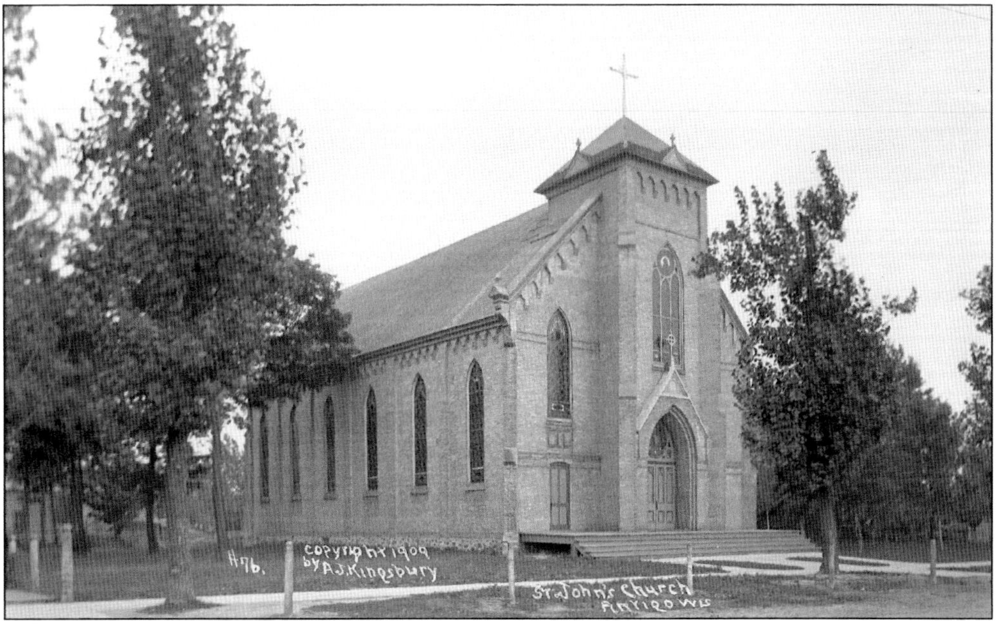

At first, the Deleglise family made their house available to hold Mass. In 1882, on land donated by the Deleglise family, Antigo's first Catholic Church held services. The original wood-frame church was destroyed by fire in May 1883. This new, larger church on the same site held its first services in 1884 but was not completed until 1886. The church shown here was replaced in 1957.

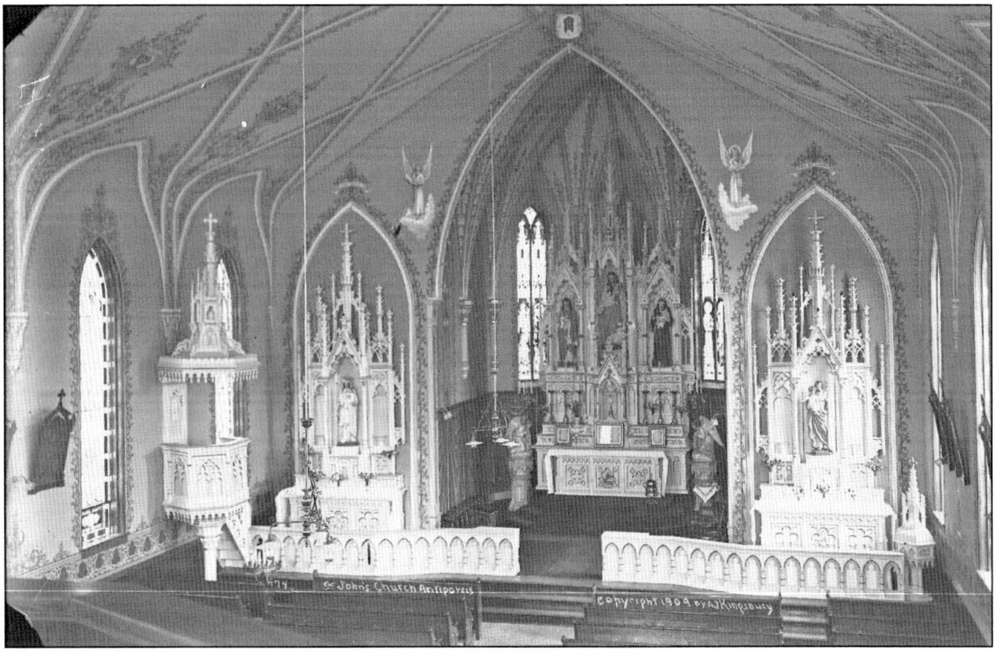

The church interior was unfinished when services were first held. By 1888, work on the interior began in earnest. Paul N. Klose of Milwaukee was commissioned to do frescoes, and E.B. Brielmaeir, also from Milwaukee, designed and supervised the building of the Gothic-designed alter. He also designed the baptismal font and pulpit. This was, by far, the grandest church in the city.

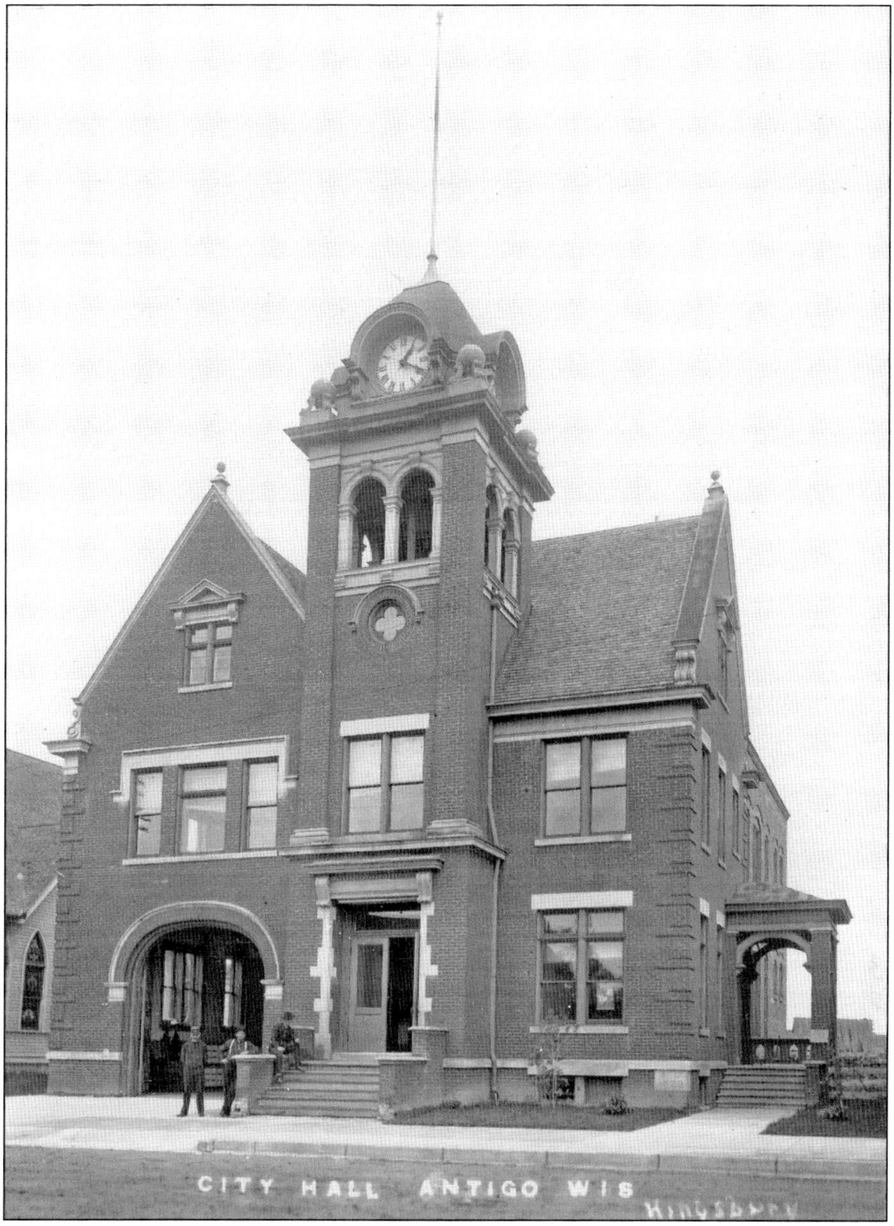

When Antigo was incorporated in 1885, the city took over a property used as a skating rink and built a frame structure, which served as city hall and the fire department. It served until 1901, when a new brick building housing both city hall and the fire station was erected; bids went out in 1899. Architects Van Ryan and De Gelleke of Milwaukee were awarded the commission, and local builder Charles F. Dahlman was granted the building contract for $9,250. Dahlman is the same contactor who built many structures in Antigo, including the Carnegie Library in 1905. In fact, by the time of his death in 1921, Dahlman was responsible for more buildings in Antigo than anyone else to that point. The city hall and fire station served Antigo for almost a century. In the mid-1990s, a new city hall was built, and the building depicted here was torn down in 1996 after first removing and preserving the clock faces and bell. Interestingly, the cost of the building's razing in 1996 was about five times that of its construction.

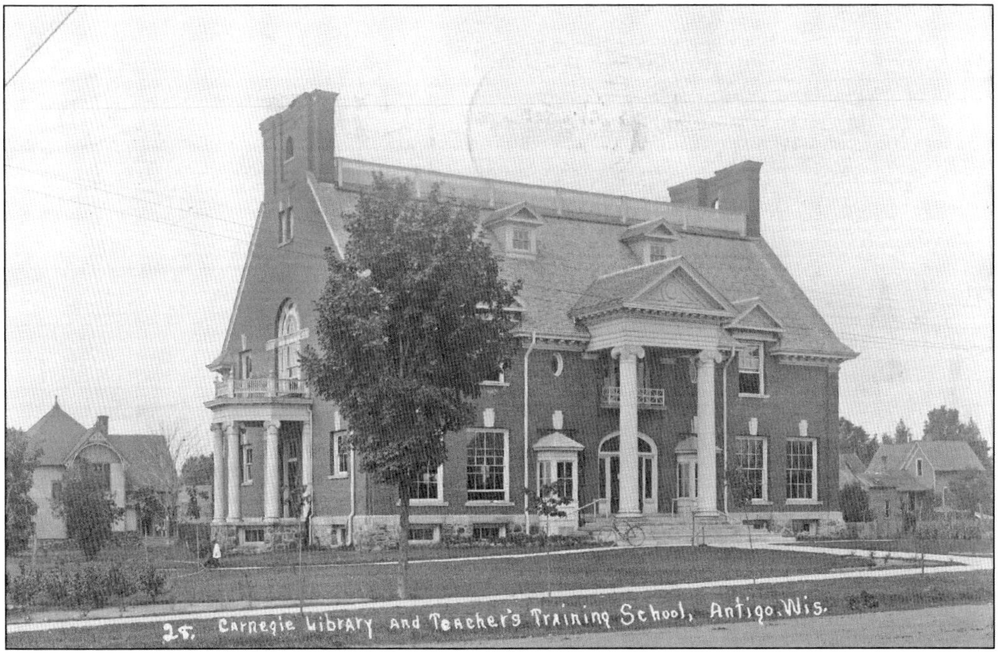

Andrew Carnegie funded more than 1,600 libraries nationwide and some in Canada under the belief that his access to books as a young man was important to his development. There were 63 Carnegie Libraries in Wisconsin alone. Many of them have been destroyed or radically modified. This one, built in 1903 to 1905, continued to serve as Antigo's library until 1997.

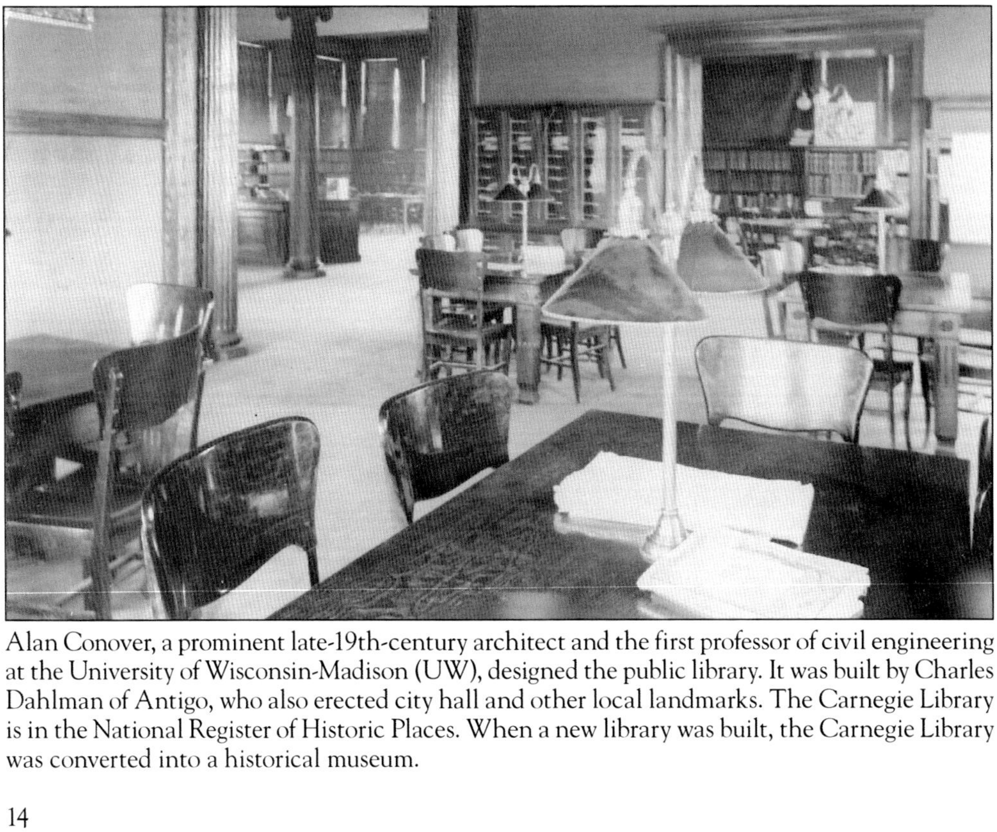

Alan Conover, a prominent late-19th-century architect and the first professor of civil engineering at the University of Wisconsin-Madison (UW), designed the public library. It was built by Charles Dahlman of Antigo, who also erected city hall and other local landmarks. The Carnegie Library is in the National Register of Historic Places. When a new library was built, the Carnegie Library was converted into a historical museum.

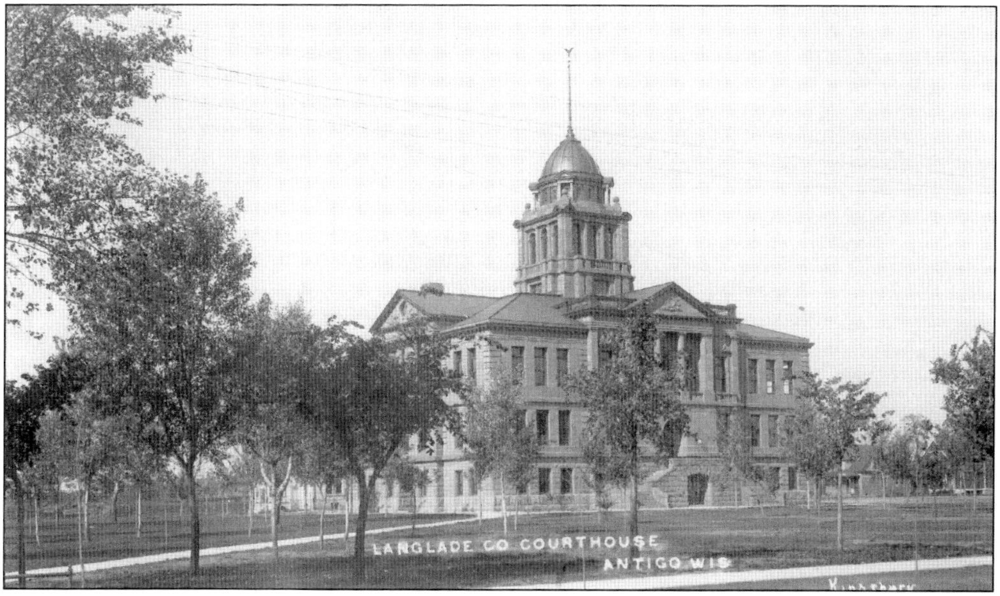

In 1879, New County was created and later renamed Langlade. Antigo became county seat in a highly contentious election. This is Antigo's second courthouse, constructed in 1905. It was built by a Minneapolis company that primarily used Port Wing brownstone. Interior murals were designed by A.E. Soderberg of LaCrosse, who had worked on the 1893 Chicago Exposition and the Swedish king's summer palace in Uppsala.

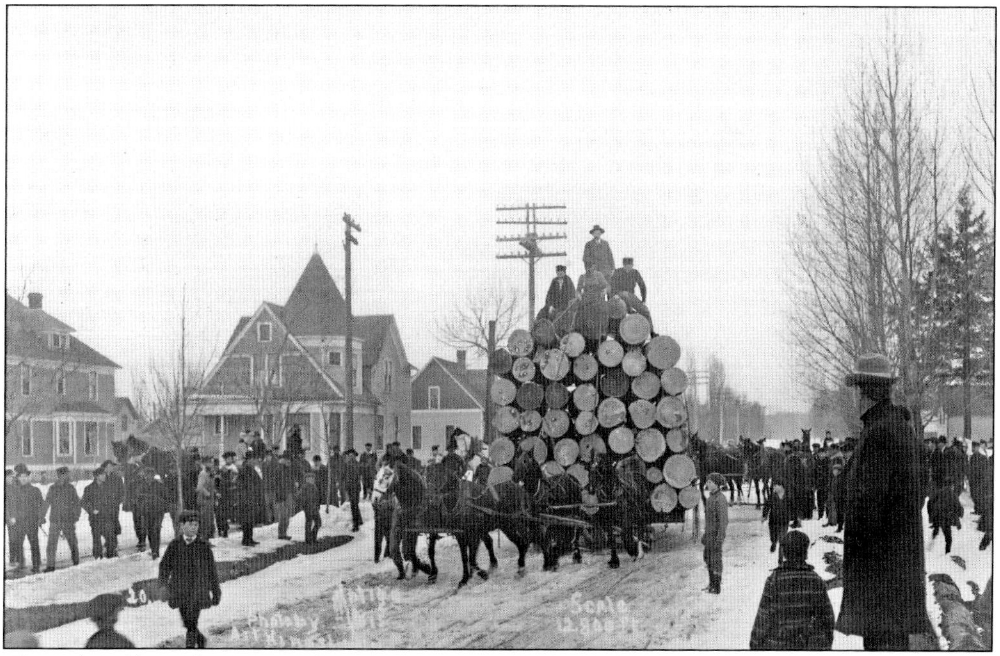

The railroad brought most timber into Antigo to the sawmills and factories. Horse-drawn sledges were used, and contests often developed to see which team could haul the largest load through the streets of Antigo. These displays were documented in many photographs.

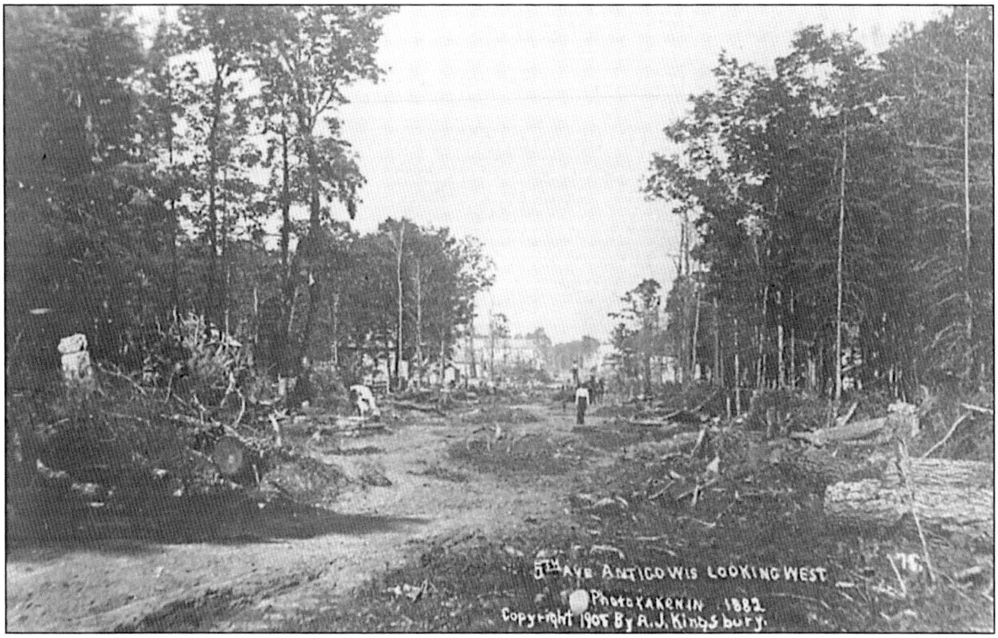

When Deleglise settled in Antigo, Willard Ackley already had established a trading post seven or eight miles to the west. The Ackley family helped the Deleglise family in many ways, and the path between the two cabins was well travelled. Eventually, this wooded path was cleared and it became Fifth Avenue. Kingsbury sold this 1882 image on postcards, even though it was shot by an unknown photographer.

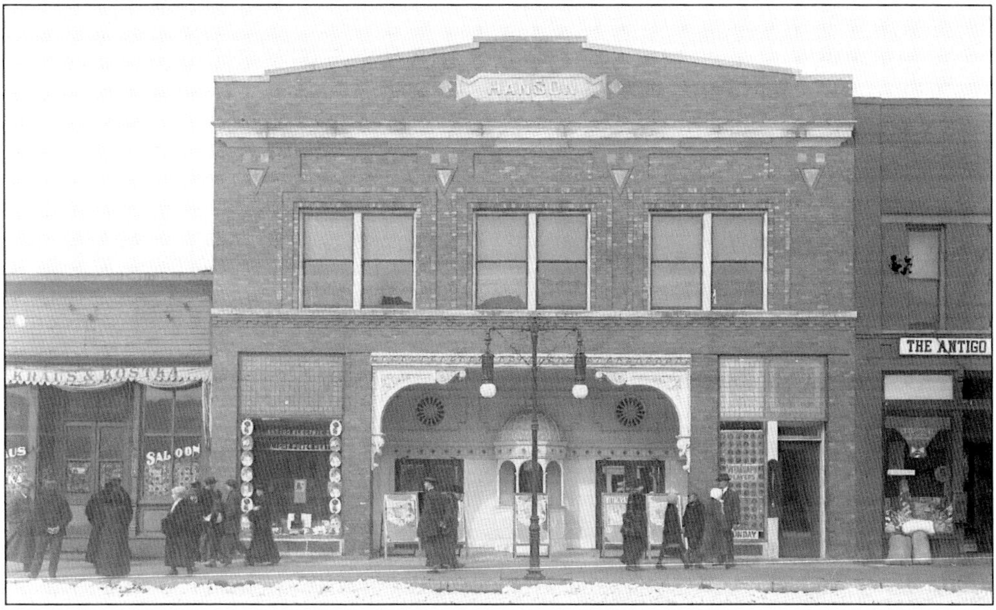

The *Antigo Daily Journal* reported on January 22, 1916, "Last summer many paid as high as a dollar to see a film called the *Birth of a Nation.* I admit the thing was well advertised by the various attempts at censorship. . . . But why it drew a dollar per seat when other motion picture houses charged but ten cents for equally meritorious productions, I am at a loss to explain. Ellis Usher, Milwaukee."

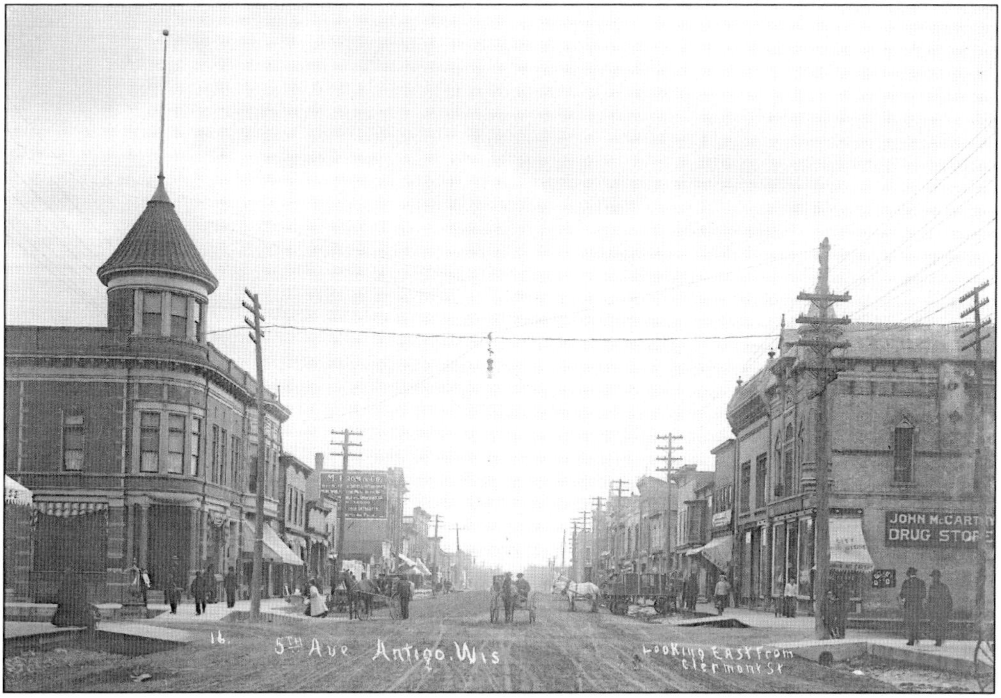

From the beginning, Antigo's main thoroughfare was Fifth Avenue. When Antigo was incorporated in 1885, merchants campaigned for the construction of board sidewalks on Fifth Avenue. Road improvements were also advocated so that rural settlers could easily come downtown. The building in the right foreground, John McCarthy's Drug Store, is an Antigo landmark. Built in 1888 as a grocery, it was a pharmacy from 1901 to the late 1990s.

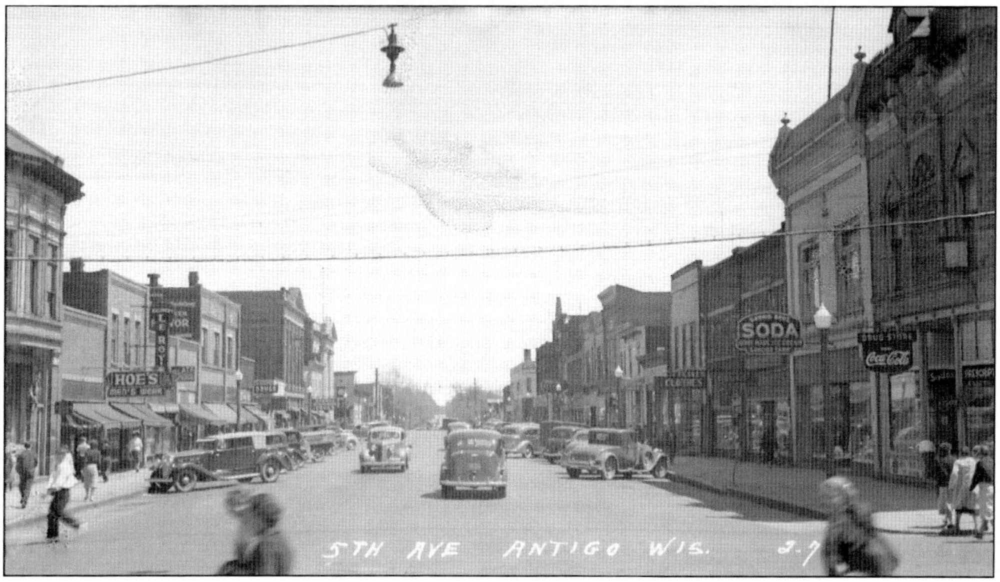

In the 1940s and 1950s, downtown Antigo, and Fifth Avenue in particular, was a bustling shopping area. Antigo was an important railroad hub. Older residents still recall a ritual from their childhoods: the family went downtown on a Friday evening to the depot to greet arrivals or just look, and then they would go shopping or meet up with friends.

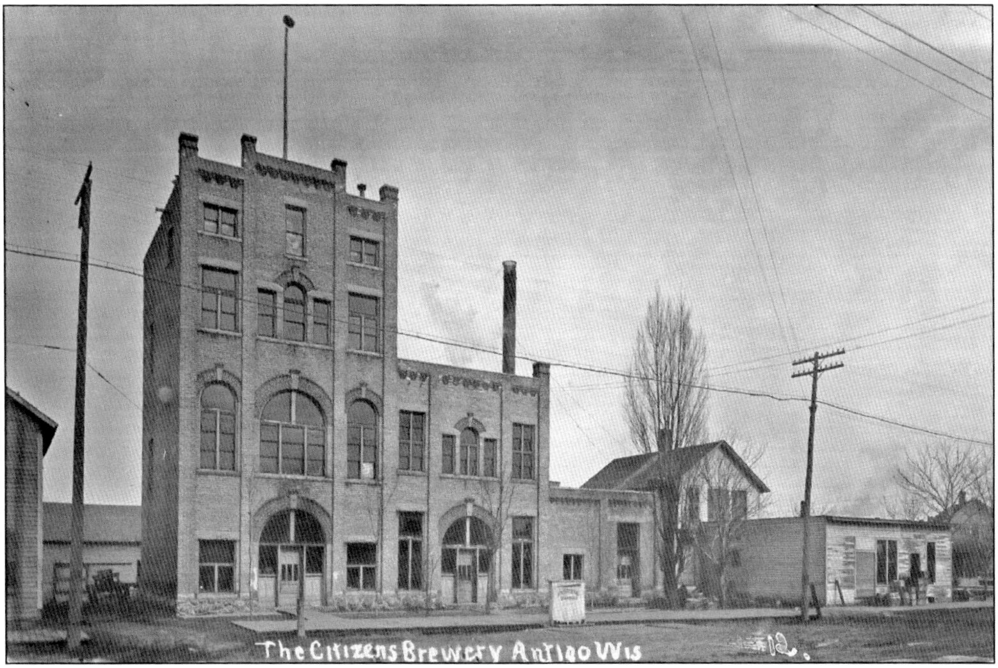

Citizen's Brewery was one of two Antigo breweries established after the death of temperance advocate Francis Deleglise. The first legal sale of liquor took place in 1885, when Antigo was incorporated as a city. The dries, however, won the 1886 elections and outlawed liquor again. By the early 20th century, beer was once more brewed and sold in Antigo.

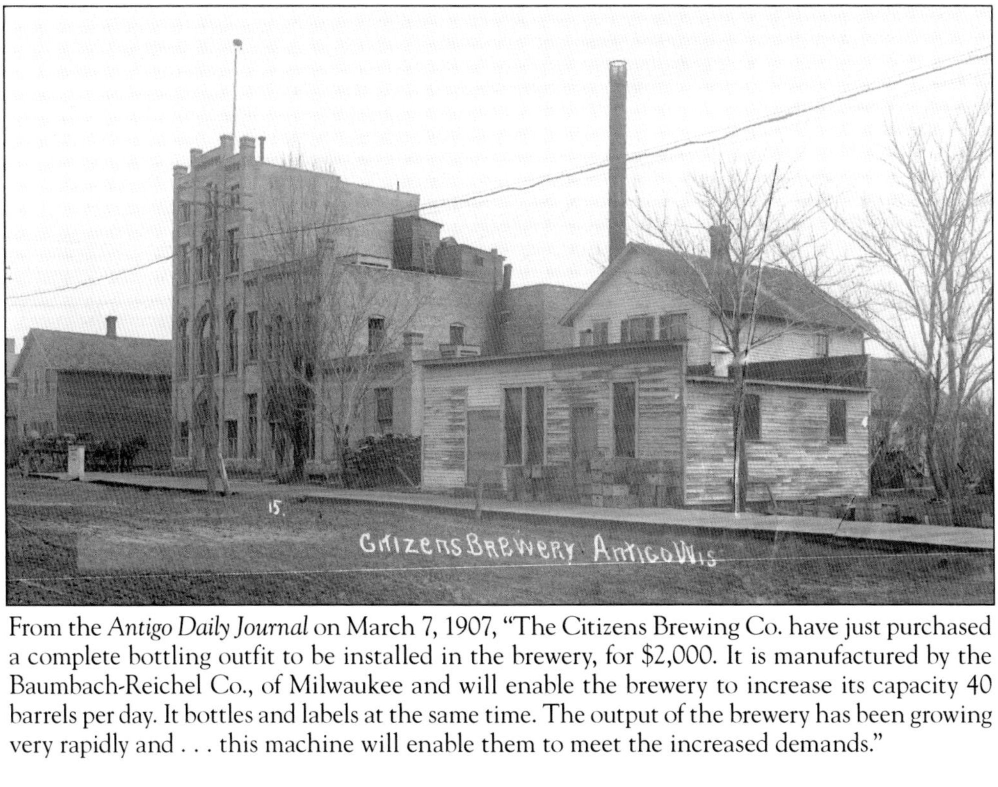

From the *Antigo Daily Journal* on March 7, 1907, "The Citizens Brewing Co. have just purchased a complete bottling outfit to be installed in the brewery, for $2,000. It is manufactured by the Baumbach-Reichel Co., of Milwaukee and will enable the brewery to increase its capacity 40 barrels per day. It bottles and labels at the same time. The output of the brewery has been growing very rapidly and . . . this machine will enable them to meet the increased demands."

As in many towns, the Fourth of July is an occasion for parades and celebrations. The Citizen's Brewery was only too happy to enter its proudly patriotic float and pony cart in this grand holiday parade. A.J. Kingsbury was there to photograph this entry and many more in parades over the years.

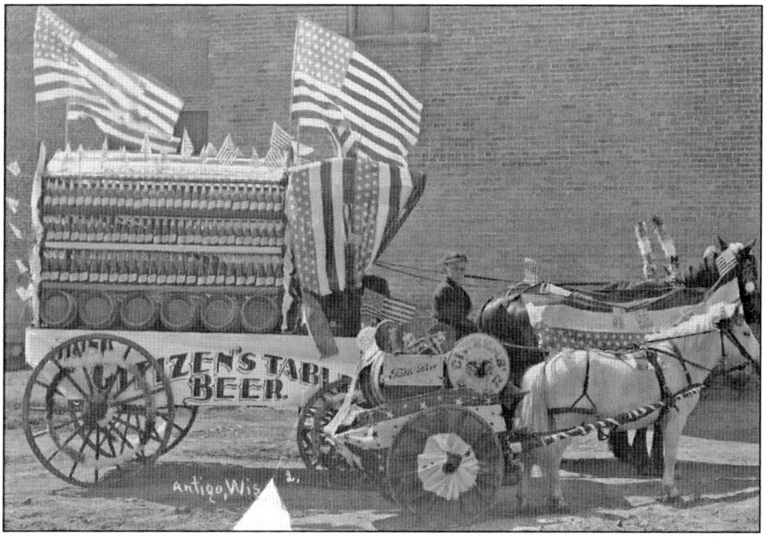

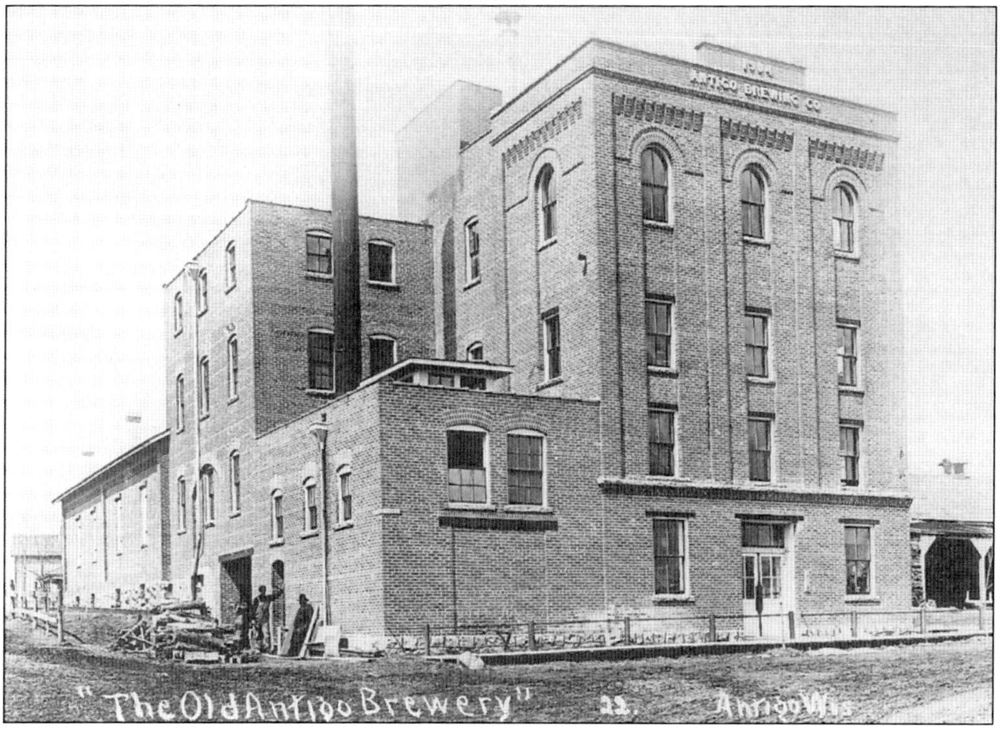

The Antigo Brewery was closed because of Prohibition. The Kraft Cheese Company bought it in 1922, when it sought to expand beyond its northern Illinois home base. This plant became a major cheese production center for Kraft and a major Antigo employer. Although Kraft left in 1992, cheese production continues under the Sartori Cheese Company. In 2008, Antigo-produced cheese Raspberry Bella Vitano won "Best New Cheese in the World" at the World Cheese Awards in Dublin, Ireland.

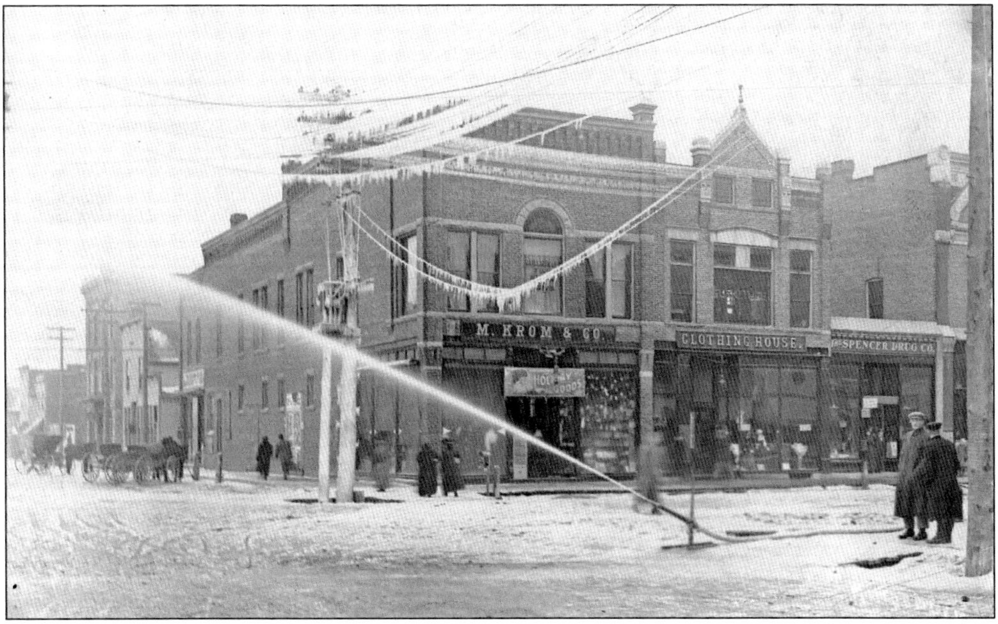

Amid busy Christmas shopping on December 15, 1910, one of Antigo's worst fires occurred at Krom's Department Store, a major local retailer. Work on a basement gas pipe caused an explosion and fire. The fire department quickly extinguished the blaze, and it seemed under control. However, the fire reignited, and in 15 minutes, the building was an inferno, raging out of control and threatening nearby buildings.

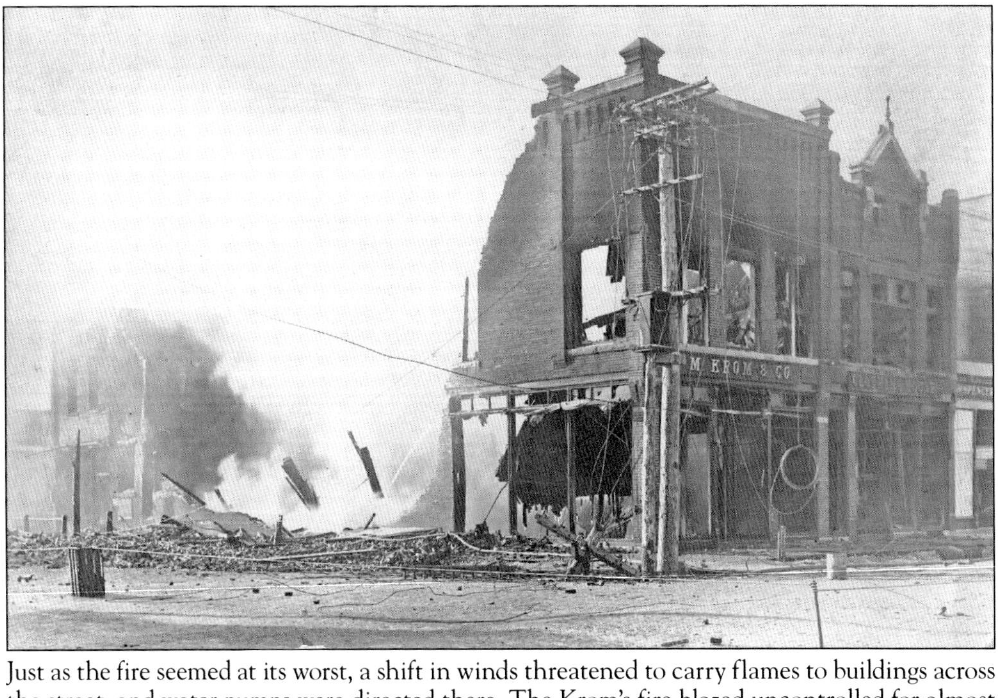

Just as the fire seemed at its worst, a shift in winds threatened to carry flames to buildings across the street, and water pumps were directed there. The Krom's fire blazed uncontrolled for almost an entire day, in part because the water pumps used to fight the conflagration lacked sufficient force to reach the second floor and roof of the building. The fire caused over $100,000 damage.

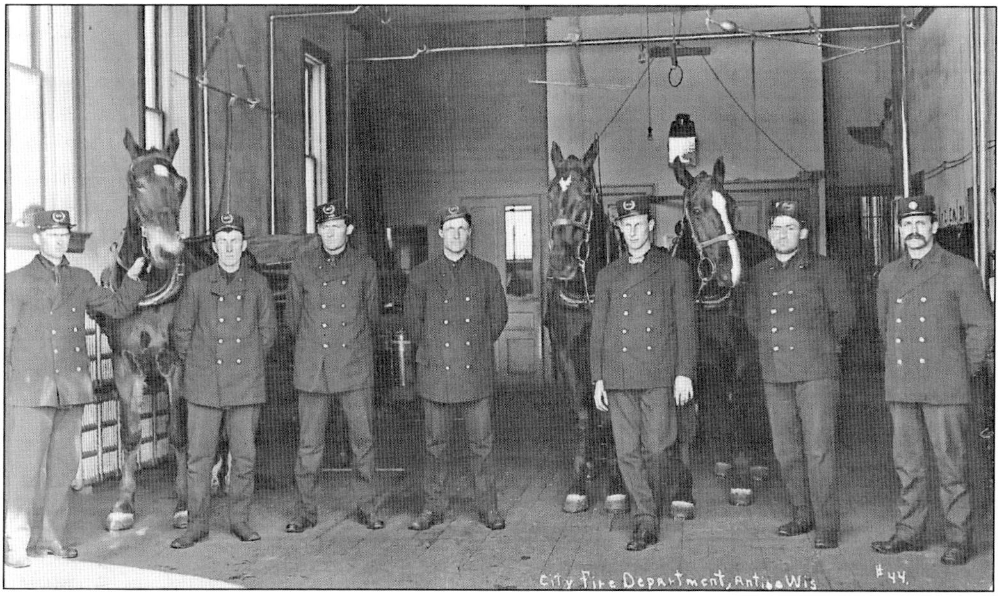

City officials, realizing their fire department had inadequate equipment, purchased a new horse-drawn fire wagon, which arrived in 1911. Here, firemen pose with the horses. Harnesses were suspended from the ceiling, and when the alarm rang, the horses stepped underneath them and were hitched up. When fire trucks replaced the horse-drawn wagon, firemen continued to use the old wagon in the winter since horses were more reliable on snow-covered and icy streets.

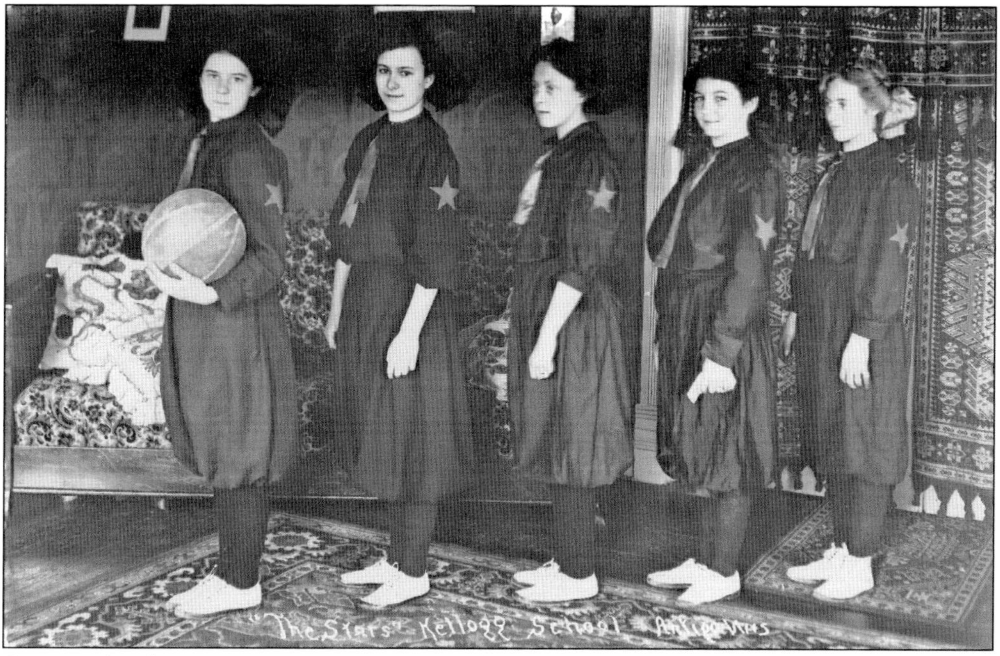

Organized girls' sports were uncommon in the early 20th century. The Antigo High School yearbook of 1919 states, "This is the first year in which girls have taken an active part in high school athletics. A tournament was held, but no definite decision was reached due to evenly matched abilities." The following year, the senior girls' team bested the women's faculty team with a final score of 12-2.

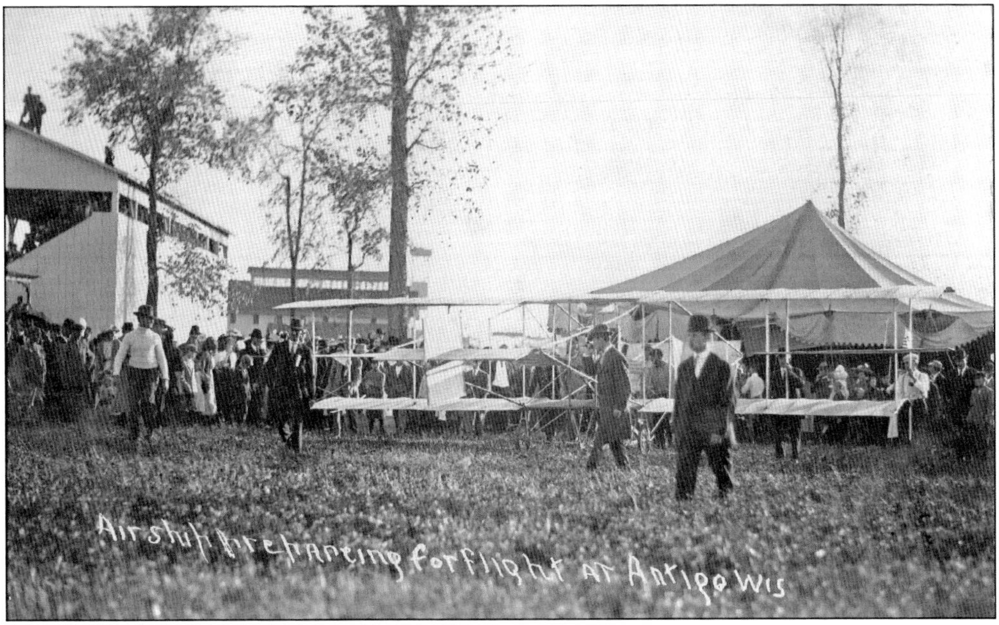

In 1909, airplanes made their first flights in Wisconsin. Wausau's 29-year-old John Schwister brought his *Minnesota–Badger*, Wisconsin's first home-built airplane, to the Antigo fairgrounds in September 1911. In doing so, he became the first Wisconsin pilot to be paid to fly. Around 6,500 fair attendees witnessed the exciting demonstration of this modern machine.

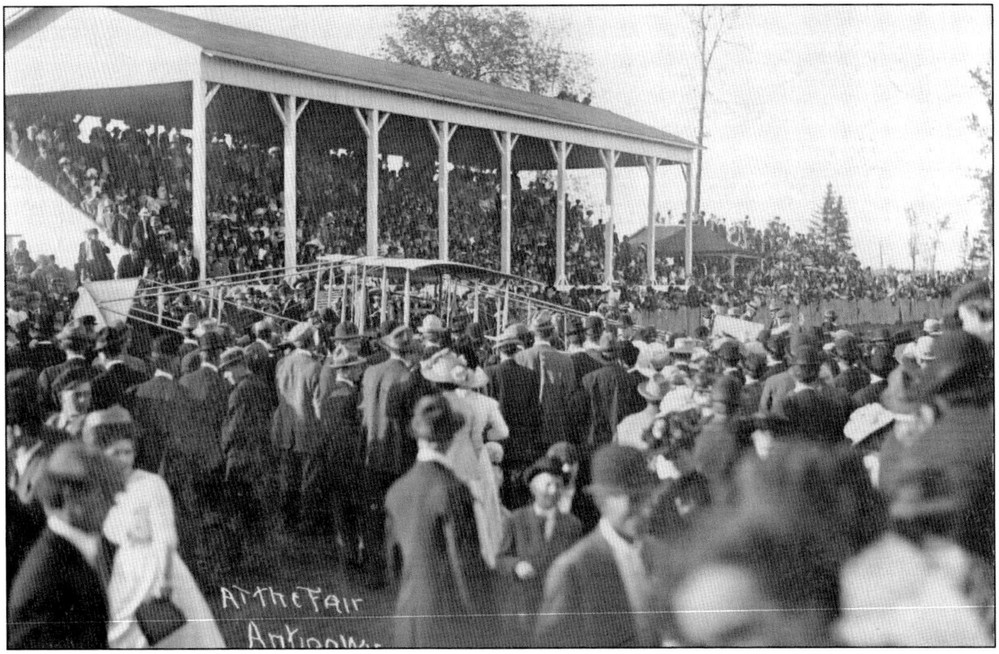

On September 8, 1912, local residents got another look at a flying machine. County officials hired a barnstorming pilot, Lincoln Beachy, to make three separate flight passes over the grandstand at the fairgrounds. Area schools were closed so that students could witness the event, towns along the railroad line sent citizen delegations, and more than 10,000 people came to watch the flights. Thirty months later, Beachy died when another one of his planes crashed.

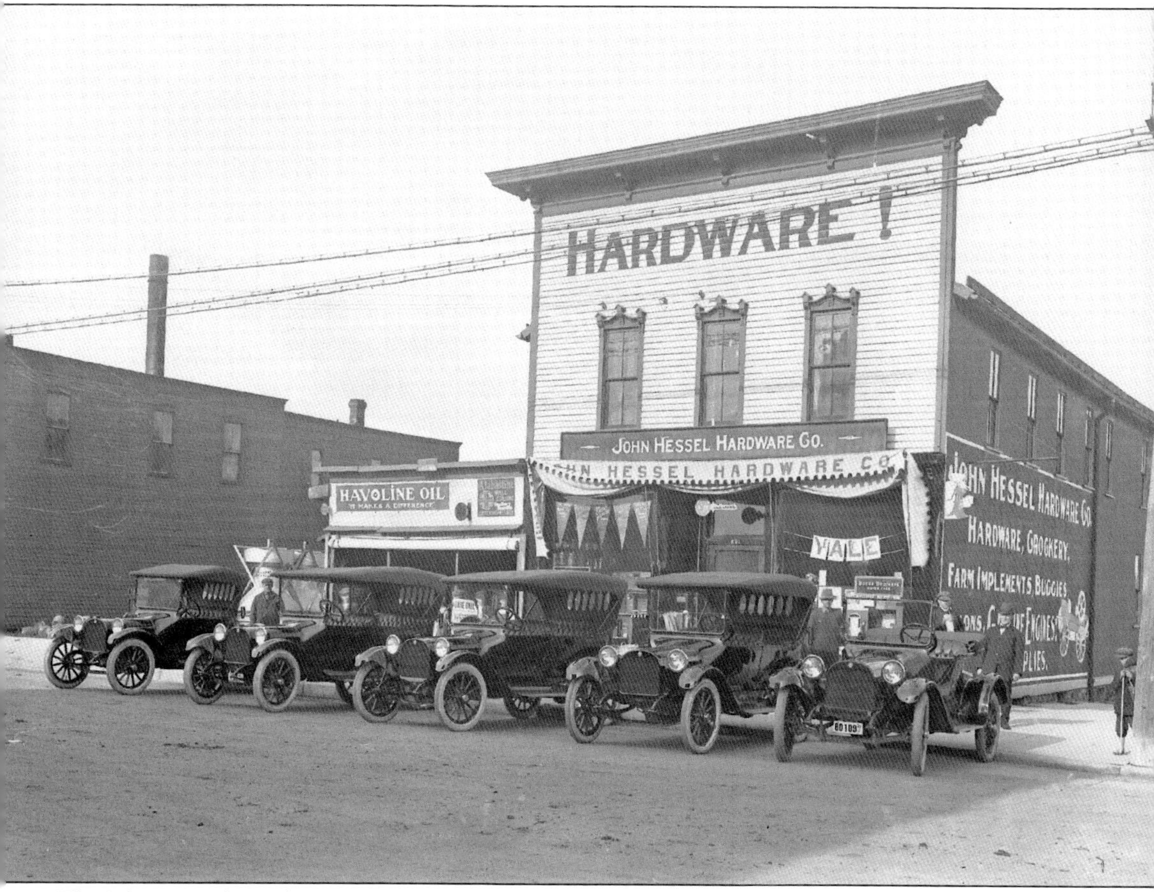

The John Hessel Hardware Company sold cars, buggies, and groceries in addition to hardware. In 1912, when barnstorming pilot Lincoln Beachy was hired to fly at the fairgrounds, it was a major event. Beachy purchased gasoline for the flight at Hessel's. John Hessel took out a large ad in the newspaper proclaiming, "Gas has never been higher in Antigo." The cars lined up in this photograph were 1916 Dodge Brothers Motor Cars. The Dodge brothers, John and Horace, were respected manufacturers of automobile parts before they built their first complete car in late 1914. The brothers' good reputation and the fine quality of their cars sparked rapidly growing sales. Over 70,000 cars were sold in 1916. In that year, Dodge's new Touring Car (or Roadster) cost $785 plus shipping from Detroit ($1,100 plus shipping in Canada) and a winter Touring Car, including regular mohair top, was priced at $950 plus shipping ($1,335 plus shipping in Canada). The cars were tough and dependable and were used by the US Army in World War I as staff cars and ambulances.

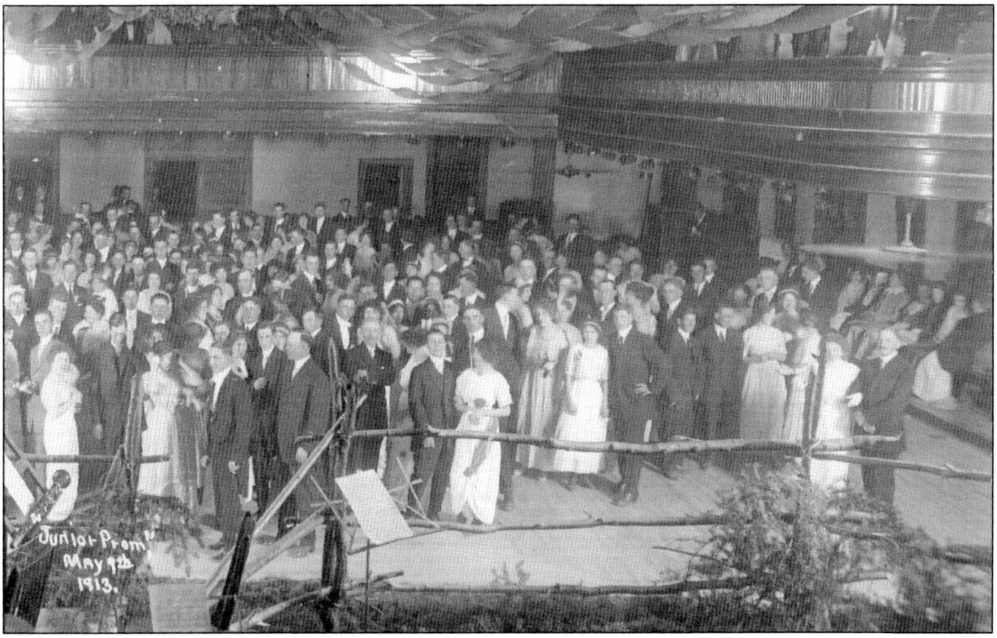

Antigo's second opera house, built in 1904, was converted for this evening into a dance hall. With the stage taken over by an orchestra and the audience seats removed, the area was reconfigured for dancing. Shown here is the high school's May 1913 junior prom dance. On other occasions, the main floor of the Opera House was sometimes used for roller-skating.

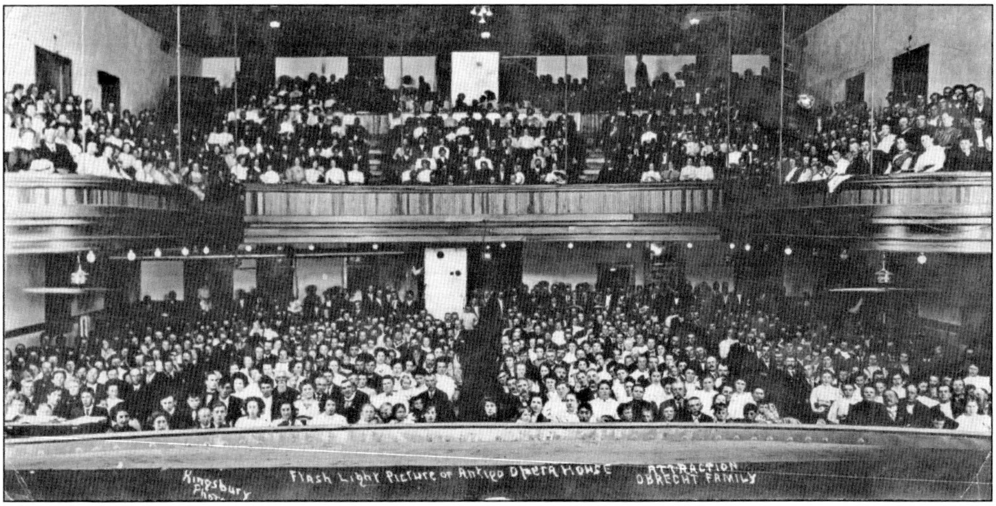

The Opera House in Antigo, like several throughout the state, presented a variety of entertainment, including vaudeville shows, stage dramas, concerts, silent movies, and eventually talkies. The stage could accommodate 50 people together with two railroad cars of scenery, and the building could seat an audience of 1,100. Years ago, the structure was converted into apartments.

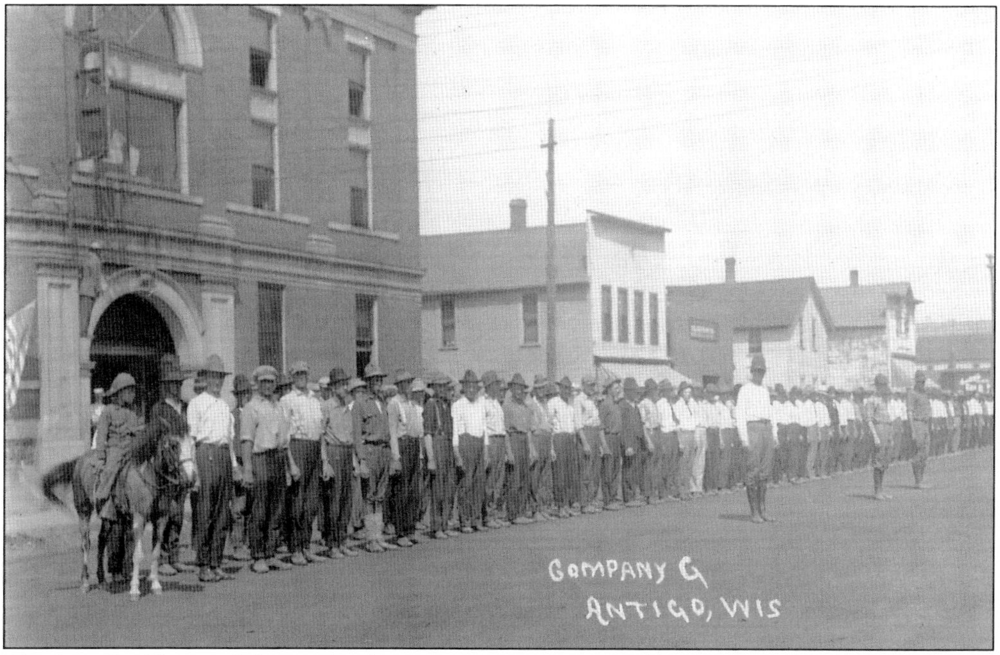

The large building at left was the Opera House. During World War I, wealthy Antigo resident John Hanousek purchased the Opera House and donated it to the city and county for use as an armory. This group of recruits trained there. They were formed into Company G, 107th Trench Mortar Battery Company and went on to see action in Belgium and France.

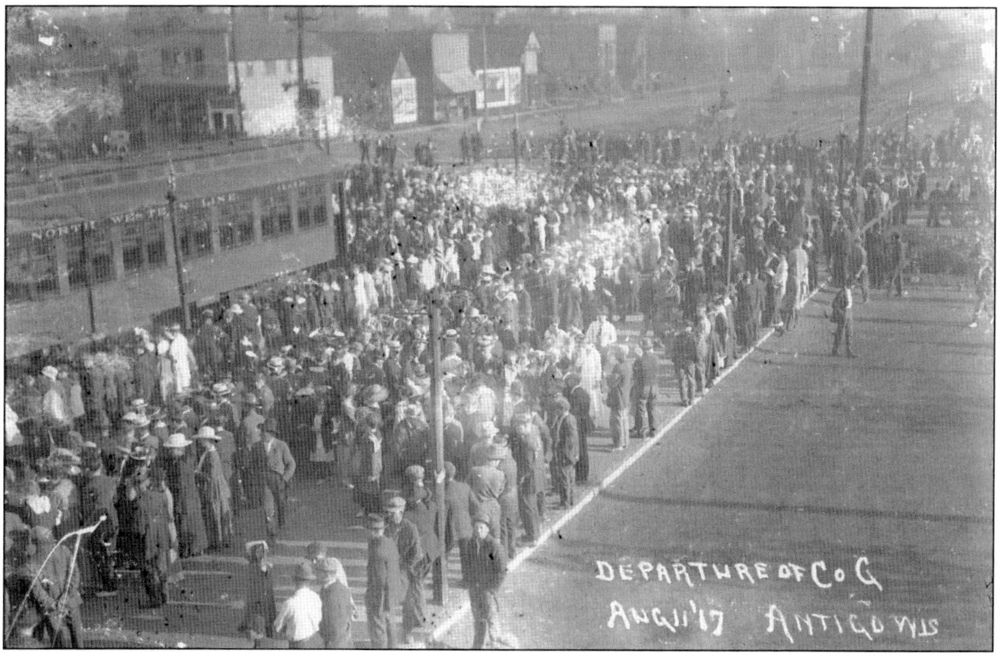

The 107th Trench Mortar Battery Company first trained in Antigo at the Opera House, followed by Wisconsin's Camp Douglas, and then in Texas before shipping out to see action in Europe. The departure of soldiers from the Antigo depot drew a large crowd of family and well-wishers, as did their eventual return.

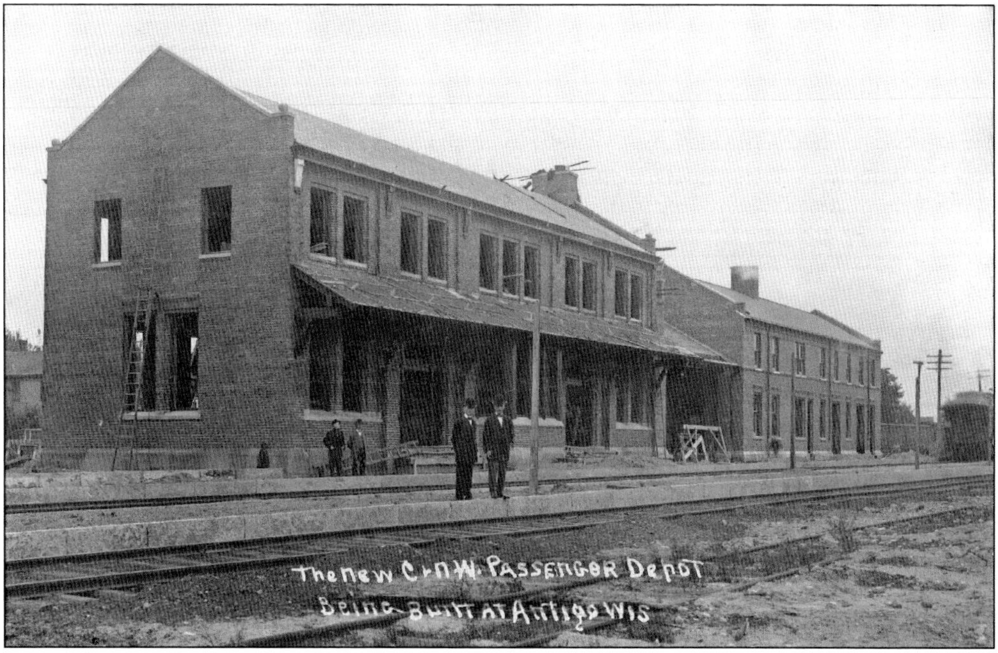

Antigo became headquarters for the Ashland division of the Chicago & North Western Railway in 1907. Extensive expansion included construction of this new railroad depot. For over 40 years, two major passenger trains arrived daily at noon. Southbound No. 116 and northbound No. 117 appeared within minutes of each other, laying over for 55 minutes while crews checked the trains and passengers enjoyed lunch.

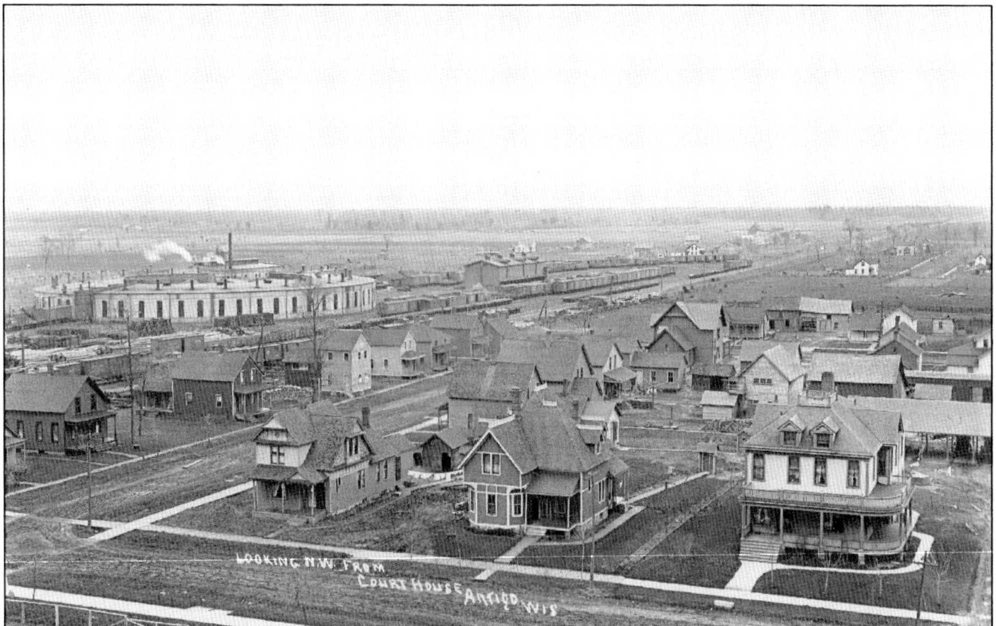

Part of the rail yards, including the huge roundhouse, can be seen from the courthouse roof. The rail yards stretched for a length of over 10 city blocks once Antigo became a major freight and passenger hub. (See page 116 for a closer look at this roundhouse.)

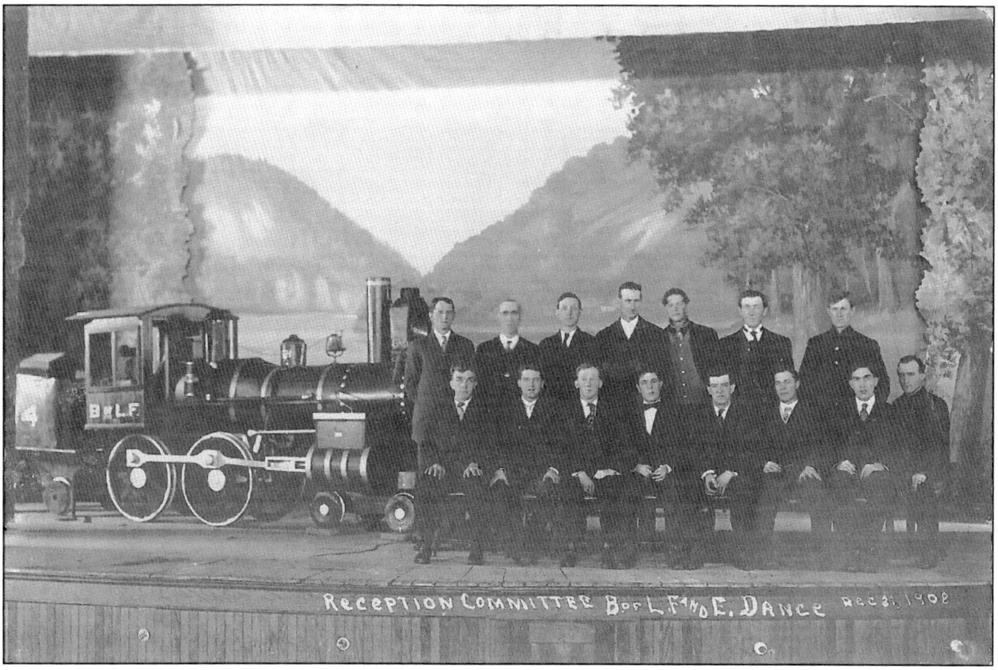

The Brotherhood of Locomotive Firemen and Engineers was an important union in a railroad town such as Antigo. Here, union officials and a locomotive prop pose on the stage of the Opera House prior to a dance.

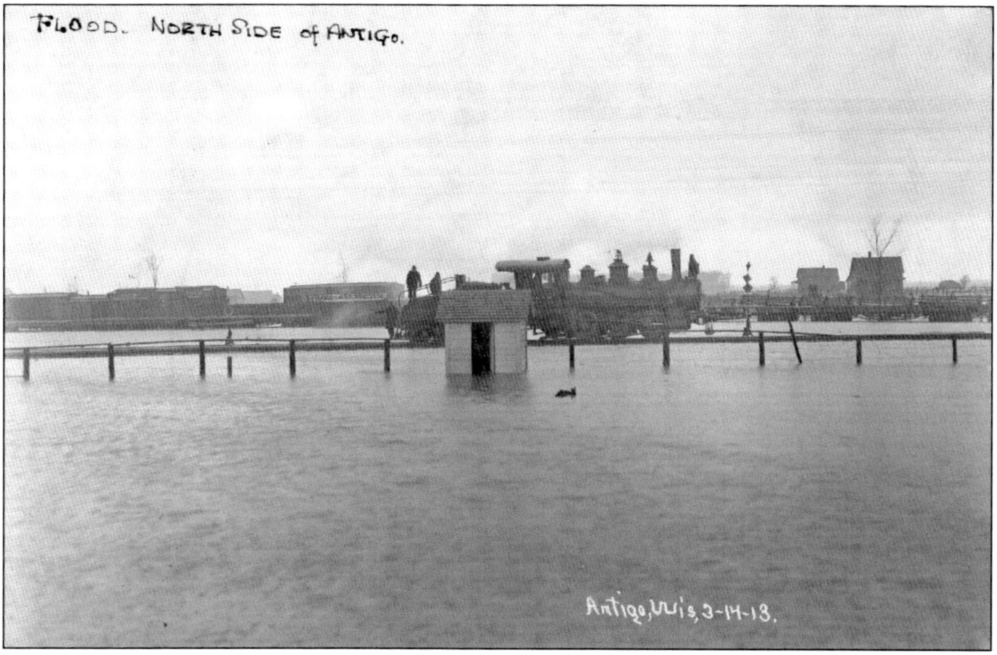

Downtown Antigo's many sawmills and wood-product factories were vital to the city's growth. Railroad spur lines carried timber from the lumber camps into downtown Antigo's mills. Here, the railroad trestle that passed over the edge of Kellogg's Pond is completely surrounded by the springtime floodwaters of 1913.

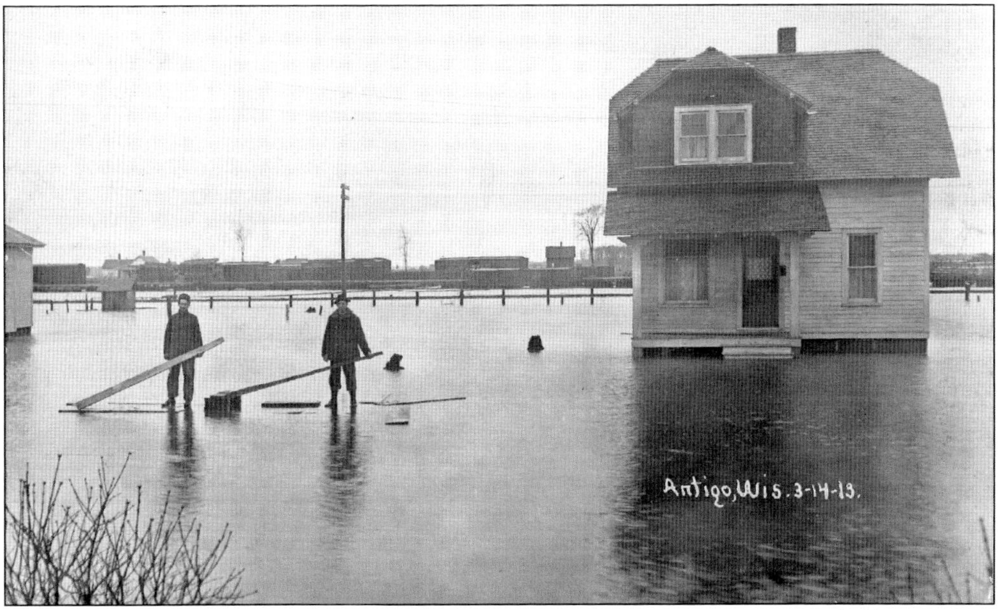

Antigo is located on a flat plain, the bottom of a former glacier lake, and is bounded by terminal moraines to the north and east. Periodic spring floods occur due to rains and snowmelt, causing Spring Brook to overflow, resulting in the flooding of downtown streets. Images of the March 1913 flood were captured by Kingsbury.

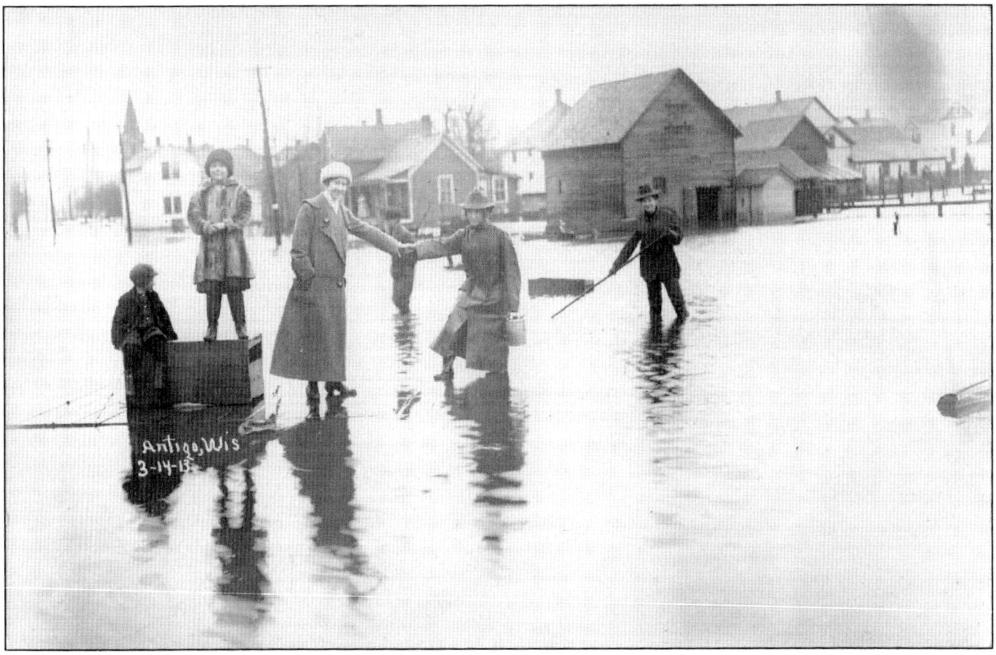

Spring floods still occasionally happen, but they were a regular spring event in the early 20th century. The floods of 1913 were some of the worst. The fire department was called upon to aid beleaguered residents. Water was so high in regions of downtown, some people would visit their neighbors in rowboats.

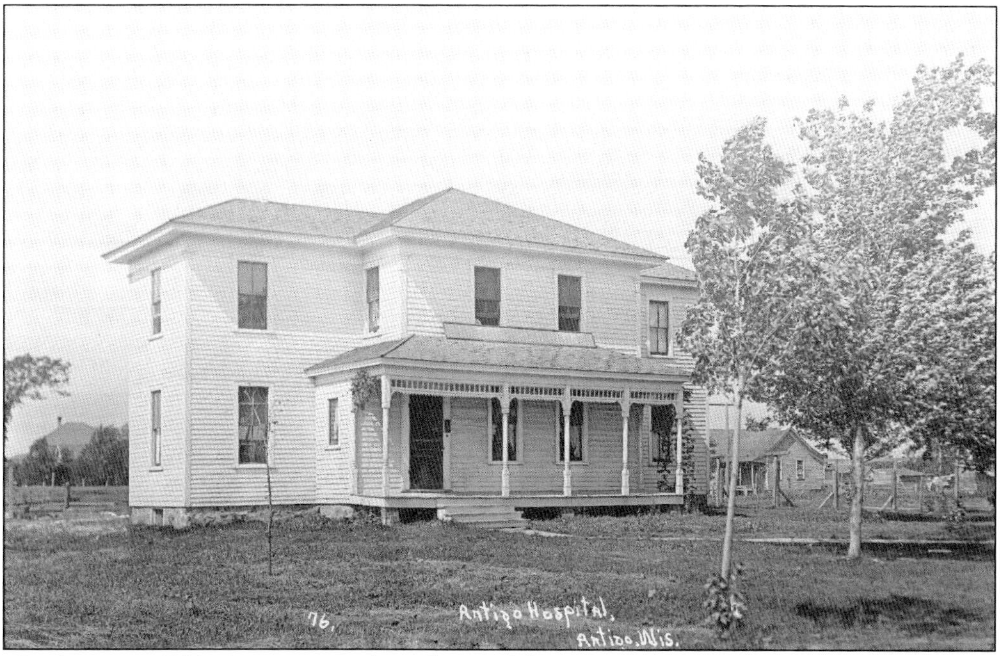

This home on Fifth Avenue served as a hospital from 1897 to 1933. Originally run by doctors I.D. Steffens and G.E. Moore, Dr. G.W. Moore joined his uncle when Steffens retired. Antigo hospitals were based in houses; this was the oldest of three in operation. When the city constructed a large hospital, these small hospitals reverted to other uses. This building still stands, although remodeled.

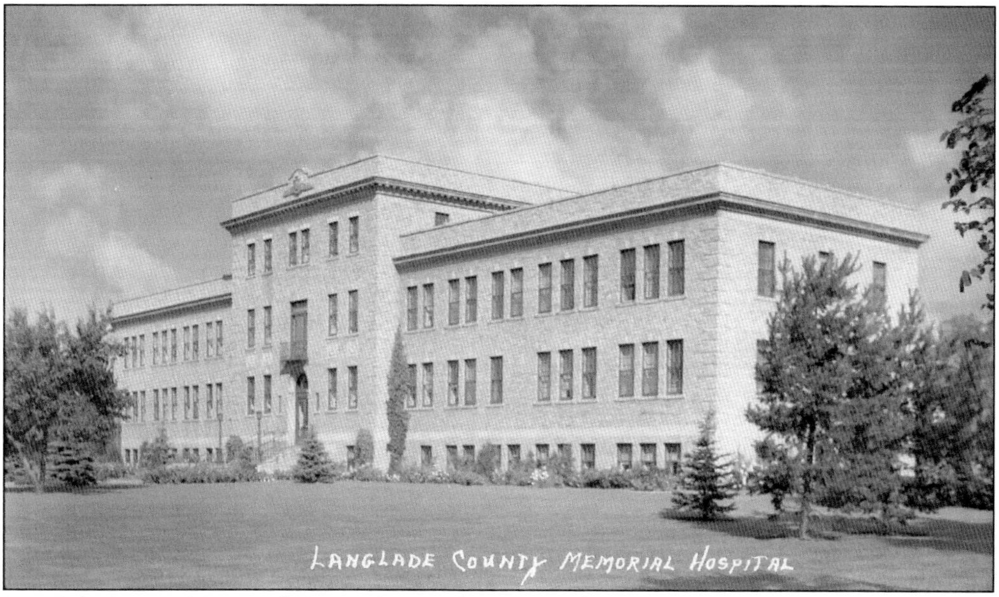

Langlade County Memorial Hospital opened in 1933. When the county first decided to build this new hospital, the Great Depression halted construction. Civic leaders convinced the Religious Hospitallers of St. Joseph to come to Antigo and run the hospital. Building additions were made in 1954, and a clinic was added in 1992. Continued expansion is planned and the complex is becoming a major part of the Antigo community.

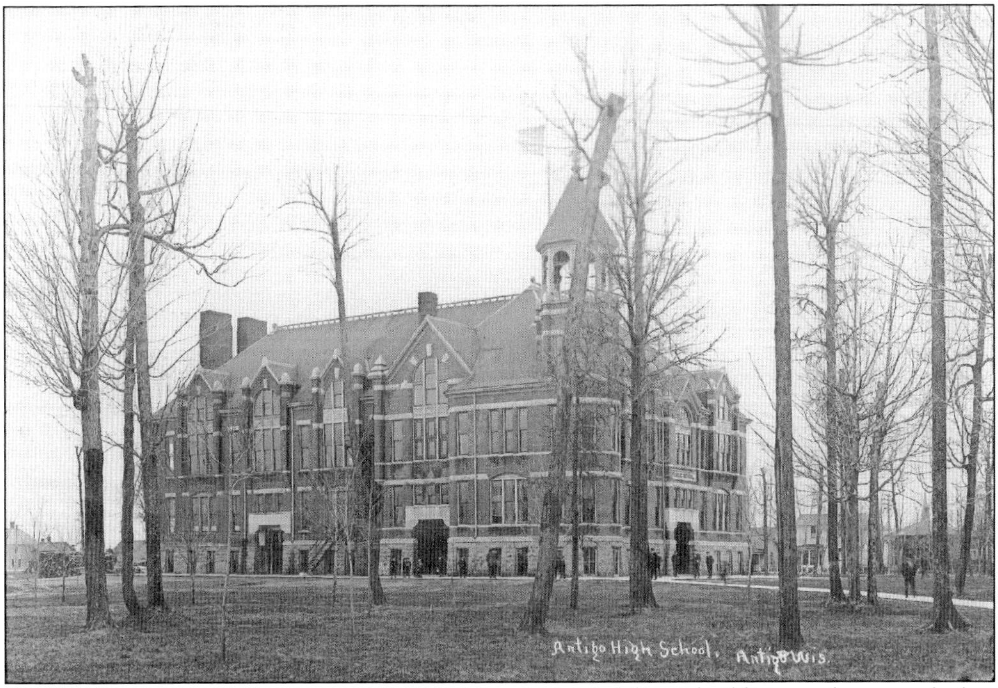

Antigo's first high school was erected in 1883. It was a wood-frame building on the grounds that later became the Carnegie Library's site. It had an enrollment of 41 pupils. In 1890, this large brick schoolhouse was built at a cost of $16,500. This school was destroyed in a fire in 1916.

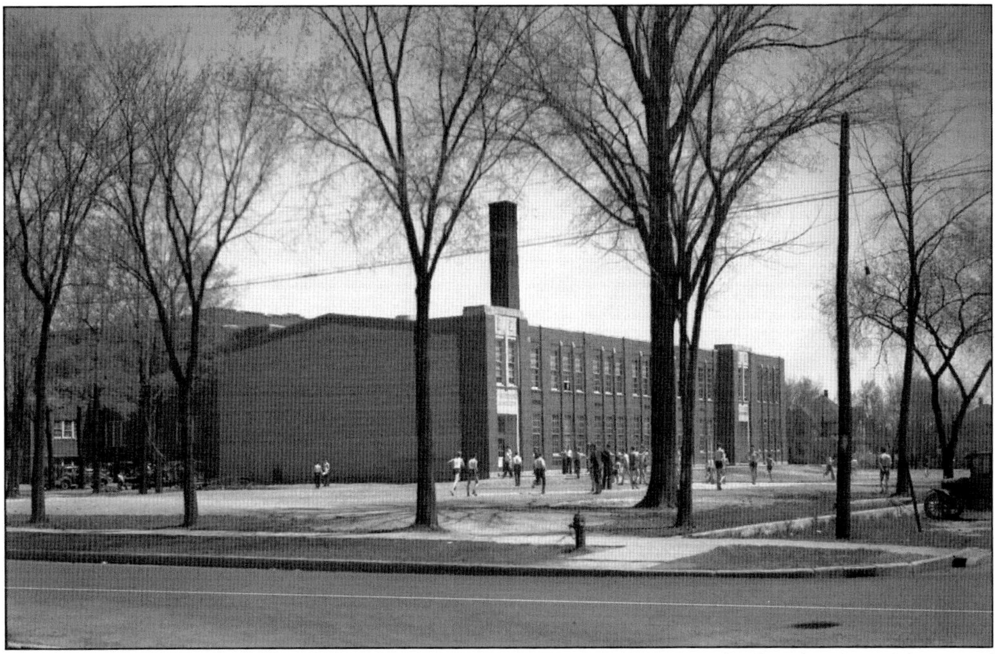

Milwaukee architect Robert Messmer was chosen to design the new high school, and by April 1916, plans were ready for the new structure to be situated on the old school site. In July 1916, the cornerstone was laid. The school was first used in the spring of 1917. In the 1990s, Antigo built a new high school, and the 1917 building, with modifications, became the middle school.

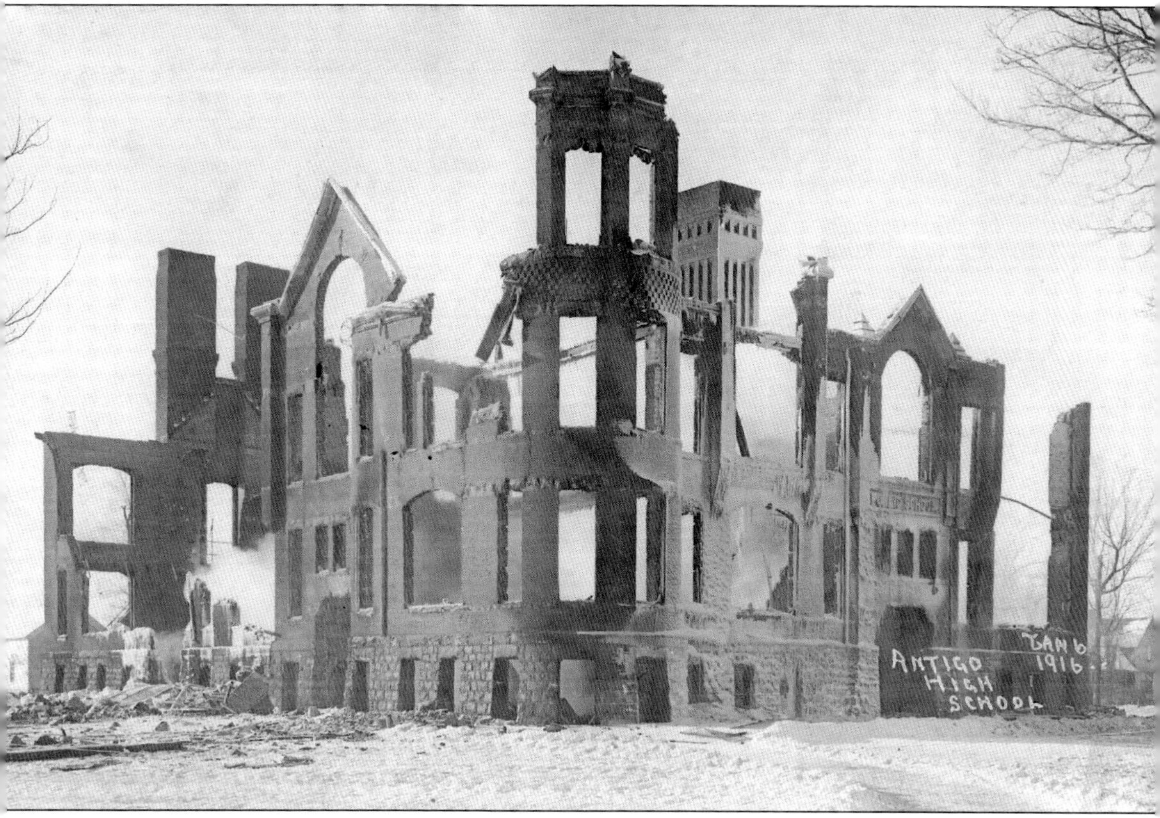

At about 2:45 a.m. on January 6, 1916, a fire broke out in the high school. The *Antigo Daily Journal* reported that an Antigo Gas Company employee heard an explosion and discovered the fire. Firemen arrived quickly, but the building was soon a blazing inferno. With flames gushing from nearly every window, burning bits of the building were carried for blocks by a strong northwest wind. "The extreme low temperature [minus 22 degrees] and the presence of snow and ice on roofs was all that prevented a widespread conflagration . . . firemen fought the blaze under great difficulties. It was necessary to change shifts at the nozzles frequently to prevent the firemen's hands becoming numb from cold," asserted the newspaper. Fire chief Elwin Billings stated, "Not all the fire apparatus in Chicago could have saved the high school building from destruction." The building and all contents were a total loss. Immediately after the fire, citizens, businesses, fraternal lodges, and churches came forth to offer classroom space. With students dispersed, the school year continued while officials laid plans for a new school.

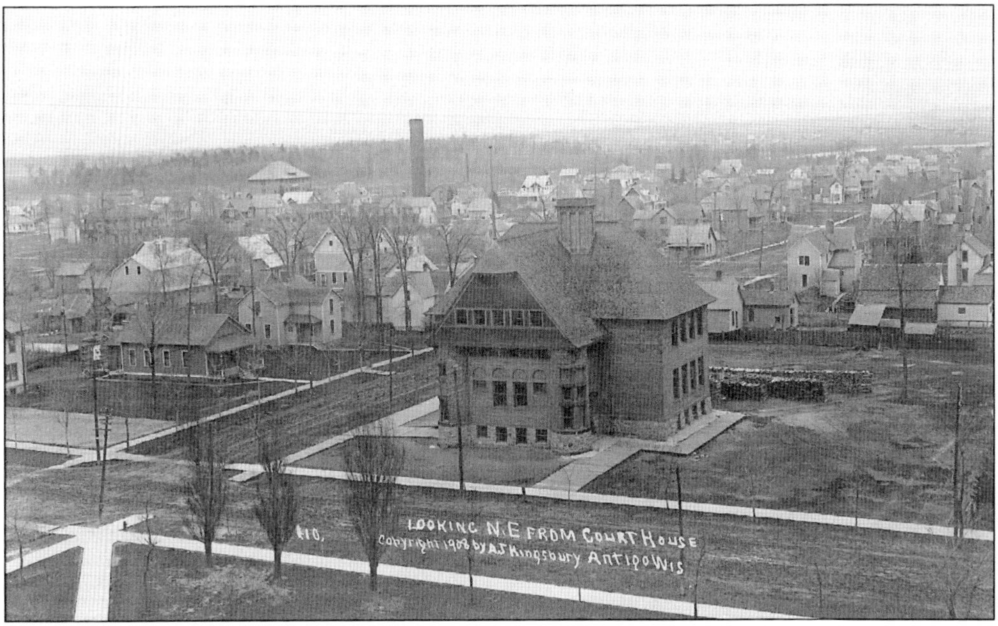

Directly across from the courthouse was the second ward elementary school, one of six elementary schools in Antigo. All of the elementary schools were built in similar styles between 1896 and 1906. This school was the first and was built at a cost of $6,868. It was designed by the Madison firm of Conover and Porter. Alan Conover was also the architect who designed the Antigo Library building.

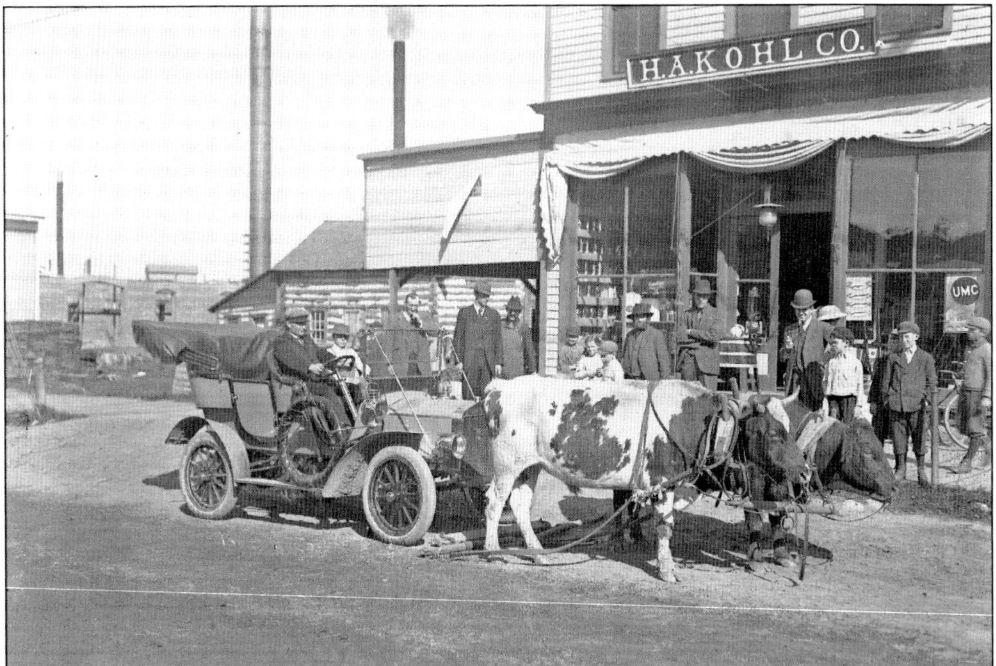

Modern modes of transportation such as the automobile were not always reliable. This was particularly true in northern Wisconsin, where roads could be very poor, particularly after heavy rains. Drivers sometimes had to revert to the old ways.

Two

A.J. Kingsbury, Photographer

A.J. Kingsbury maintained a successful commercial photography business for 46 years. Primarily dependent on retail sales, Kingsbury's shop offered a growing inventory of his favorite product, real-photo postcards, as well as many practical supplies for amateur photographers.

Although Kingsbury's Antigo storefront changed locations many times, he remained in the heart of the business district. To build name recognition, both the firm's store name and advertisements always included the words "Kingsbury" and "Kodak" until at least 1926.

During the early 1930s, Kingsbury was a member of the Antigo Camera Club. William Grosnick, also a member then, fondly recalled the club as a relaxing social setting during the lean years of the Great Depression.

Pat Kolz had been a clerk in Kingsbury's shop from 1935 to 1940. In a 1996 telephone interview, she stated that except for store employees, all of whom addressed the owner as "Mr. Kingsbury," nearly everyone else just called him "A.J." Pat remembered that during her employment, Kingsbury's manner was never rushed, he truly enjoyed his work, and he spent a lot of time behind the camera. In fact, she found him easy to work for because he spent so much time out of town.

Each summer in the late 1930s (and possibly earlier), Kingsbury traveled to Arkansas's Ozark Mountains to take pictures for several resorts. He would work there for a couple weeks and then return home to develop the films and make prints. He then shipped the finished photographs back to the Ozark resort managers.

Over the decades, he built a large portion of his business by taking pictures for resorts in northern Wisconsin, particularly in the areas around Woodruff and Minocqua. Most of this involved the resorts hiring Kingsbury to shoot attractive scenes on their properties, from which he would print an agreed-upon number of photograph postcards. The resorts then purchased them to resell to visiting tourists.

Kingsbury's later years were spent less behind the camera and more in the store's retail business. Photograph postcard demand had diminished, competition had increased, and the local newspaper hired its own photographer.

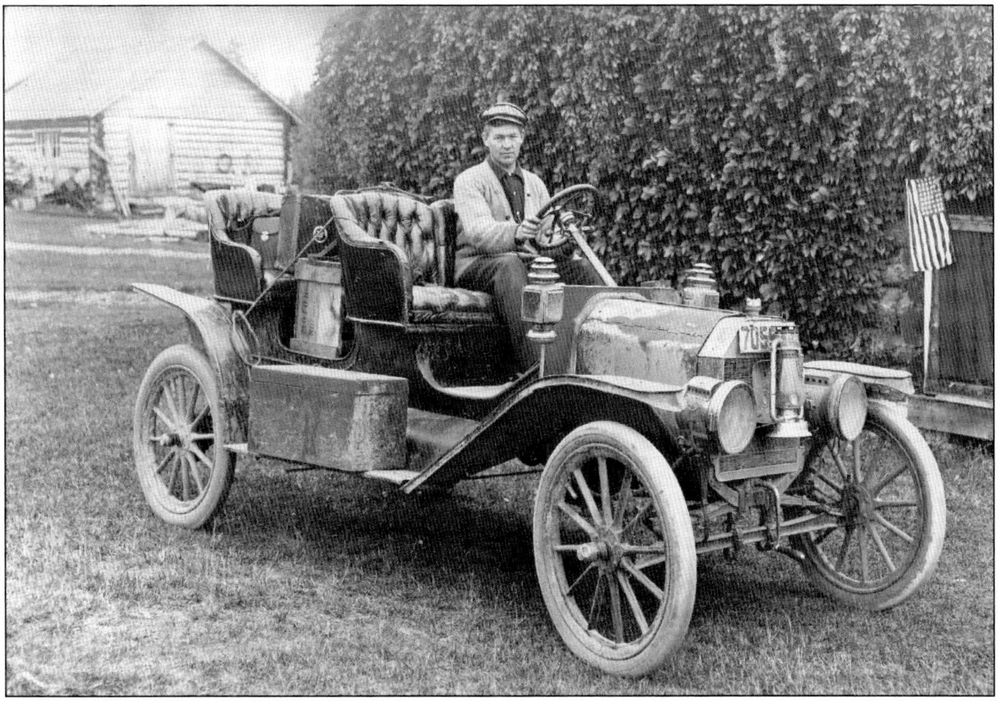

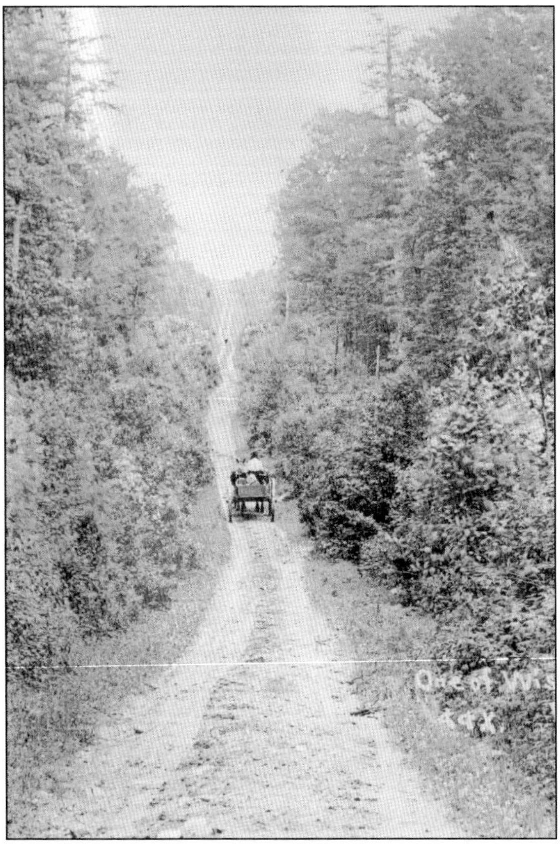

With his professional equipment carefully piled and roped into his topless, hand-cranked c. 1908 Model T Ford, Kingsbury navigated the rutted dirt and gravel roads of northern Wisconsin, occasionally crossing into Michigan's Upper Peninsula. Many of his most popular 1908 and 1909 photographs of Indian tribes were acquired in spite of the poor roads between villages. But Kingsbury never let nature stop his wanderings.

Several years later, the *Weekly News Item* newspaper wrote this news piece: "A number of automobile accidents was reported Monday. A.J. Kingsbury had a collision on his way home from Woodruff receiving cuts and bruises not serious though his car was badly damaged." (Courtesy of Prestor Pictures.)

Still early in Kingsbury's career, he parked his Ford automobile in front of his shop. He had customized the vehicle by removing the back seat and adding a very practical storage box that advertised, "Photographs and Post Cards Kodak Film Developed." Note that a c. 1913 portable outboard motor (probably an Evinrude) is attached atop the rear box.

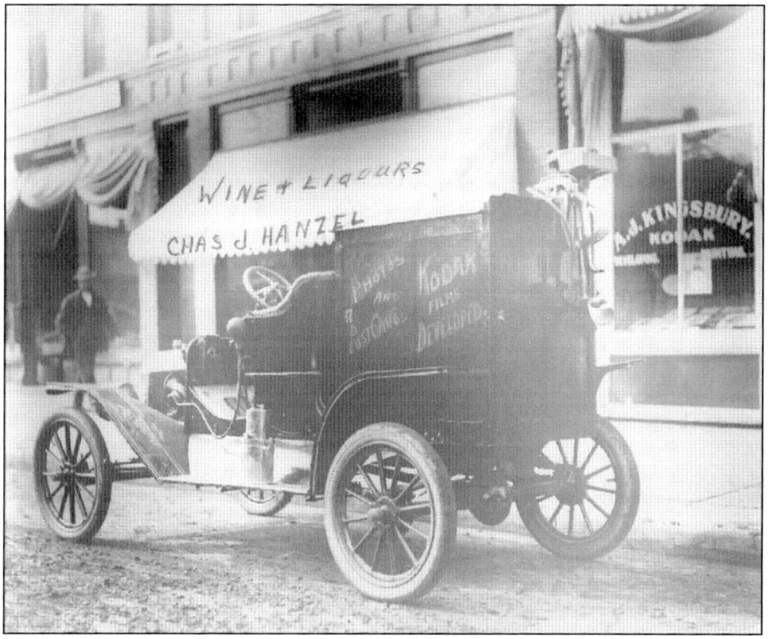

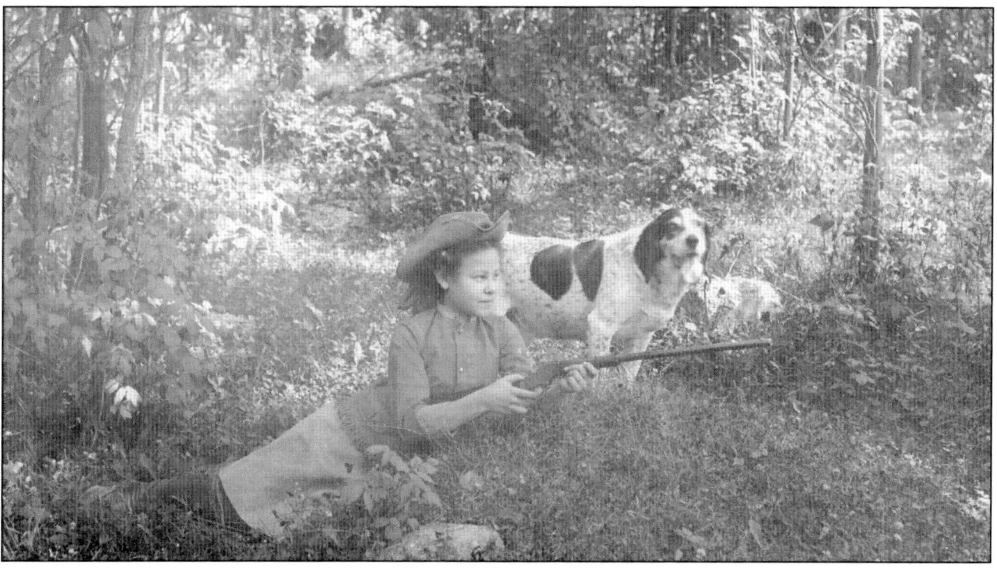

Sometimes, local residents and visitors would hire Kingsbury to photograph them for special occasions, much as this young lady did. She sent this undated real-photo postcard to David Duffey in Marion, Wisconsin. Her exact message on the back of this card was, "Dearest Dave, this picture I had taken a week ago. Hope you like. am always thinking of you darling. With 10,000 kisses. Please write. Beunka." (Courtesy of Prestor Pictures.)

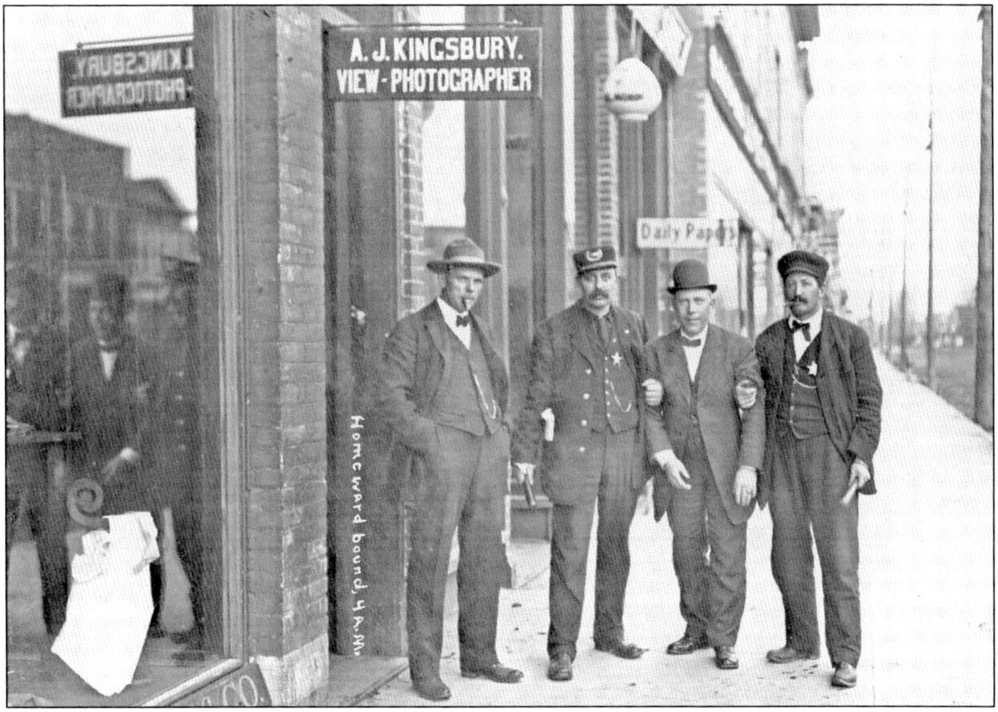

Notwithstanding this gag photograph on June 29, 1921, the *Antigo Daily Journal* wrote that Kingsbury purchased "a complete outfit for photographing finger prints . . . [he] seized an opportunity to put his outfit to service during the recent robbery. He obtained a cash box which had been rifled by the criminals and photographed a number of finger prints left. . . . These photographs would have been sufficient to convict the men of their crime even if further evidence was lacking."

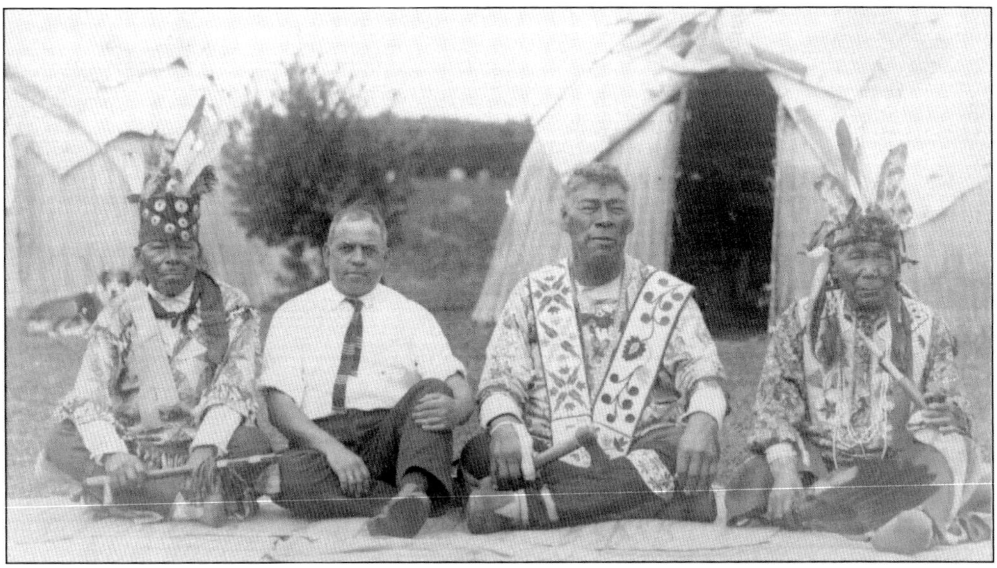

Kingsbury sometimes referred to himself with the nickname "Happy," and happy he was when immersed in Wisconsin's northern life. Here, he sits with three Ojibwe men. It seems that Kingsbury respected the tribes he photographed, but it is likely that he also paid more for people to pose for him than some other photographers did.

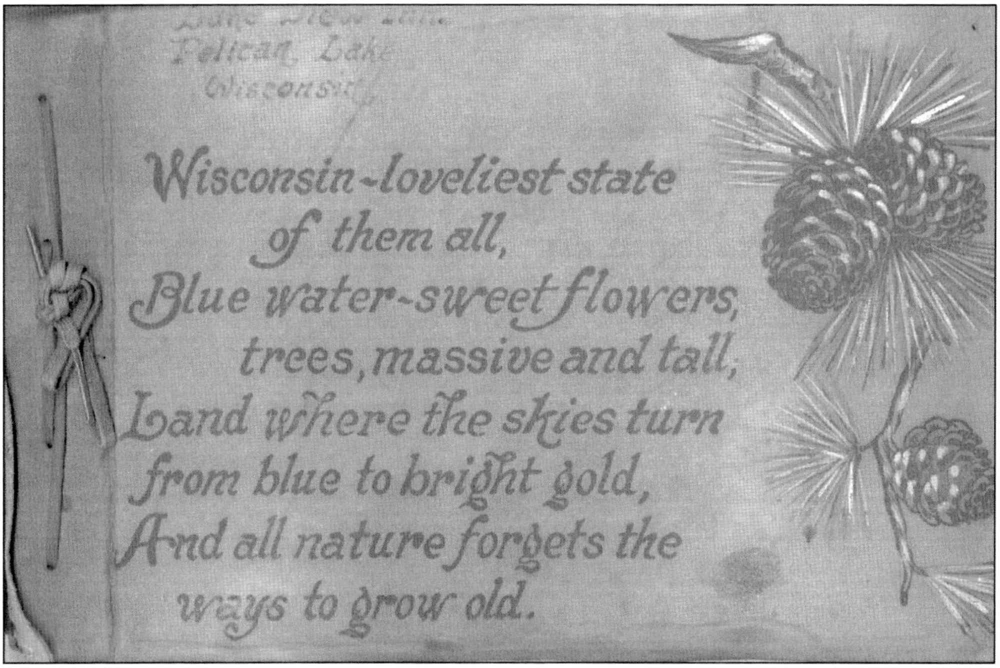

A fine example of Kingsbury's work is this display album. He presented it to the Lake View Inn, a hotel that opened in 1924 on Pelican Lake in Oneida County. With 72 postcards on standard 9.5-inch-by-6.5-inch black pages, it is covered with soft deer hide. The pine needles are hand painted green with white highlights. The album, available for casual viewing in the inn's lobby, advertised Kingsbury's services. (Courtesy of Prestor Pictures.)

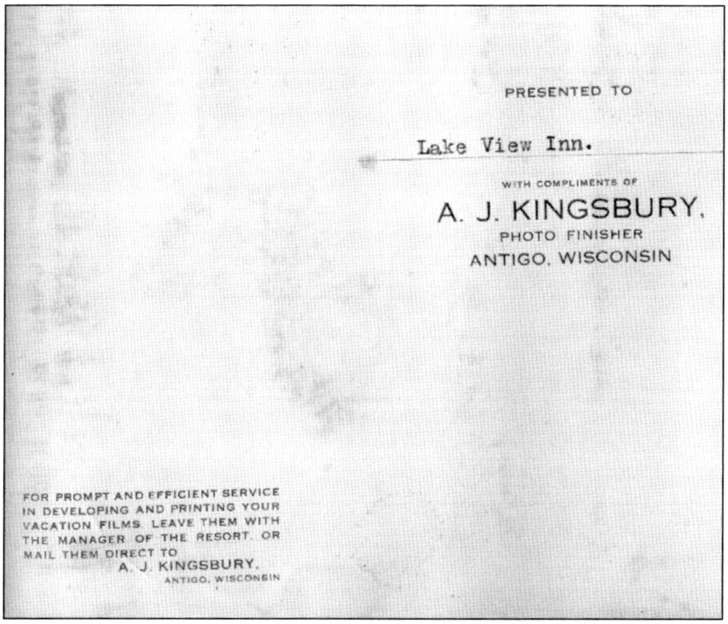

Here is a portion of the album's title page. The name "Lake View Inn" is manually typed in, which indicates that Kingsbury probably made similar albums as marketing tools. The album contains a variety of real-photo postcards, including shots of cabins, country and lake scenes, live wild animals, various fish and deer game trophies, and over a dozen images of Indians posing for the camera. (Courtesy of Prestor Pictures.)

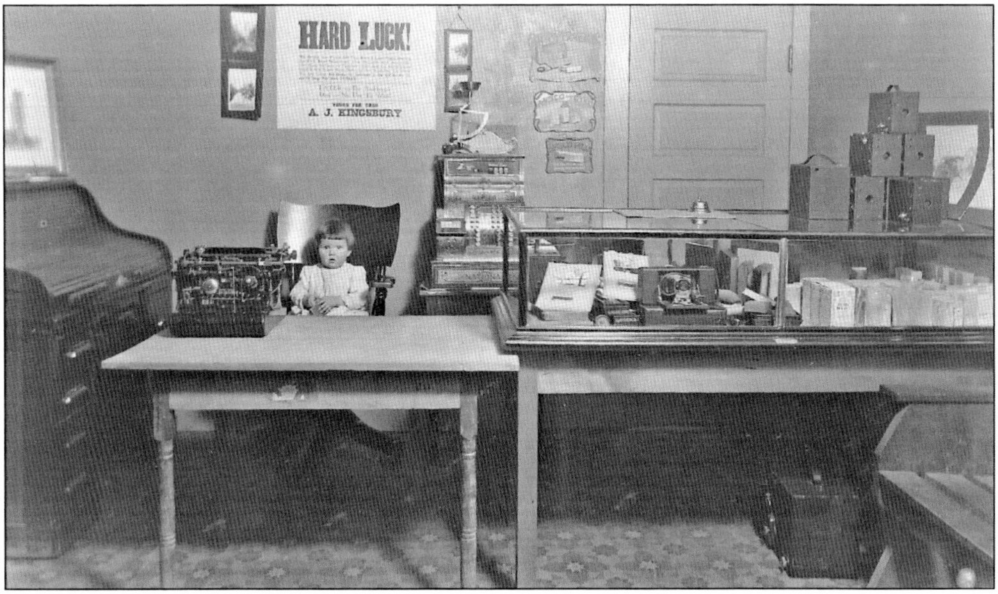

This may be Kingsbury's very first store. The simple display case exhibits a small selection of new cameras, film, and picture developing chemicals. Hanging on the wall near the fine National cash register are three tin plaques advertising Ansco cameras, chemicals, and Ansco film. This is a bit of a surprise; it was thought he sold only Kodak merchandise in the early years. The little girl in the photograph may Kingsbury's only daughter, Doris.

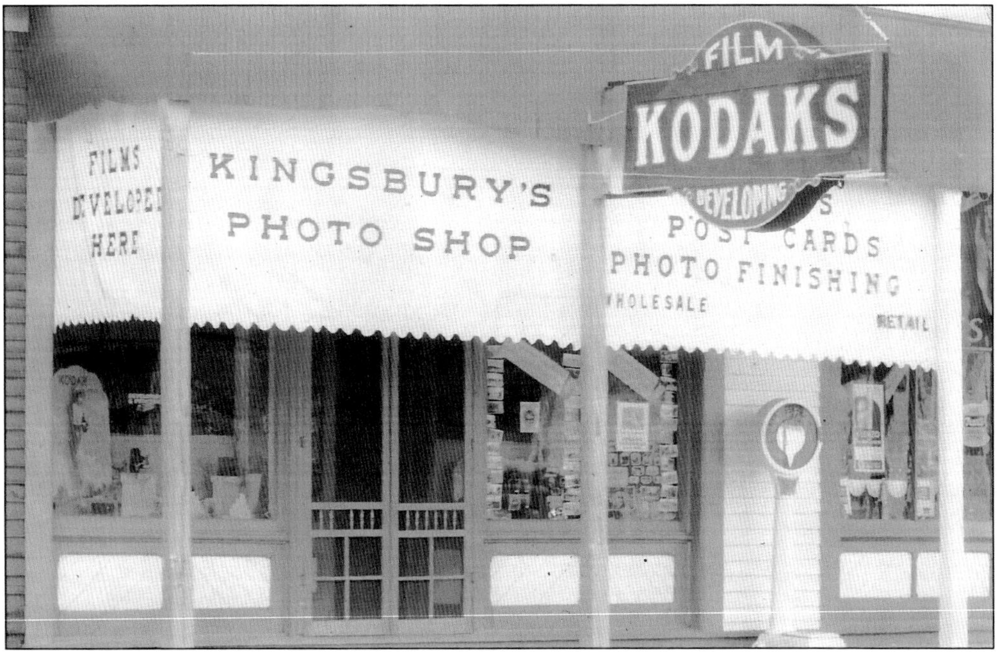

This 1920s Kingsbury store had canvas stretched between posts over the sidewalk to prevent direct sunlight from damaging items in the window displays. The left window presented several new cameras, rolls of new film, and a couple of Kodak-provided advertisements. The window to the right of the double screen doors is mostly filled with photographs and real-photo postcards of area scenes and people.

By the late 1930s, the Antigo Camera Club had faded away, further reducing Kingsbury's income. His business continued on through the Depression, although he found it necessary to sell his Minoqua shop in 1940. Here is a newspaper ad of that era, probably from the fall of 1940, when he moved into a more modern location. It was at this 705 Fifth Avenue store that Kingsbury began selling greeting cards year-round.

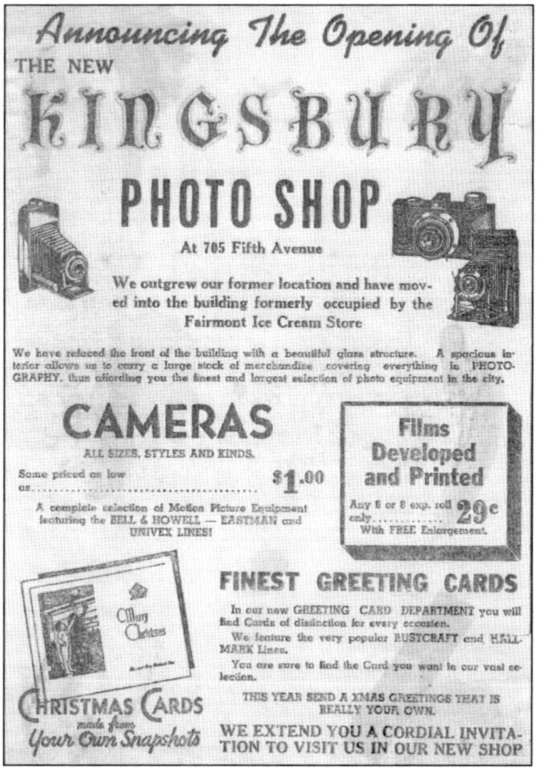

Announcing The Opening Of

THE NEW

KINGSBURY

PHOTO SHOP

At 705 Fifth Avenue

We outgrew our former location and have moved into the building formerly occupied by the Fairmont Ice Cream Store

We have refaced the front of the building with a beautiful glass structure. A spacious interior allows us to carry a large stock of merchandise covering everything in PHOTOGRAPHY, thus affording you the finest and largest selection of photo equipment in the city.

CAMERAS

ALL SIZES, STYLES AND KINDS.

Some priced as low as $1.00

A complete selection of Motion Picture Equipment featuring the BELL & HOWELL — EASTMAN and UNIVEX LINES!

Films Developed and Printed

Any 6 or 8 exp. roll only 29c

With FREE Enlargement.

FINEST GREETING CARDS

In our new GREETING CARD DEPARTMENT you will find Cards of distinction for every occasion.

We feature the very popular RUSTCRAFT and HALLMARK Lines.

You are sure to find the Card you want in our vast selection.

CHRISTMAS CARDS made from Your Own Snapshots

THIS YEAR SEND A XMAS GREETINGS THAT IS REALLY YOUR OWN.

WE EXTEND YOU A CORDIAL INVITATION TO VISIT US IN OUR NEW SHOP

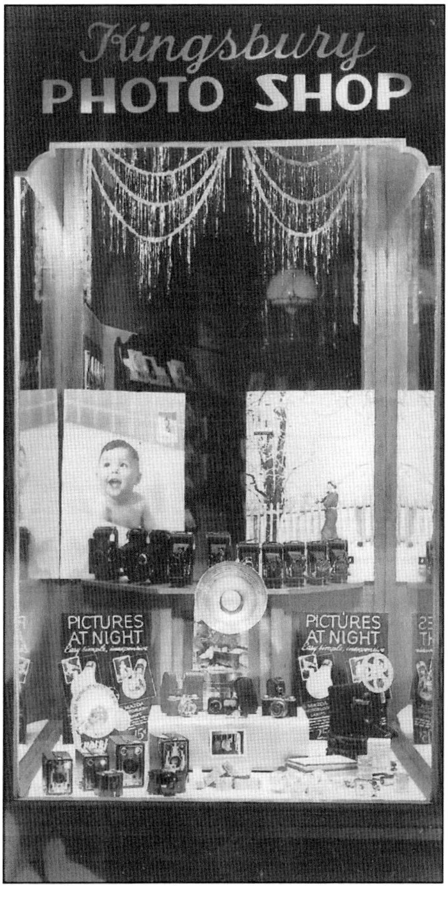

Here is a 1940s store window before Christmas. Besides a variety of still cameras for sale, Kingsbury offers movie cameras and projectors. The "Pictures at Night" posters are advertising Mazda photoflood lamps for 25¢ and photoflash lamps for 15¢.

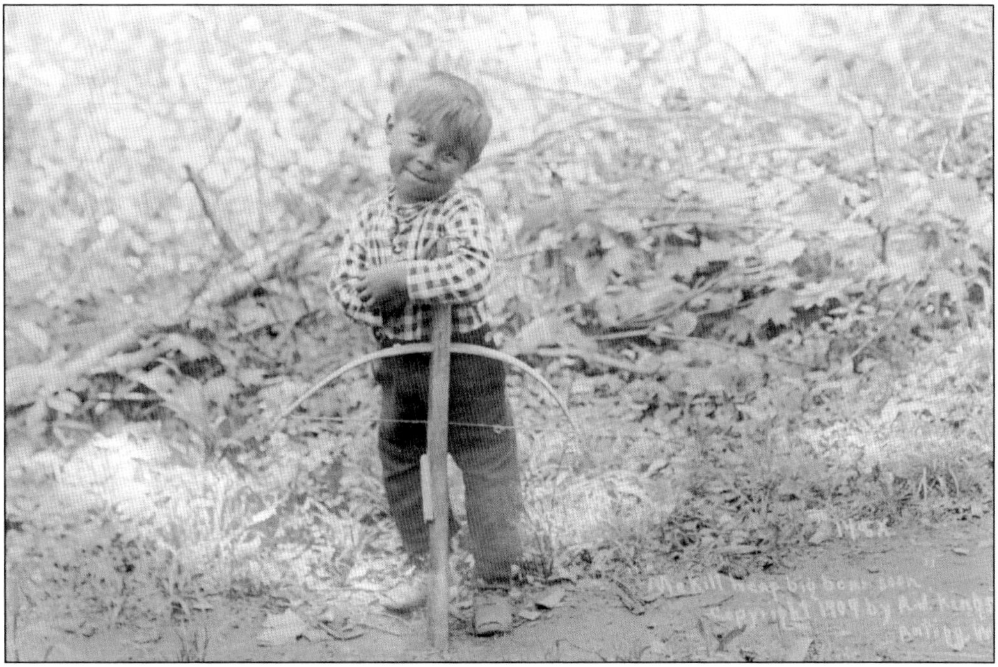

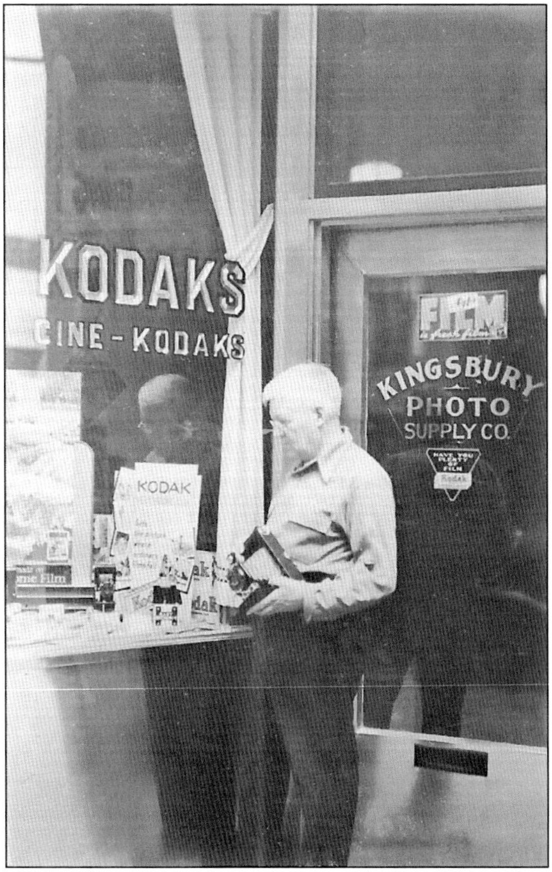

It is unknown when Kingsbury stopped driving through the North Woods or broke off his contacts with the Indian tribes. Because of the tragic 1967 studio fire, it is not possible to make an educated guess as to which photograph subjects were his favorites over the years. (Courtesy of Prestor Pictures.)

Kingsbury, who was elected vice president of the Photo Finishers of Wisconsin when that organization was created in 1924, recorded Wisconsin's northern development. In 1952, seventy-six-year-old Kingsbury sold his business. On May 22, 1956, he passed away while visiting his son Claire in Tulsa, Oklahoma. But thankfully, a wonderful Kingsbury legacy survives.

Three

Gateway to the North Woods

When Wisconsin achieved statehood in 1848, much of the North Woods was only sparsely populated, but economic development after the Civil War brought an influx of settlers to the region.

Langlade County's first white settler, Willard Ackley, set up a trading post and farm on the Eau Claire River in 1853. By 1879, settlers Charles Lazerlere and Squire Taylor convincingly argued for the establishment of New County. A year later, it was renamed Langlade after Charles de Langlade, who fought with the French in the French and Indian War. At the time, the total county population was 685, and some duties were administered by neighboring Shawano County.

County borders shifted over the next few years, but by the mid-1880s, Langlade County was well established, and by 1890, the population had grown to 9,465. Counties to the north, such as Oneida, Vilas, Forest, Iron, and Florence, were established by the turn of the 20th century.

All logging camps were close to the Wolf River in the early years, but with railroad expansion, it became feasible to log in areas around Antigo and Elcho. By the early part of the 20th century, the hardwood and conifer forests were rapidly becoming depleted. Lumber companies sold off their holdings as farmland.

Many farming settlers were Poles and Bohemians, with significant numbers of Germans and Americans from the east. One interesting group came to rural Langlade and Forest Counties from parts of eastern Kentucky. By 1903 or 1904, these "Kentucks" had formed a virtual island of mountain culture in northern Wisconsin. When Prohibition came in 1919, small family-run moonshine stills began to thrive.

Increasingly, in southern Langlade County, the plow replaced the ax, exposing fine farming soil left by the glacier's retreat. With miles of forests, thousands of lakes, and excellent fishing and hunting resources, Langlade County and other northern counties saw strong development as recreational and tourist attractions. Tourism was often linked to the resorts run by local Indian tribes, whose members were also hired out as hunting and fishing guides and sold souvenirs to visitors.

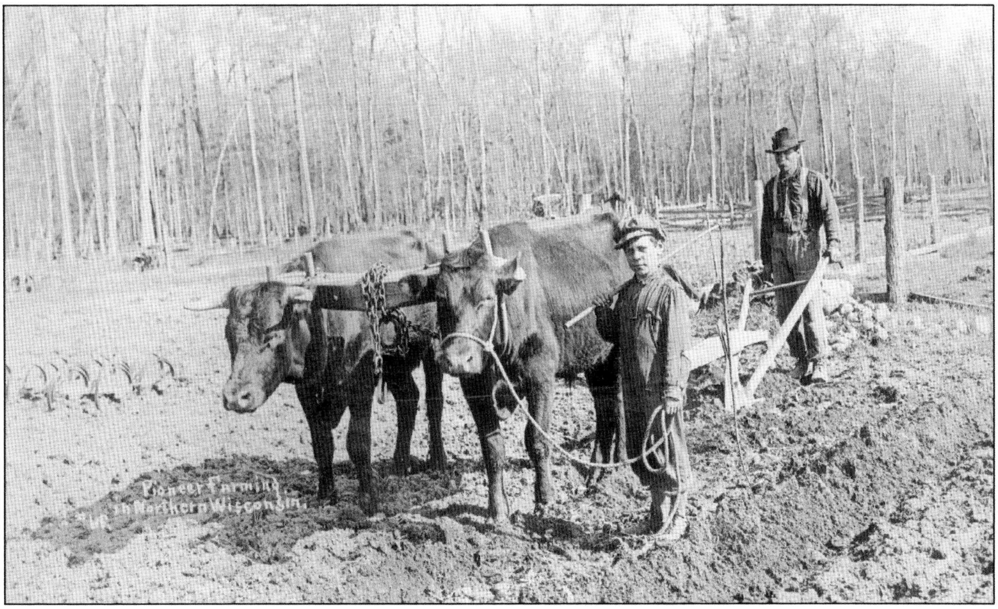

The area, known as "the Antigo Flats," contains rich soil created by glacial outwashes. In fact, Antigo Silt Loam is the official state soil. Once the forests were harvested, farmers moved in. In many cases, would-be farmers were able to purchase land on the promise of timber sales. (Courtesy of Prestor Pictures.)

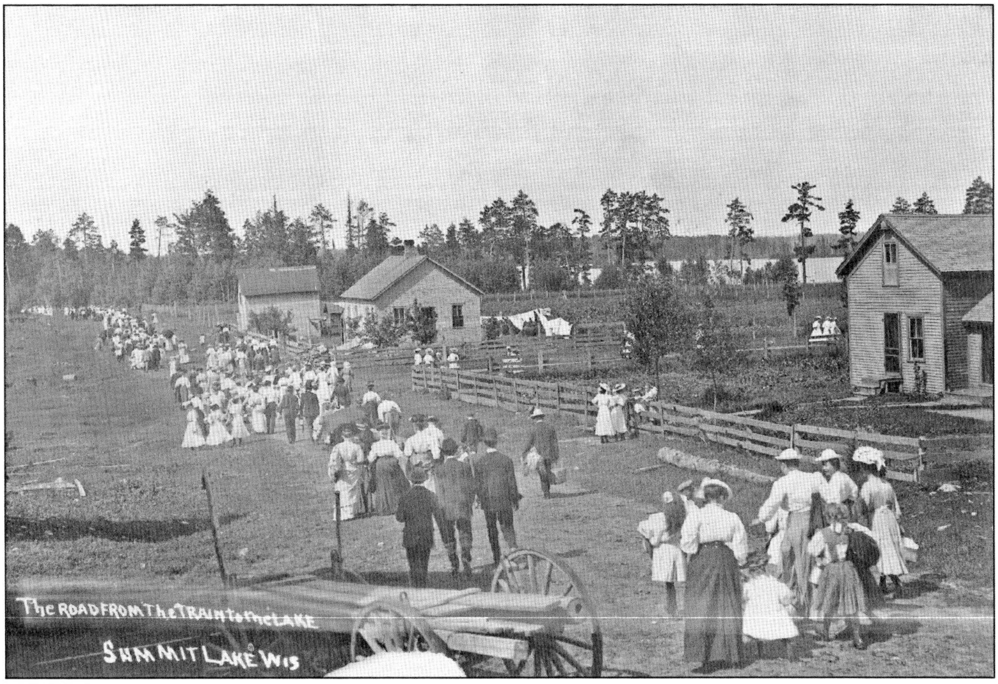

Summit Lake was, and continues to be, a small resort community about 15 miles north of Antigo in Langlade County, directly on the Chicago & North Western rail line. The people shown here are Sunday afternoon picnickers who took the train from Antigo and are now walking along the path from the depot to the lake.

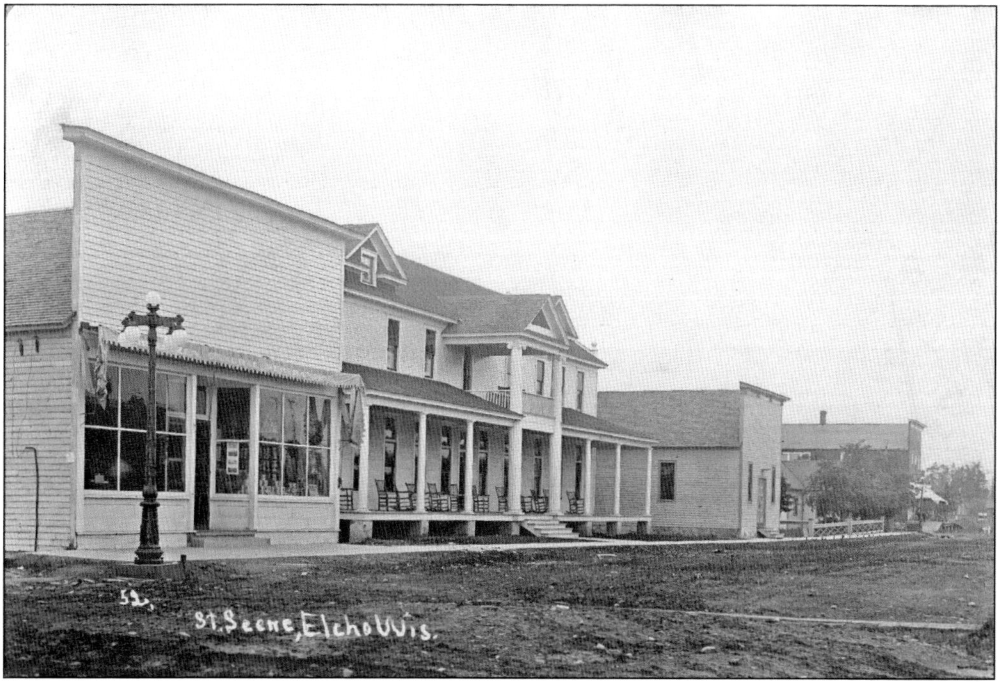

The town of Elcho, located at the northern edge of Langlade County, developed along with Antigo in the late 19th century. Charlie Fish was a Great Lakes sailor and prospector in the Klondike before he decided to settle in Elcho. His Fish Lumber Company in town was a major employer in Langlade County and one of the largest lumber companies in northern Wisconsin.

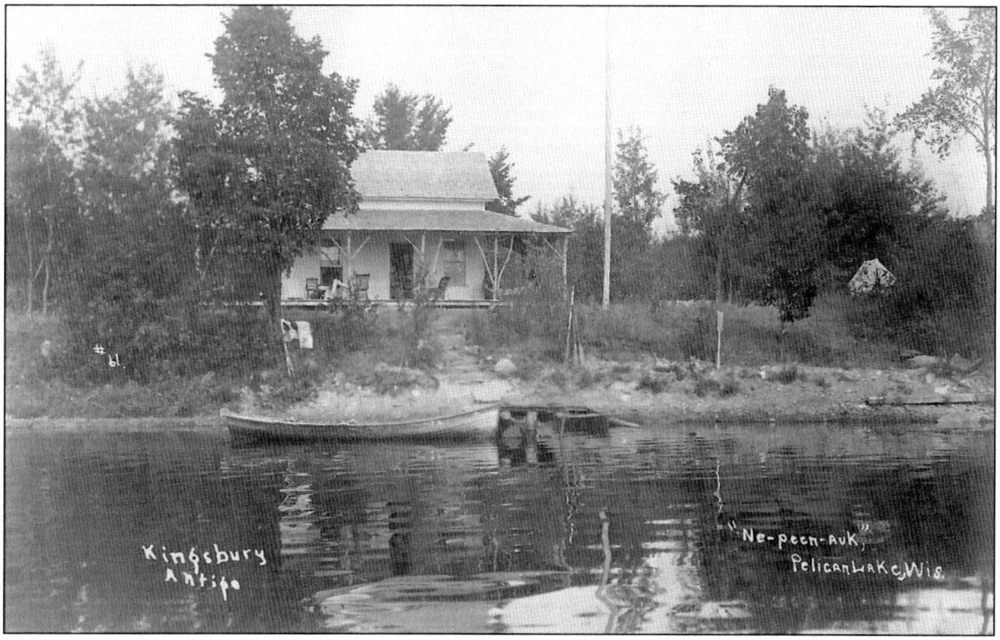

Pelican Lake in the southern part of Oneida County was ringed with cottages and a few resort hotels. In its early years as a tourist destination, there were no reliable roads to Pelican Lake; the Chicago & North Western Railway was the main way of getting there.

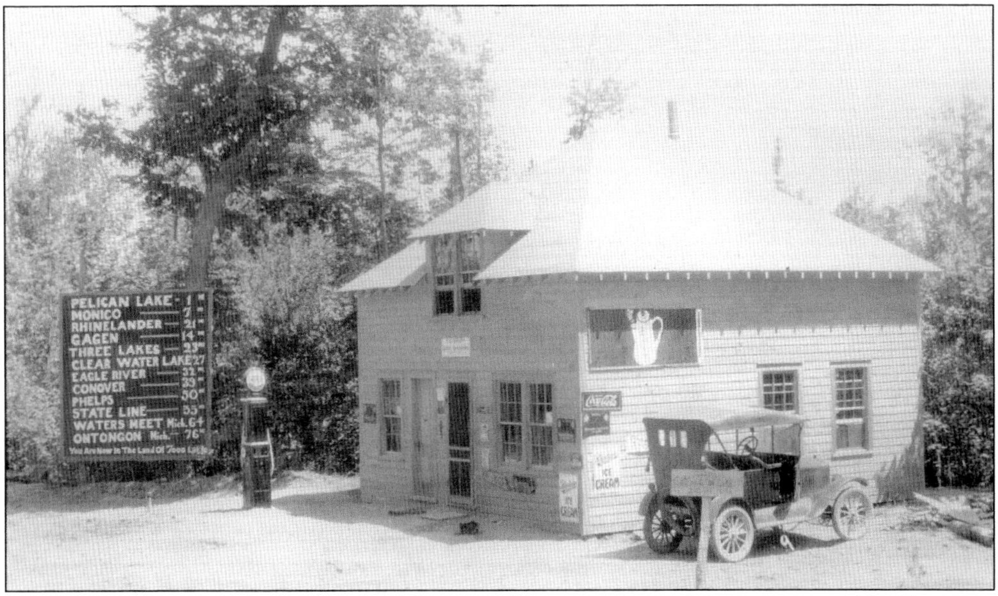

Once roadways became common, if seldom paved, one-pump convenience stores, like this 1924 business, were established. The huge sign showing distances was a useful aid when maps were unreliable. Notice the building's two narrow doors. The right door led into the Coffee Pot, a small restaurant providing lunch, sandwiches, soda pops, and Rhinelander Ice Cream. The left door may have been for a gasoline attendant or for living quarters. (Courtesy of Prestor Pictures.)

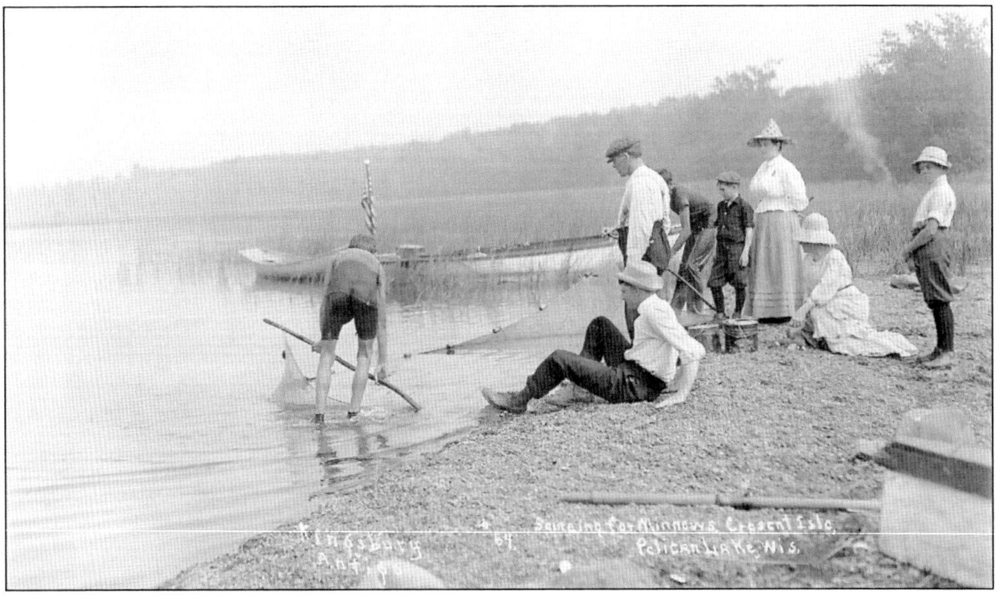

At the dawn of the 20th century, the *Antigo Weekly* newspaper noted that the land around Pelican Lake and its islands were "worthy of a place in the history of Wisconsin" for being the former home of the Ojibwe. Although the Indians coexisted peacefully with vacationers who established cottages in the area, they eventually moved on.

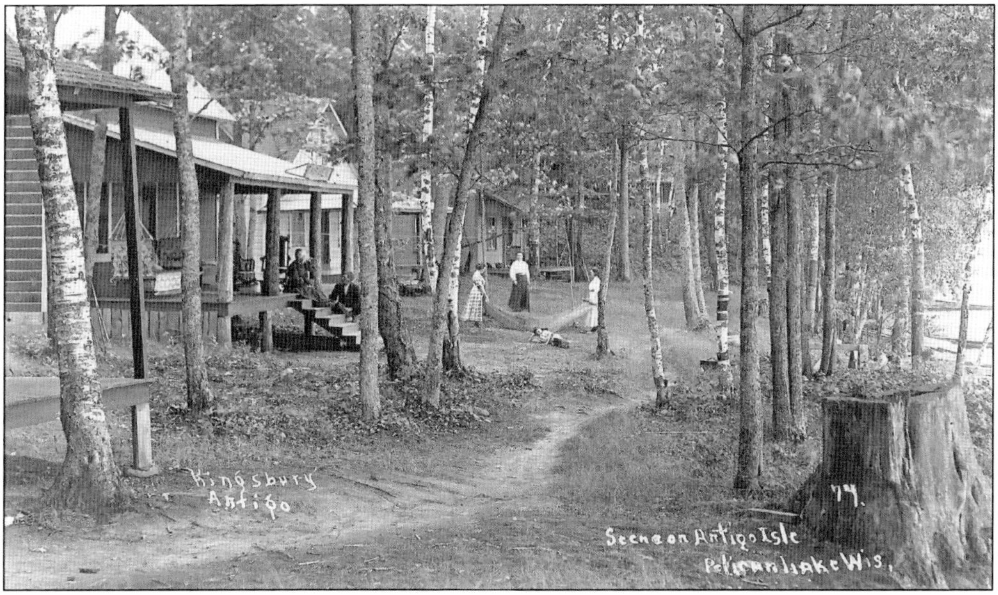

Antigo Island in Pelican Lake contained an association of cottage owners, including many important residents of Antigo who have used the island since the late 19th century. The association had a clubhouse for group activities. Relatives of A.J. Kingsbury owned one of the 18 cottages. Several of those cottages are still in use.

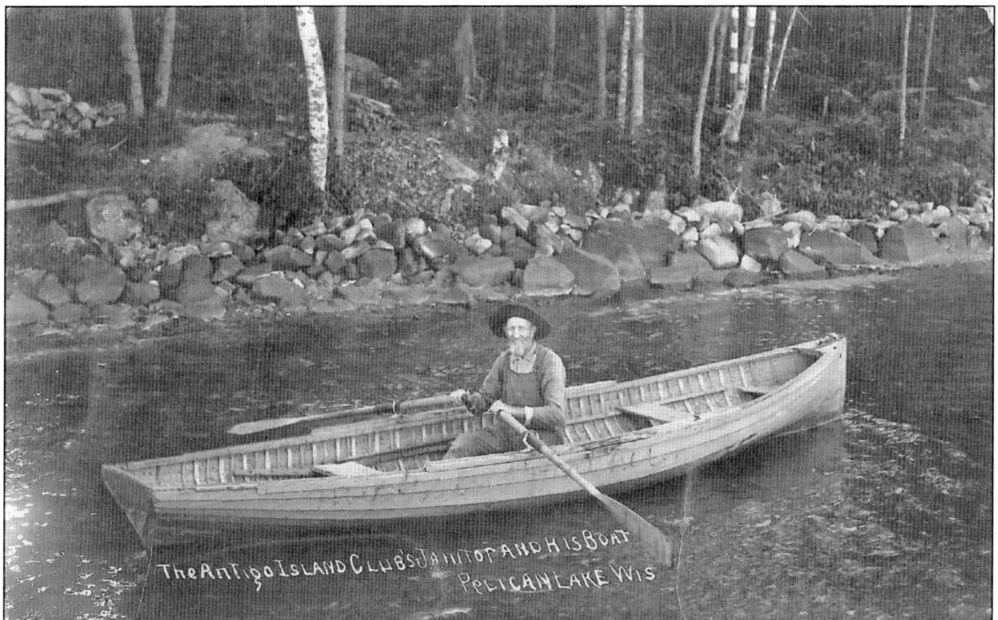

Antigo Island is a 23-acre wooded summer retreat, established in 1896. In 1897, Ed Resing was hired as a janitor for the sum of $300 a year. In addition to maintaining the grounds of the individual properties, he also tended to the single path around the island's perimeter. A 1996 listing showed 18 cottages, one clubhouse, and about 10 boathouses still in use on the island.

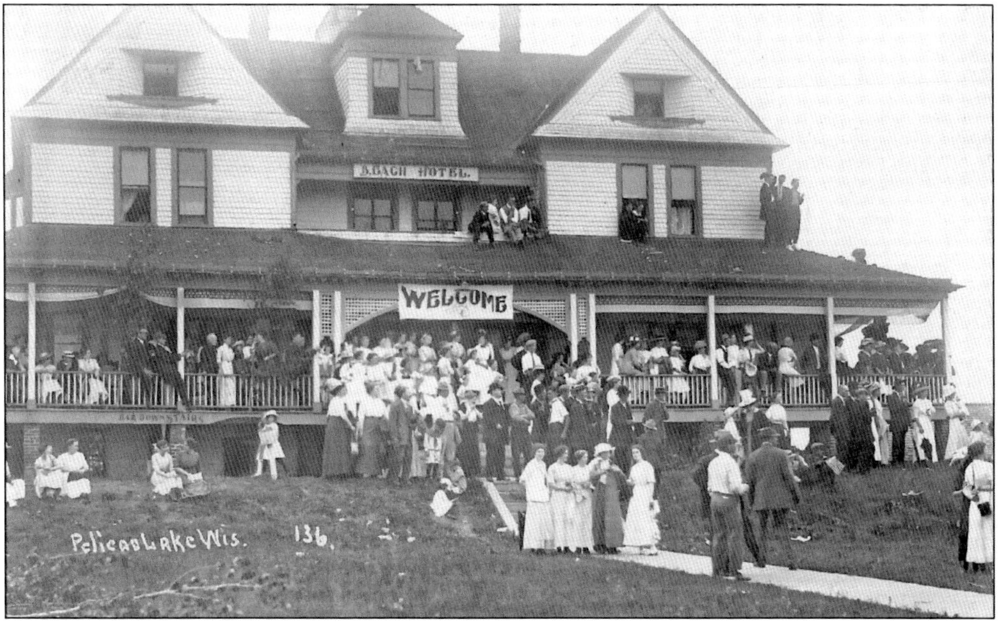

The Beach Hotel on Pelican Lake, built in 1898, was one of the larger hotels in the area. The hotel staged a variety of entertainment for hotel guests and locals. It is thought that the crowd shown in this photograph is observing a boxing match taking place just off to the right. This hotel was severely damaged by fire in 1927 but was rebuilt a year later.

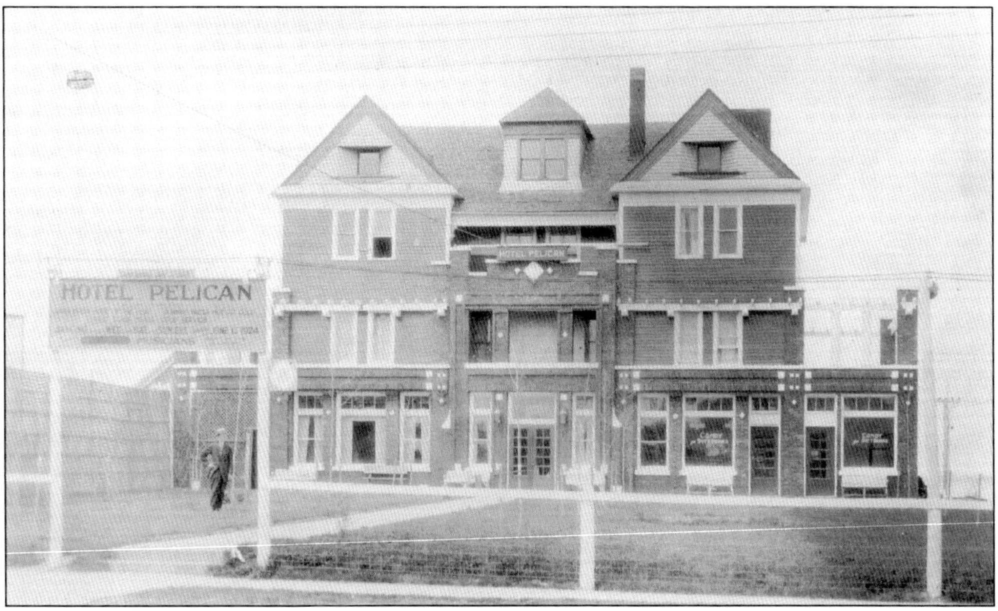

Another fine choice for temporary visitors was the Hotel Pelican. The hotel held its grand-opening party on June 1, 1924. The sign advertises, "Open Every Hour of the Year, First Class Meals, Running Water Hot and Cold, Good Service, Dancing Every WED. and SAT. and SUN. EVE." (Courtesy of Prestor Pictures.)

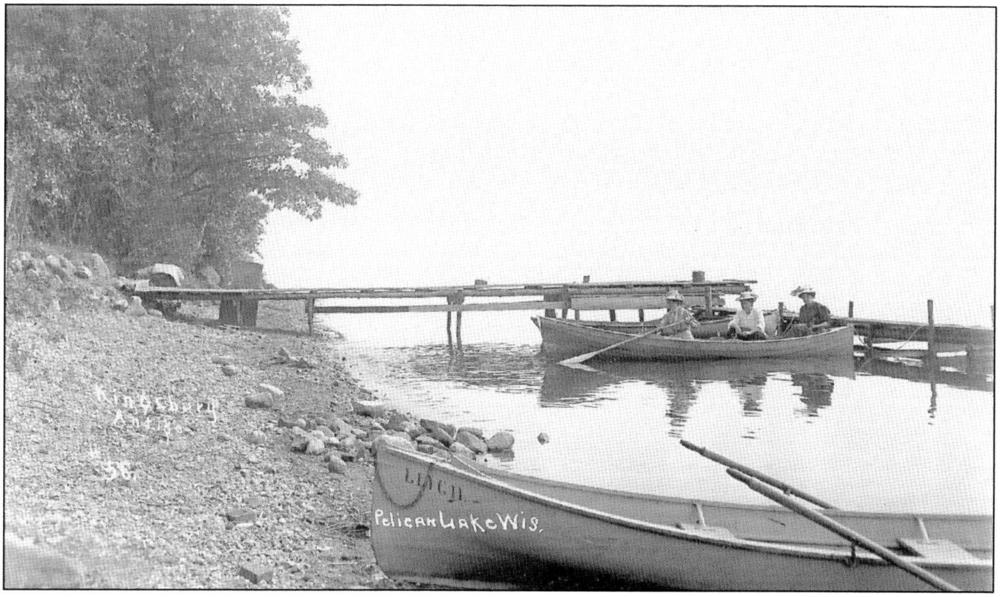

It is interesting to see the formal, and somewhat impractical, clothing worn by men and women as they participated in leisurely activities at the lake. These ladies are having fun in a rowboat on Tomahawk Lake.

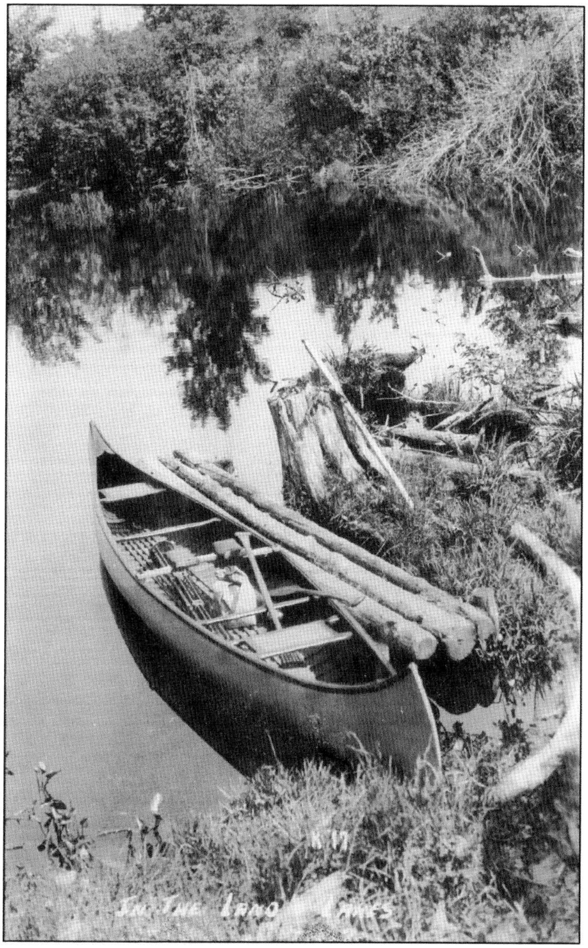

Here is a typical canoe that Kingsbury sometimes used in his searching for new photograph subjects. His large camera tripod lays in the bottom of the canoe, alongside a crumpled brown paper bag. Is it equipment or his lunch? Notice the three logs laying on the shore side of the canoe. Someone, maybe Kingsbury, has attached the three logs together to form a relatively stable and dry stepping platform. (Courtesy of Prestor Pictures.)

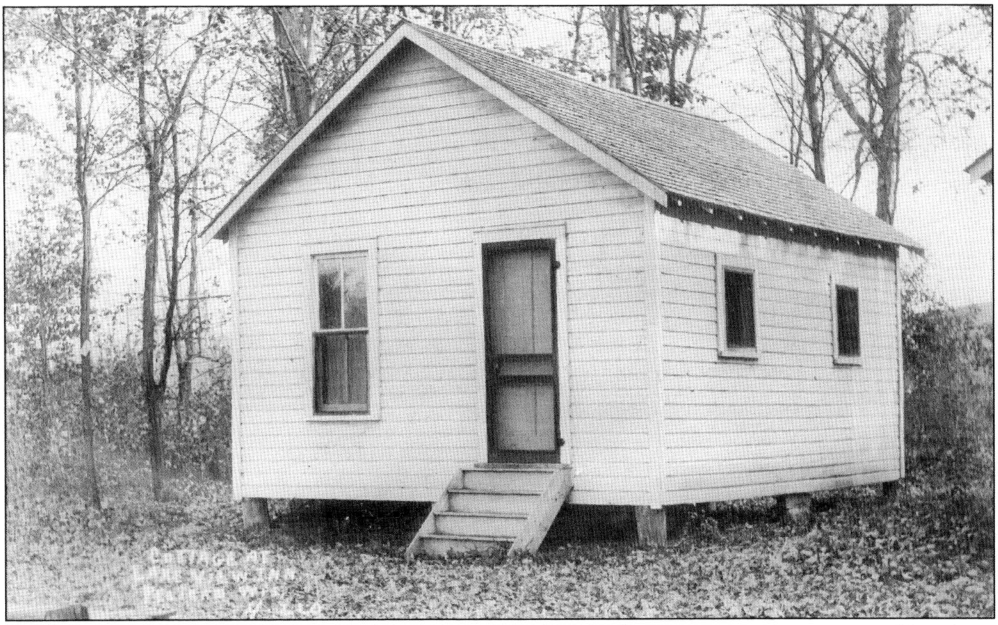

On September 29, 1922, the *Minocqua Times* reported, "Charles E. Lawton, proprietor of Rainbow Resort, situated at the south end of Minocqua Lake, is adding two cottages to his new resort. The cottages are very neat and cozy and will appeal to summer people seeking furnished cottages. The contract for the building was given to Prosper Jossart of Minocqua." The cottage pictured here is not one of the cottages mentioned in the article. (Courtesy of Prestor Pictures.)

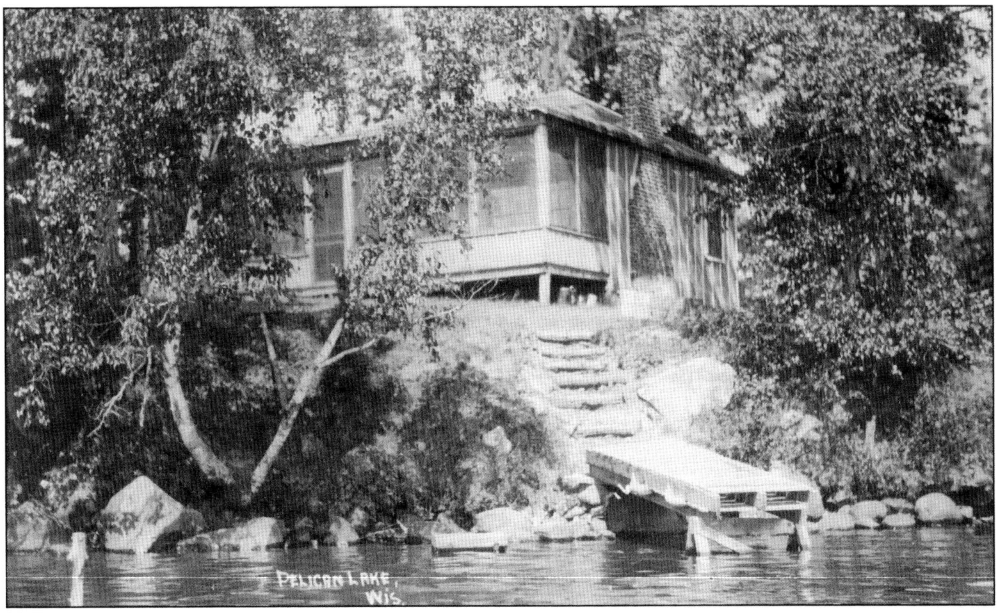

This cottage on Pelican Lake is similar to many in northern Wisconsin. For a city dweller and weekend visitor heading to a lake cottage like this, even the drive through forest- surrounded roads is calming. So, arriving at this rustic summer retreat would be cause for much joy. Light breezes rustling through white birch leaves and the soft lapping of warm waters against an ageless shoreline—it is peace. (Courtesy of Prestor Pictures.)

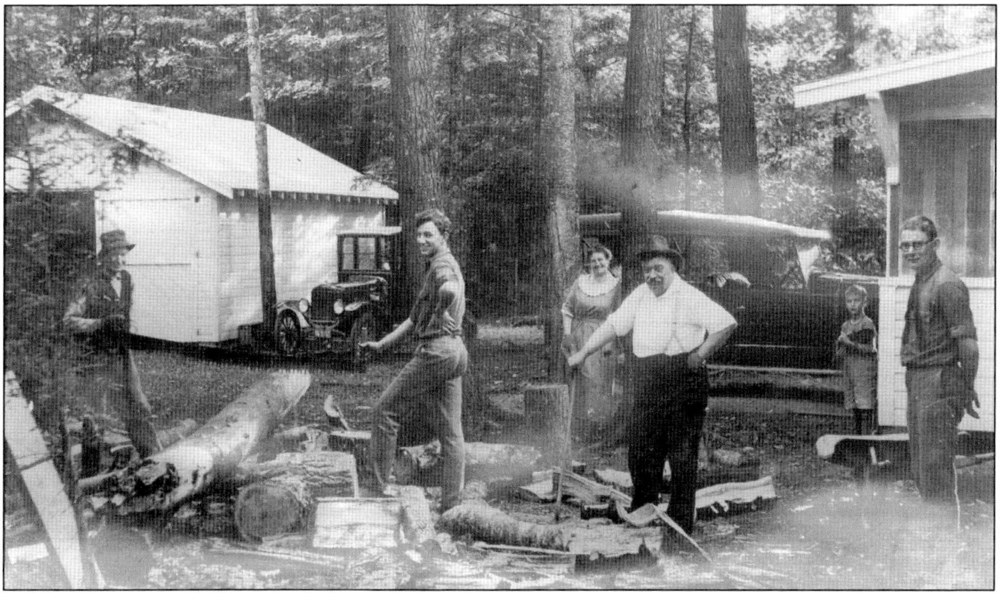

A June 30, 1927, article in the *Vilas County News-Review* read, "A steady and appreciable increase in land values in upper Wisconsin has been observed recently. The most noticeable increase has been in resort property on and near the myriad of lakes in the northern counties of the Wisconsin summerland." It also stated that there were also a "number of tourists who each year are coming into the state to make their summer homes here." (Courtesy of Prestor Pictures.)

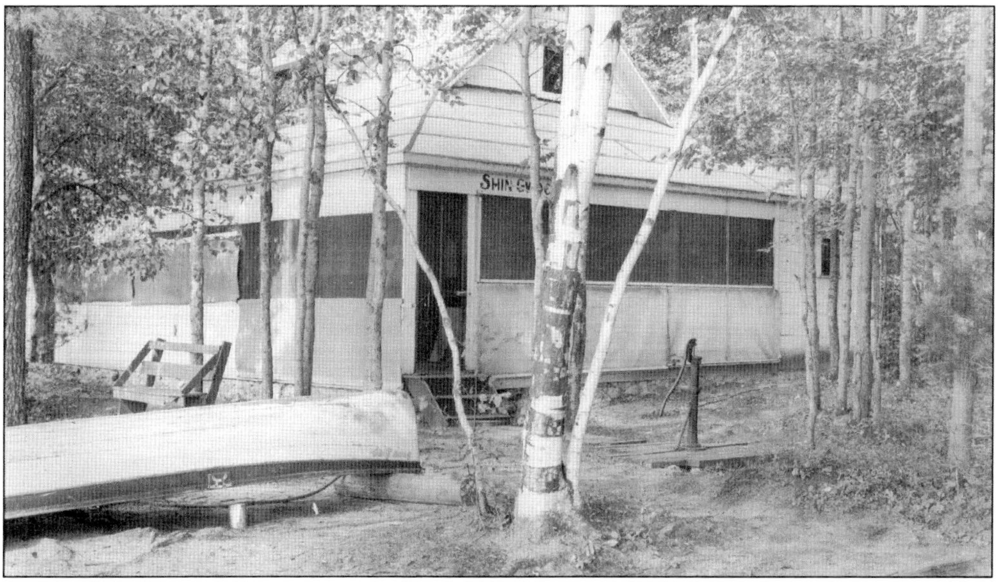

"Mr. and Mrs. Geo. Richardson and son Harold of Chicago arrived Friday at their Lake Katherine summer home [not this cottage] to spend several days. The temperature in Chicago when they left was 84 degrees, and they were somewhat surprised to find the lakes here frozen over, their summer home blocked with snow and the temperatures registering in the thirties," reported the *Minocqua Times* on. (Courtesy of Prestor Pictures.)

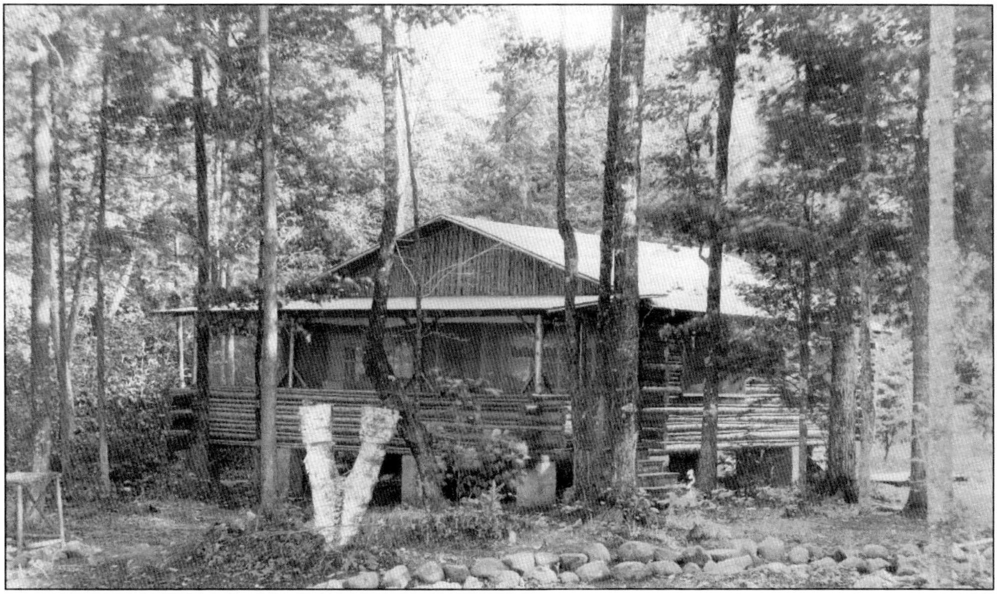

Here is a very sturdy-looking cottage whose walls display a different style, alternating small logs with larger logs. But it has none of the really big logs one usually sees in log buildings. It sports a very smooth, professional-looking roof, a building-wide front porch, and white lace curtains in the front windows. Note the birch bark planters atop the V-shaped tree stumps. (Courtesy of Prestor Pictures.)

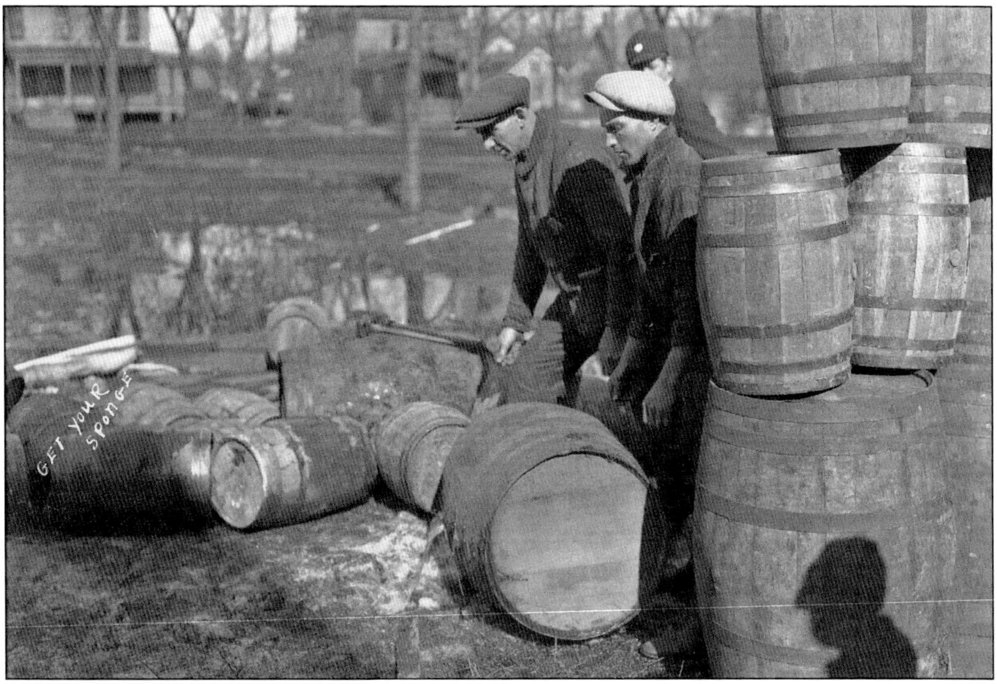

Prohibition, or the "Noble Experiment," was instituted in the United States in 1920 and continued until 1933. This created a booming business in the production of moonshine throughout northern Wisconsin. Railroad cars of sugar were shipped to isolated small towns with no questions asked. Occasionally, however, moonshine operations were broken up by police.

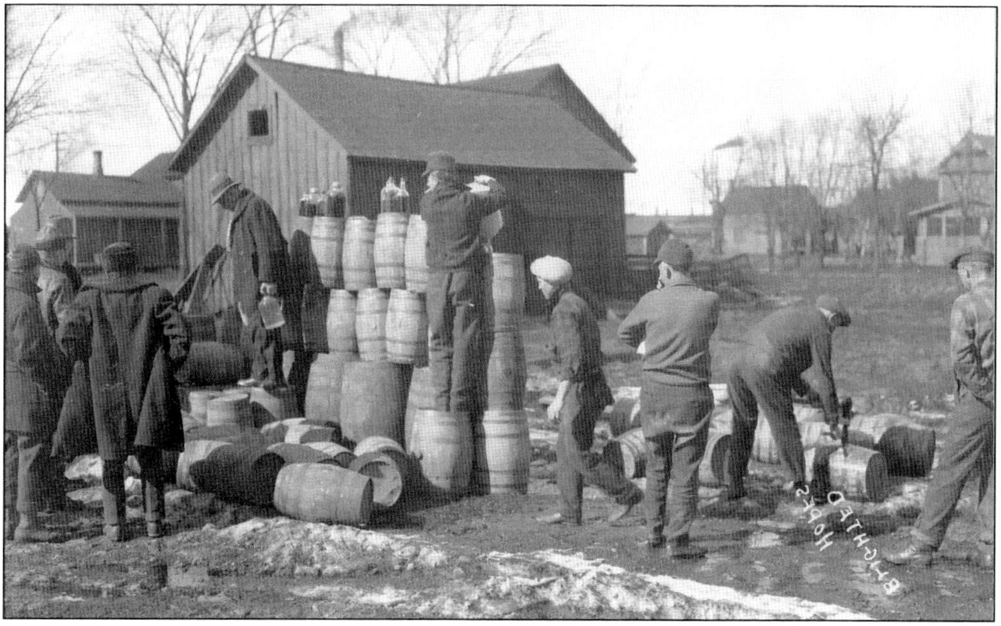

"One of the biggest moonshine raids in the history of the state was made in Forest County by four state prohibition agents. One two hundred gallon still, one two hundred seventy-five gallon still and one three hundred gallon still were confiscated. Six thousand gallons of mash were destroyed. Seven prisoners were taken. All were armed but surrendered without a fight. This district is known as the Kentucky of Wisconsin," reported the *Minocqua Times* on October 6, 1922.

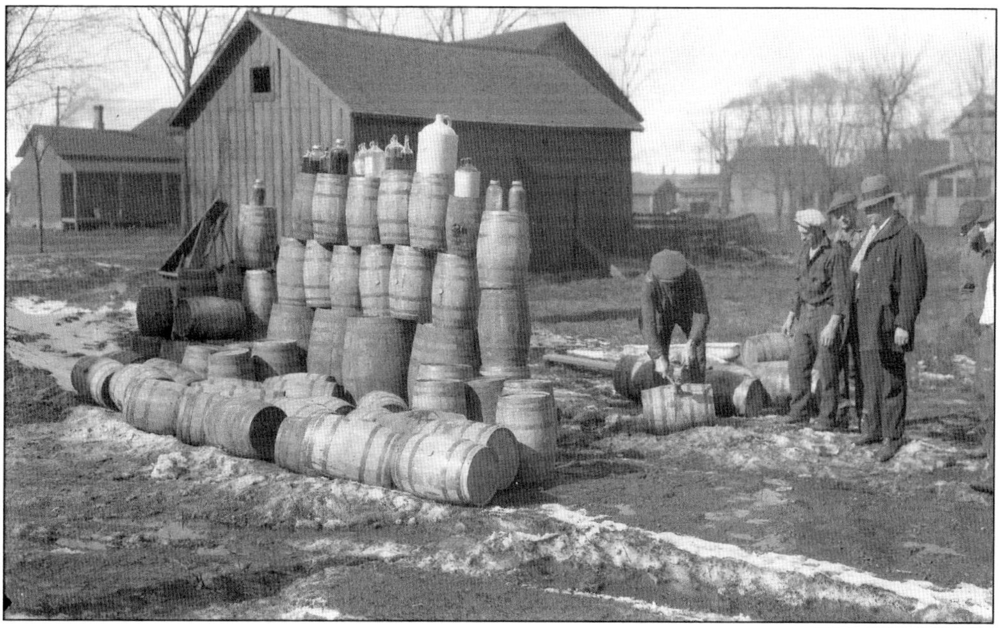

Early moonshine recipes that were brought to the English colonies by Scotch-Irish immigrants called for whatever grain was available. Langlade County moonshiners even used potatoes. Early moonshiners used very little sugar, but with improved transportation and railroads, sugar became readily available. Although this increased the volume of moonshine produced, some claimed there was a "loss of pride in the final product."

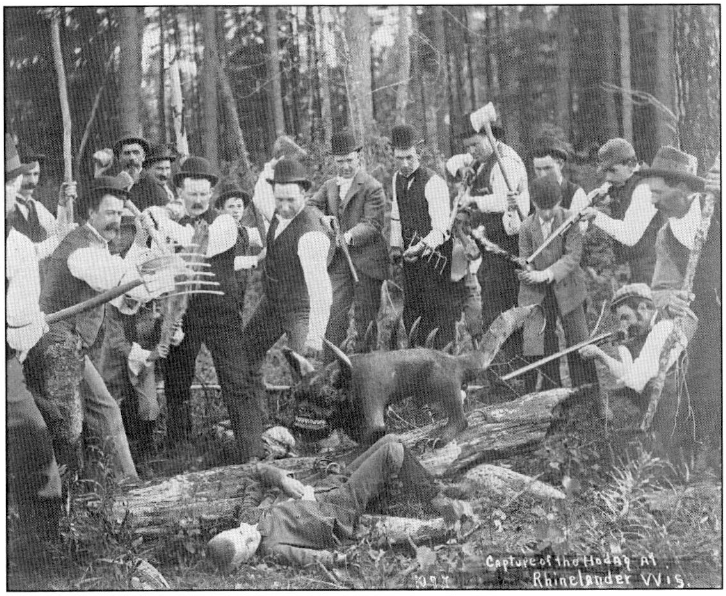

The Hodag is a mythical creature invented by a timber cruiser in Oneida County in the 1890s. Although the hoax was quickly exposed, the Hodag has become the symbol of Rhinelander. Many likenesses, in statues and on souvenirs, may be seen throughout the city. It is the mascot of the local high school sports teams. In some ways, it resembles the mythical water panther of Ojibwe legend.

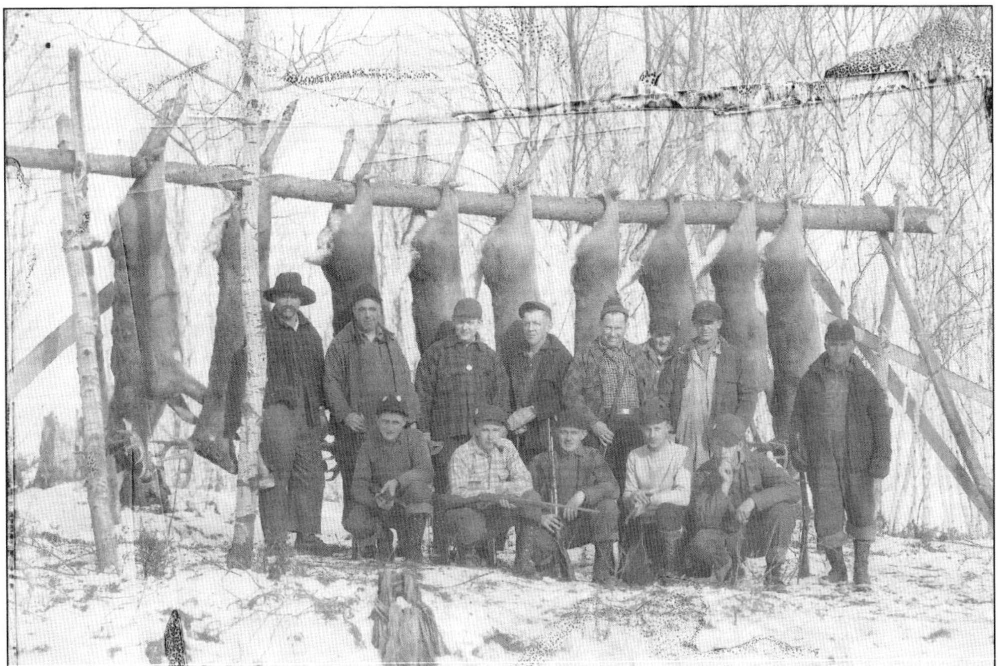

Postcards advertising the abundance of deer hunting greatly benefited the railroads with their increasing networks of rail lines and the lodges that sprang up in northern Wisconsin. But some old timers saw the trend differently. One observer noted in 1914 that over 125,000 hunters had taken up the sport, and he feared deer hunting would disappear in his lifetime.

The September 8, 1909, edition of Rhinelander newspaper the *Vindicator,* printed the following about the county fair: "Don't miss the diving horse. Those who saw it elsewhere say it's the most wonderful feat performed by an animal. The horse dives 40 feet into a tank containing ten feet of water." And on September 15, the paper reported, "The diving horse was a most unusual feature and performed his stunt without the least bit of urging, in fact seemed to enjoy it." (Courtesy of Prestor Pictures.)

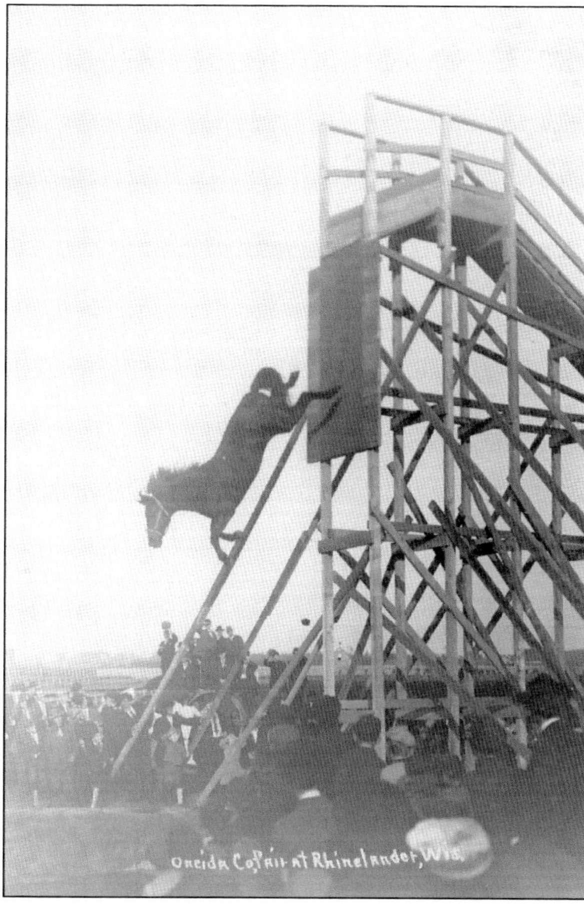

"Wisconsin, for years the leader among all states in the country in propagation and restocking of lakes and streams, is clinching its leadership this year with a record of fish production never previously approached. This year's program, which aimed at the unprecedented goal of 1 billion fish hatched and planted, has already exceeded that figure with the season's work only partially completed," reported the *Minocqua Times* on July 3, 1937.

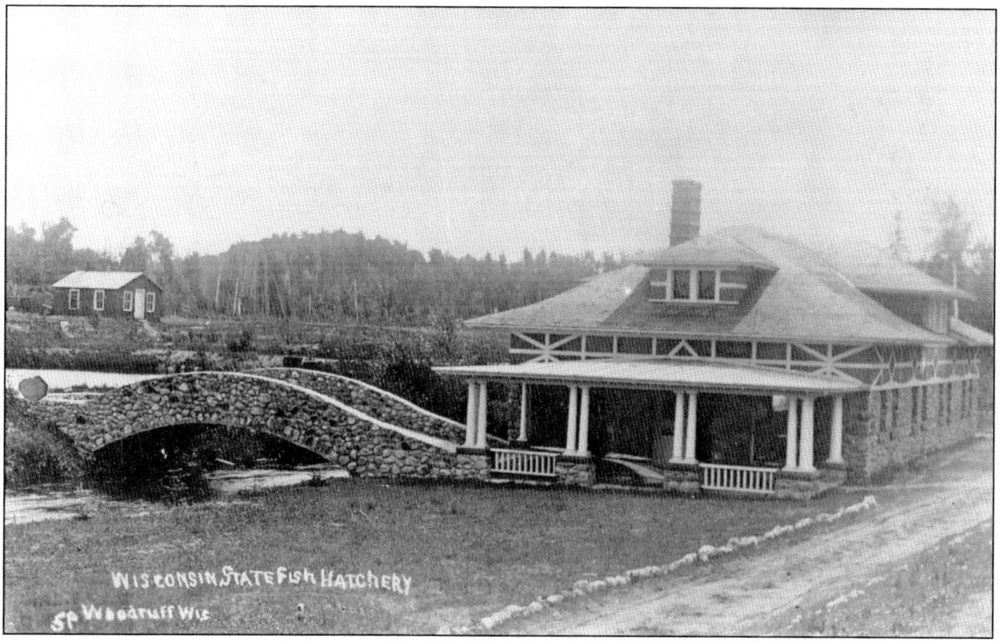

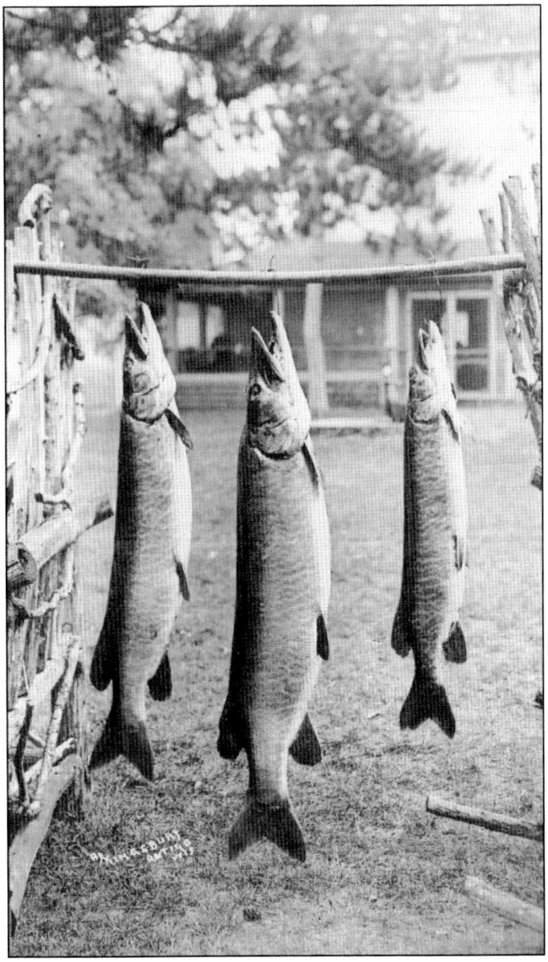

Muskies were a much-appreciated fish up north. On October 6, 1922, the *Minocqua Times* wrote, "A giant [tiger] muskellunge weighing forty one and three-fourths pounds was captured in Carrol Lake Wednesday by E.E. Wigren of Oak Park, Ill. . . . Only after a hard fought battle was the fish finally brought to gaff. It was fifty-four inches in length and twenty-two and one-half inches in girth." The fish mentioned in the article is not in this picture. (Courtesy of Prestor Pictures.)

From the *Minocqua Times* on April 23, 1937, "The following method will give you an estimate in pounds if a scale is not available. Measure the girth of the fish in inches at the thickest point. Square the girth and multiply by the length of the fish. Divide by 800. The answer is the weight in pounds." (Courtesy of Prestor Pictures.)

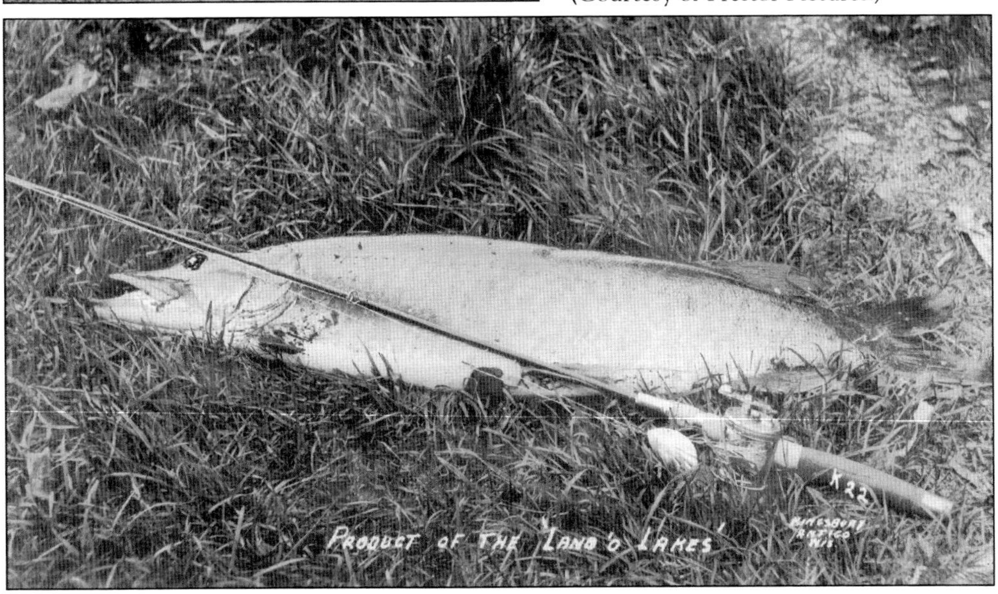

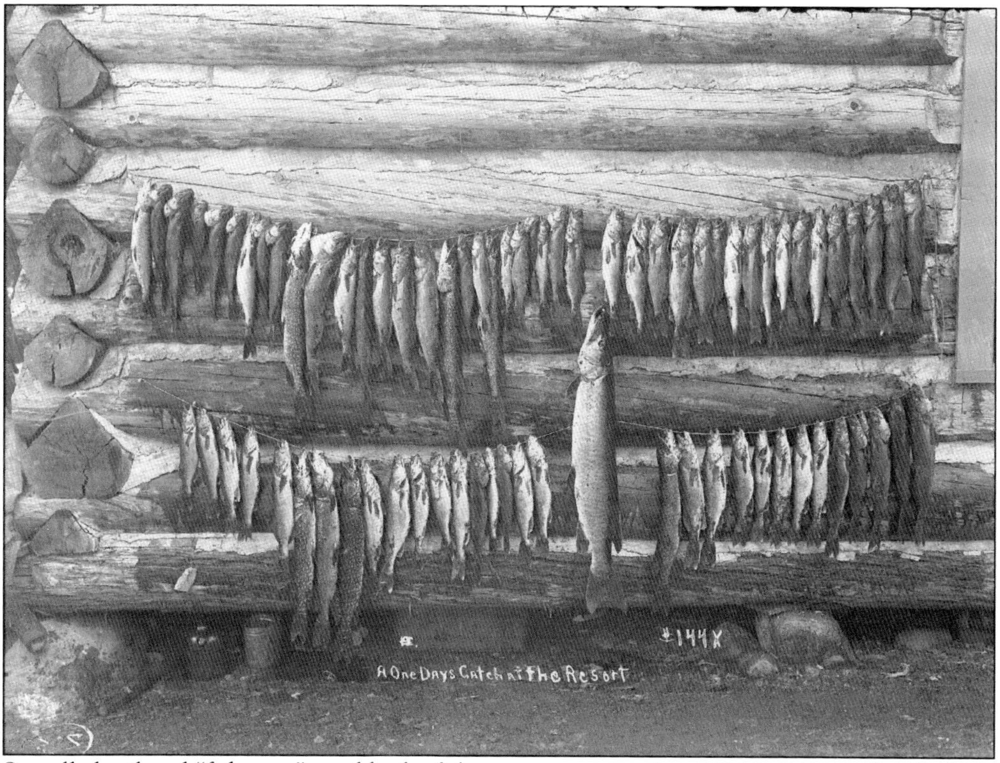

So-called railroad "fish runs" would take fishermen to resorts from Chicago on weekends, from May 1 to Memorial Day. After that, they ran every day but Monday until Labor Day and then once a week until October 1. The very last passenger coach to pass through Antigo was a fish run going to Spider Lake near Mercer in 1981.

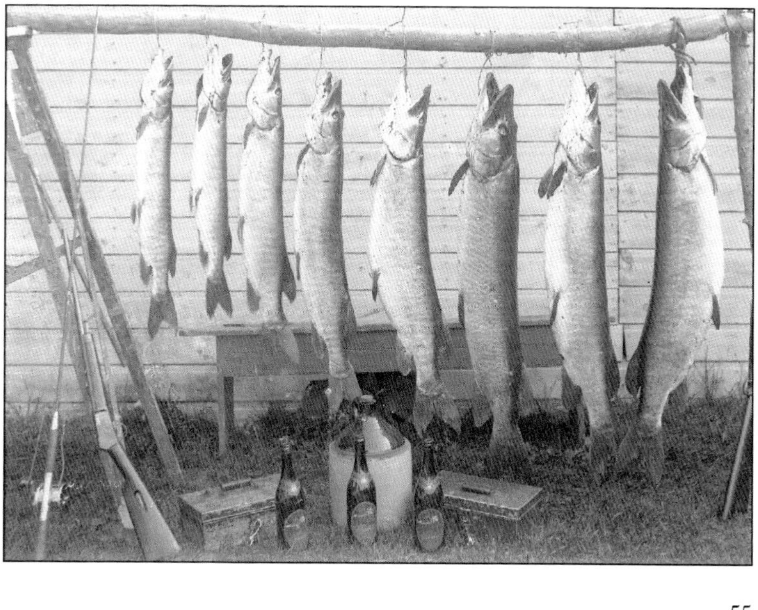

The muskie, or muskellunge, is one of the most prized game fish in northern Wisconsin. They are challenging to catch and are large enough to be trophy fish, as this photograph attests. The muskie is the largest member of the pike family. The name is thought to be derived from the Ojibwe word *maashkinoozhe*, meaning "ugly pike."

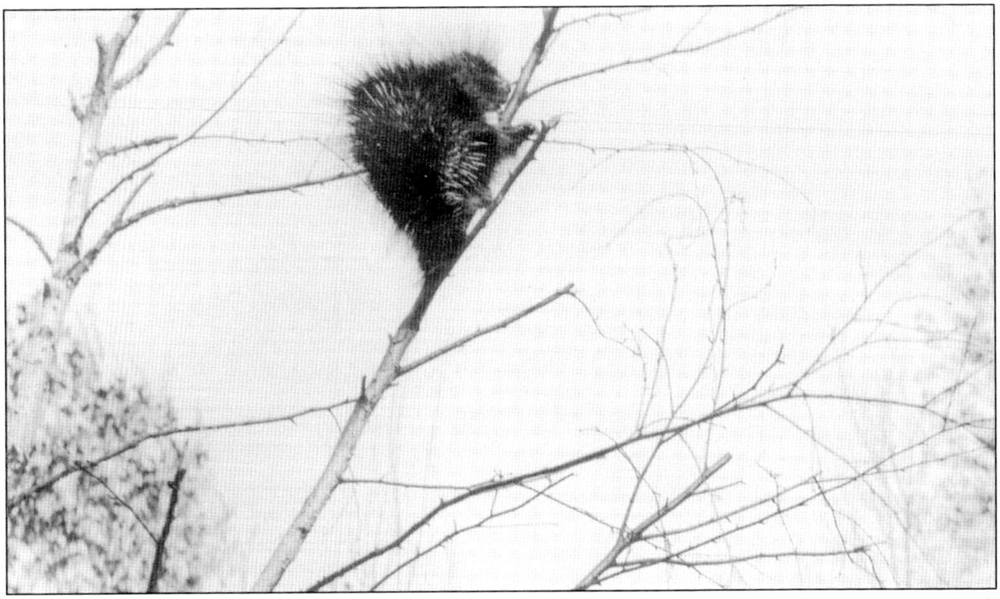

On January 3, 1916, the *Wittenberg Enterprise*, in its "Winnebago Indian Items" section, reported, "George Crane and Albert Big Thunder were hunting one day and came across a skunk trail. They followed it until it ended in an old hollow log. They chopped the log open and found the skunk living with a porcupine." (Courtesy of Prestor Pictures.)

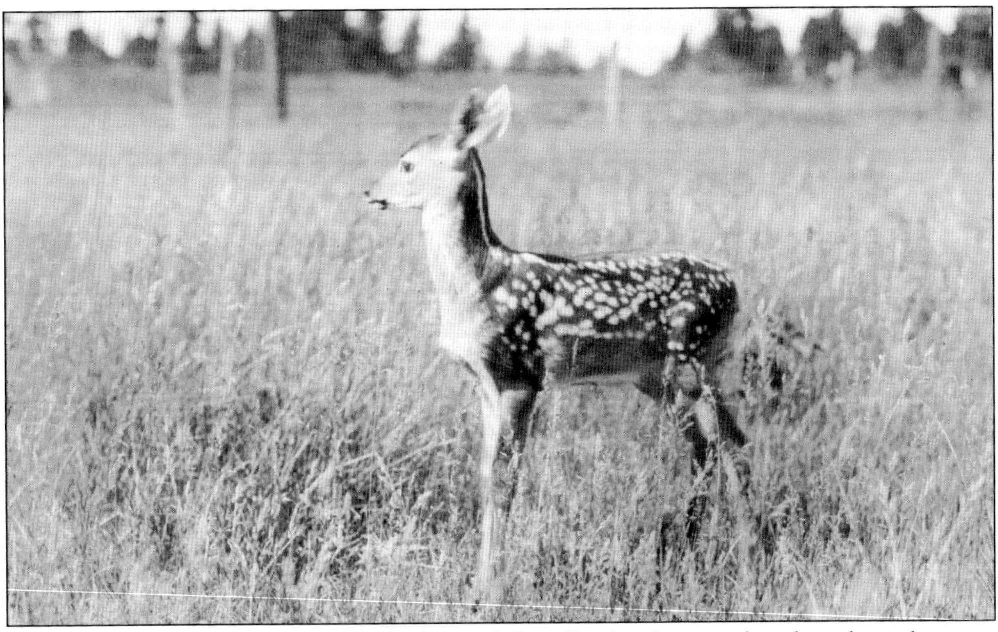

"Governor La Follette announced he had signed the official order providing for a three-day open hunting season on deer from Nov. 29 to Dec. 1, inclusive. As was the case last year, one buck will be the bag limit and only deer with forked horns may be shot. . . . He wrote, . . . 'constant vigilance must be exercised to prevent undue depletion of deer,' " the *Minocqua Times* reported on October 8, 1937. (Courtesy of Prestor Pictures.)

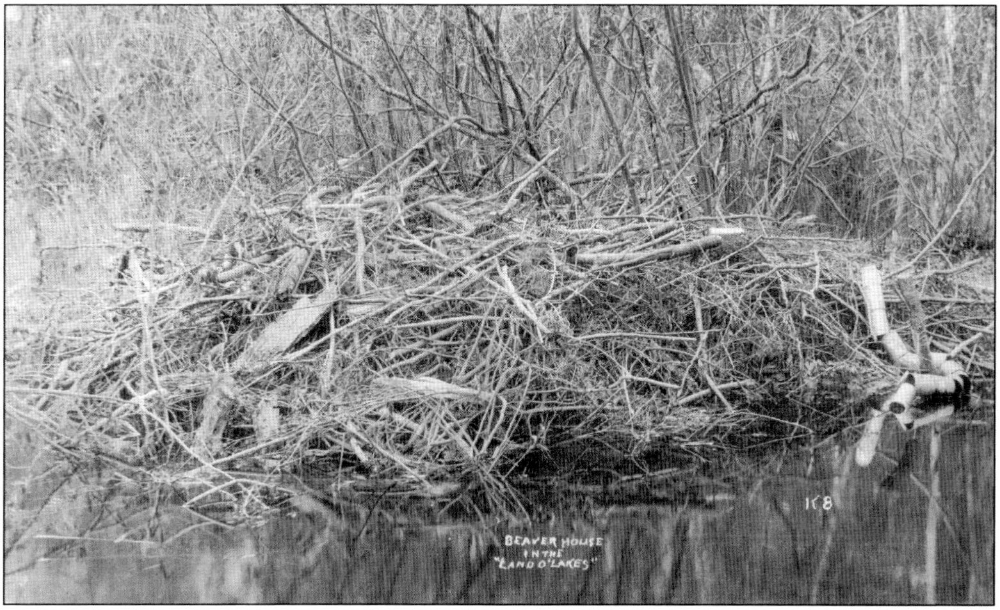

Here is a typical beaver house. Made of sticks and larger branches, it is quite difficult for enemies to dig through. The only way inside a beaver house is underneath, through an opening underwater. Once inside, there is a relatively dry floor area. Beavers live through the winter here, with a large stock of food stored underwater near their doorway. They eat plants, such as clover, grasses, and aquatic vegetation, and sometimes tree bark and twigs. (Courtesy of Prestor Pictures.)

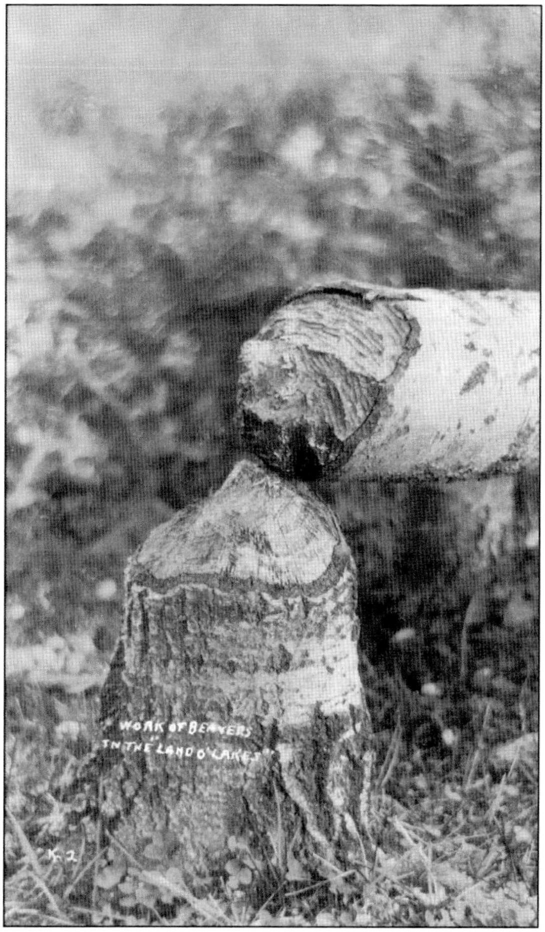

This is a nice close-up of a beaver's work. They gnaw steadily around the tree base until only a thin area of the tree's center is left, which cannot support the tree, so it falls over. Besides eating some bark, beavers use small trees to build dams that will block small streams. Then the water builds up, forming a pond. These ponds become extremely good habitats for many other animals. (Courtesy of Prestor Pictures.)

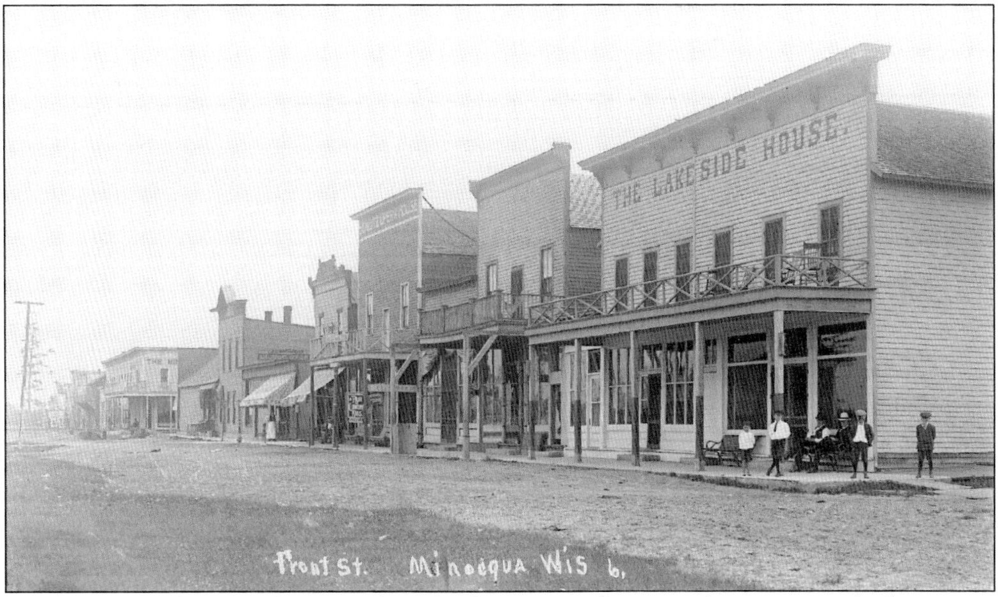

"Minocqua has the natural surroundings for skiing, snowshoeing, tobogganing and other winter sports and there is no reason why resort owners of this section should not cater to winter tourists. The winter tourist is a novelty now, but it is safe to say that the time is not far distant when the Island City will be known far and wide as a winter health resort," the *Minocqua Times* reported on December 15, 1922.

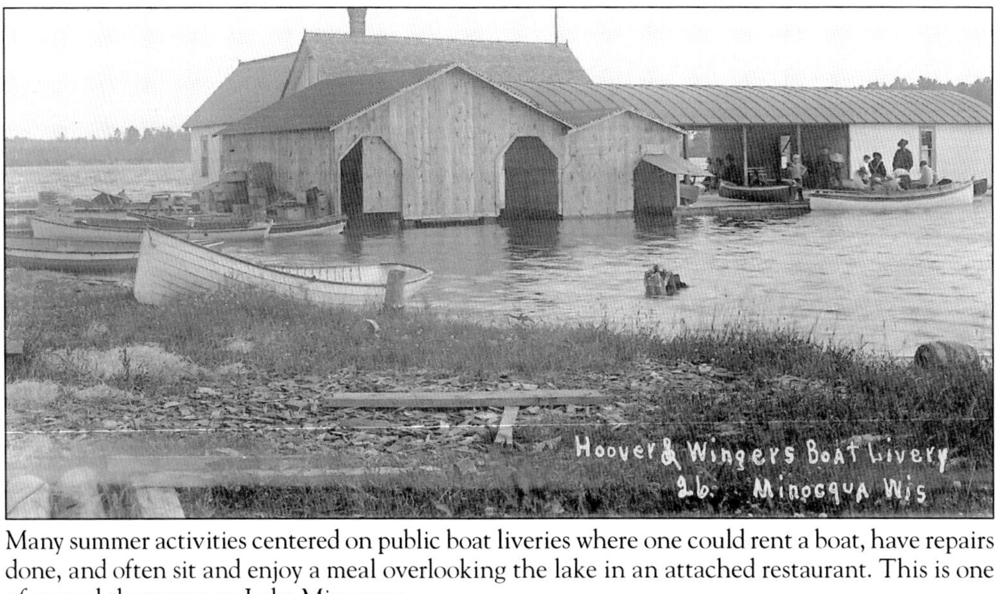

Many summer activities centered on public boat liveries where one could rent a boat, have repairs done, and often sit and enjoy a meal overlooking the lake in an attached restaurant. This is one of several that were on Lake Minocqua.

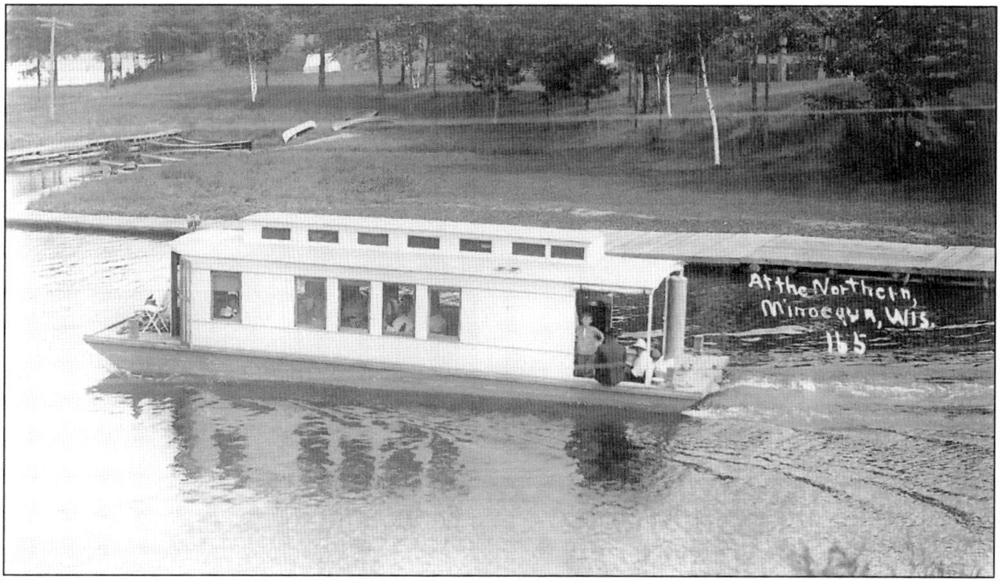

Boating on Lake Minocqua is arguably the most important activity that drew people to Oneida County and the Minocqua/Woodruff/Arbor Vitae area. Some cottages were paired with large and elaborate boathouses that could be sites of socializing, in addition to being places for boat storage.

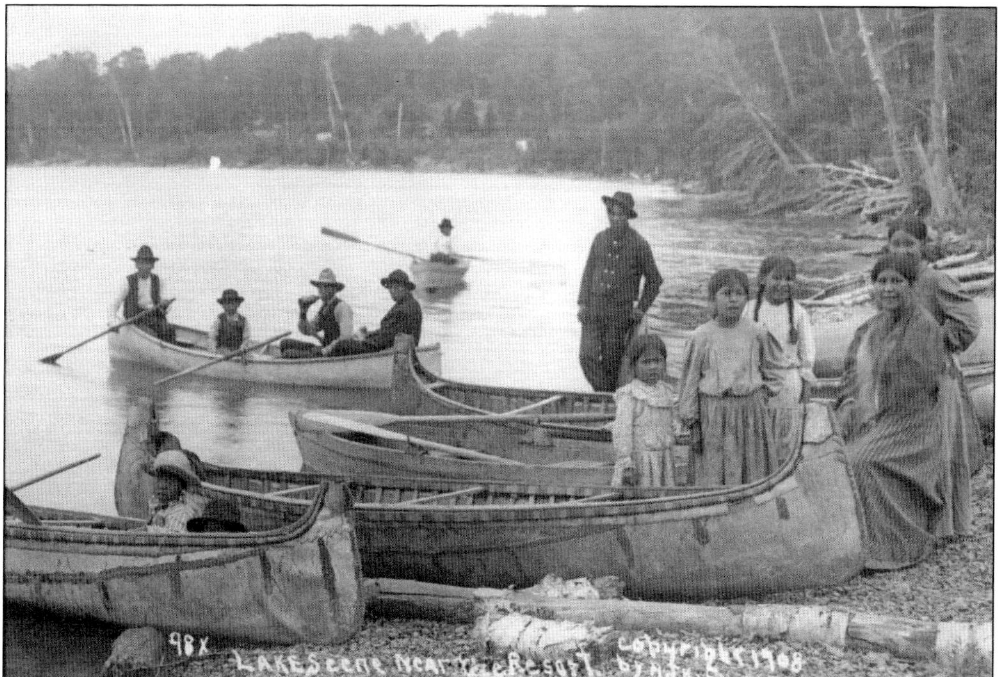

Resorts were also maintained by the Ojibwe, primarily the Lac de Flambeau. Tribal men, as well as women, worked as fish guides who would not only take anglers to favorite spots but would also prepare a traditional shore lunch for tourists.

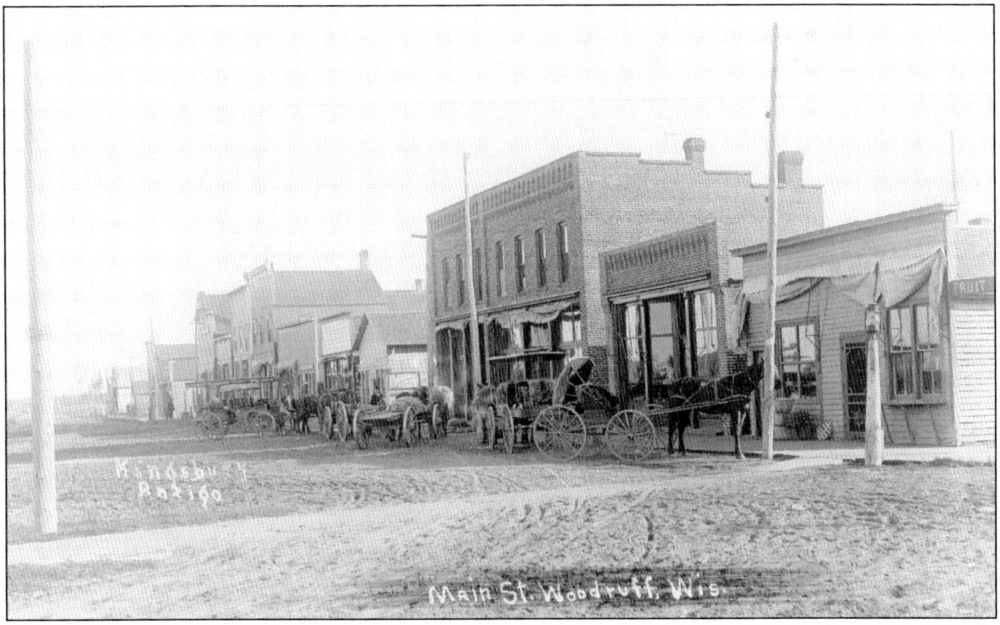

In 1953, Dr. Kate Newcomb was an Woodruff-area doctor well known for making house calls in all weather, sometimes on snowshoes. As the city grew in population, demands on her time increased. She worked with schoolchildren to raise over $17,000 in pennies. The "Million Penny Parade" became famous, and the funds raised helped create Dr. Kate's Hospital in Woodruff.

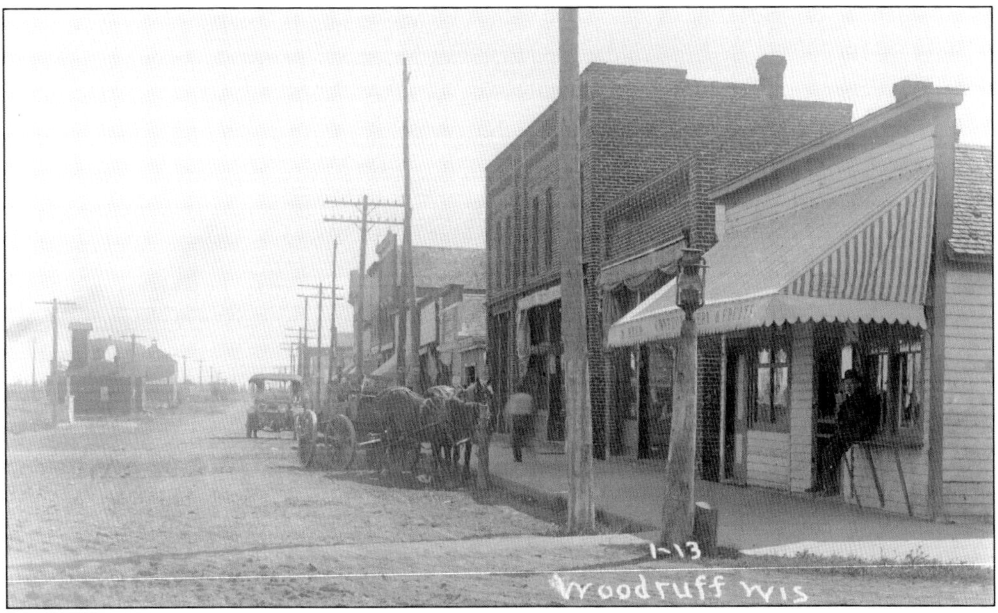

The *Minocqua Times* reported on September 22, 1922, about Woodruff, "Twenty years ago this town had a reputation. 'Woodruff beats Hurley' was a common expression. Lumber jacks from camps around sought Woodruff for pay day amusement. Today Woodruff has entirely changed its character. 'Watch Woodruff Win' is the slogan used by those building up the little northern city . . . the Woodruff rest room for tourists is the pioneer building of its order in this part of the state."

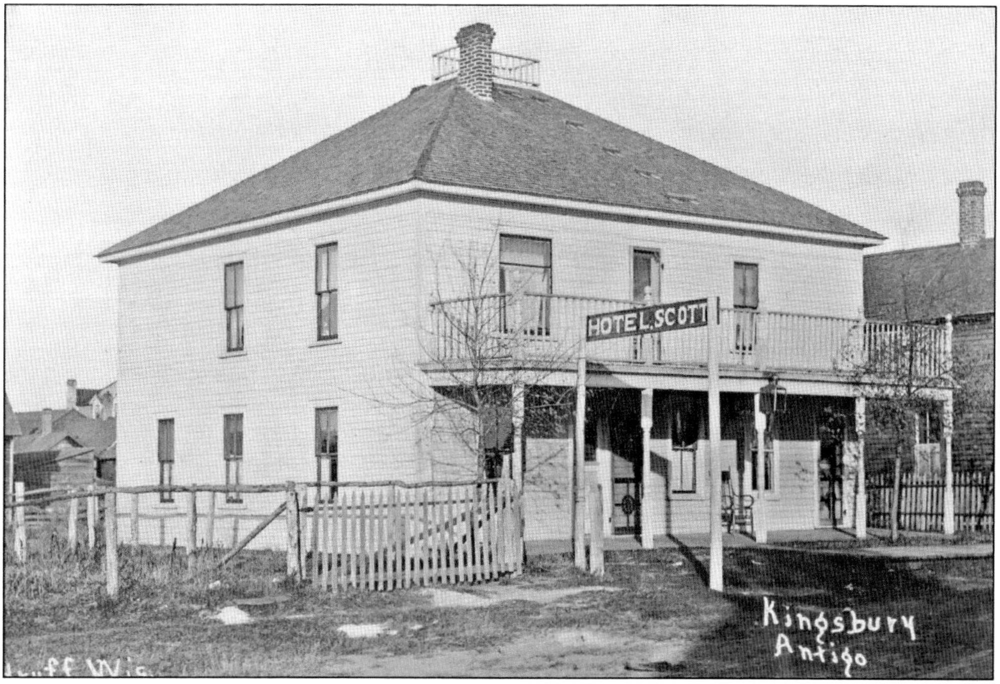

Woodruff, along with Arbor Vitae and Minocqua, form the center of a major tourist destination in Oneida County. In addition to frequenting resort hotels, many families spent summers in cottages in the area. While the families stayed all season, the wage-earning fathers would arrive for each weekend by train from their jobs in cities such as Milwaukee and Chicago.

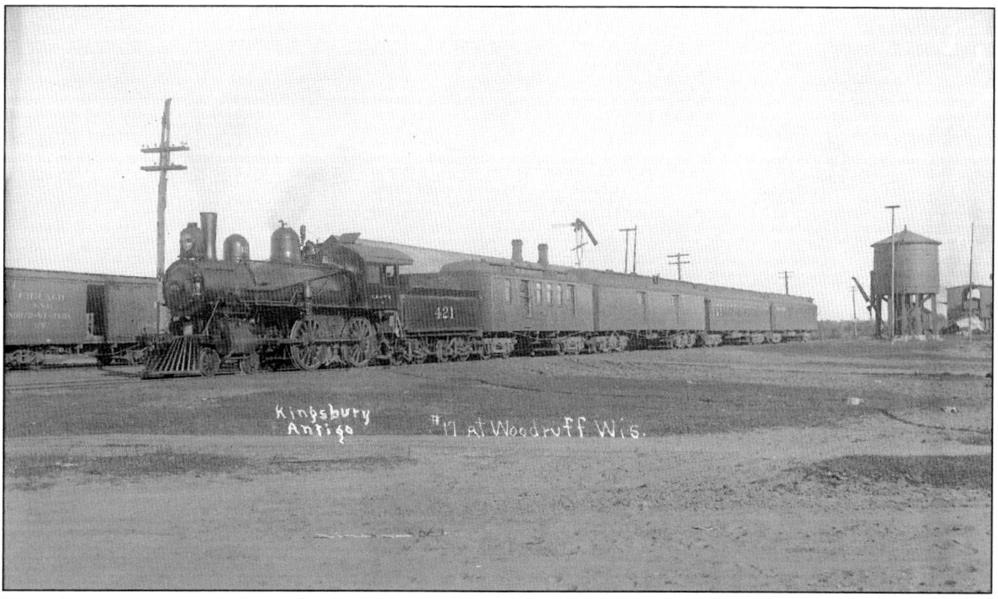

Kingsbury often used the title "Just Arrived" to label his photographs of trains in the railroad depots. This scene shows the depot area at Woodruff, Wisconsin. The busiest days at the depot were Fridays and Sundays, as men commuted from their city jobs to and from their summer homes and families.

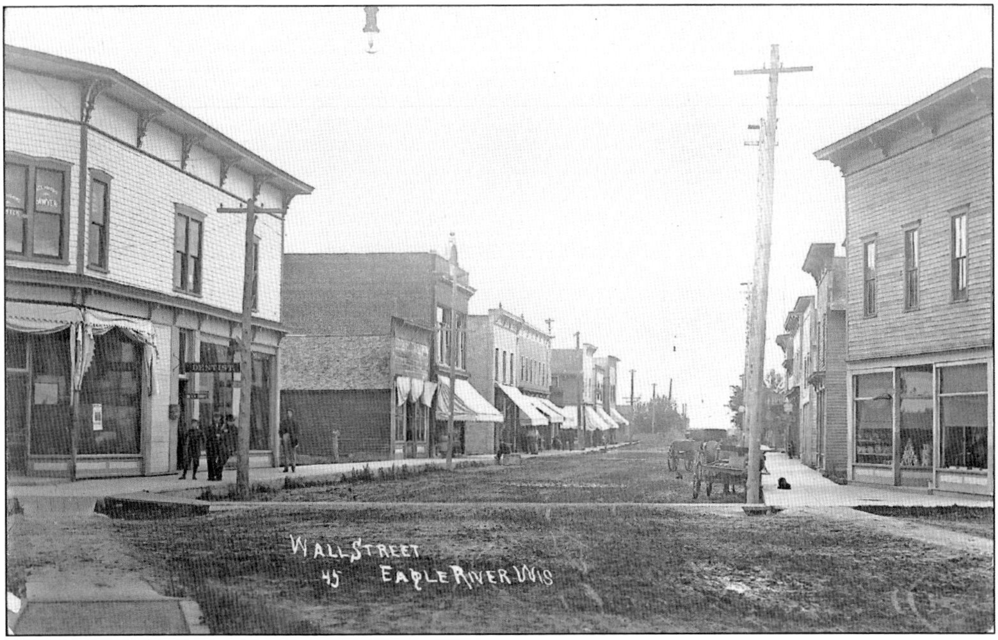

Eagle River, situated in Vilas County, used to have a small population in winter but grew in summer due to tourism and families occupying their cottages. Today's winter tourism, cross-country skiing, snowshoeing, and snowmobiling have made the area a year-round tourist destination, hosting many special events such as snowmobile races.

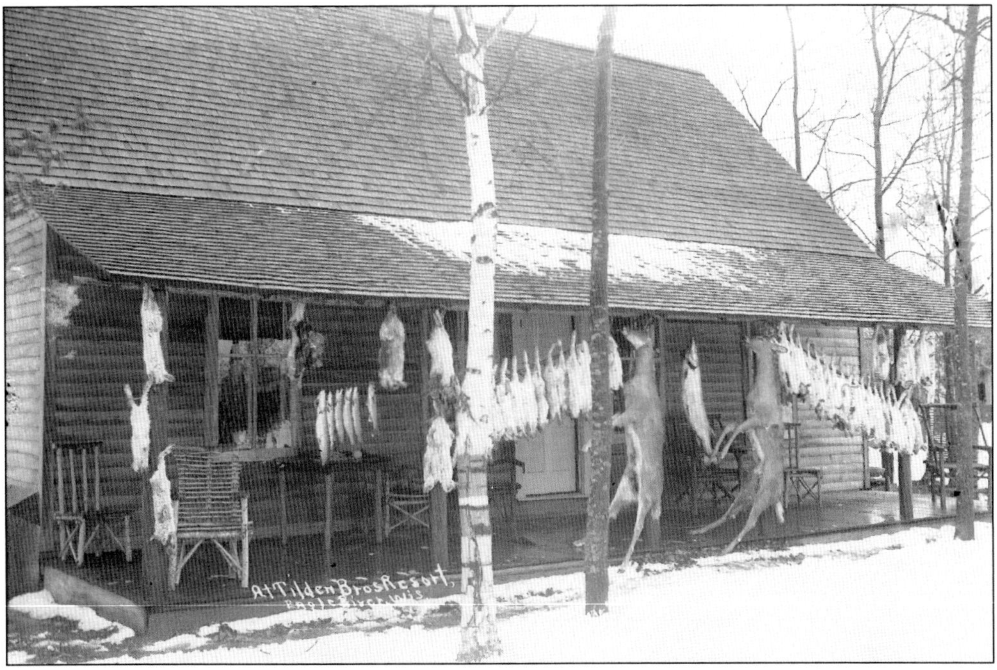

As publicity made hunting more popular, becoming part of the tourist industry, it became necessary to impose regulations in order to preserve the deer population. By 1924, the hunting season had been reduced from 20 to 10 days, and one could not shoot a buck with less than a three-inch antler or one younger than one-year-old.

Four

Menominee Tribe

According to the 2000 census, Wisconsin has one of the highest numbers of Native Americans, as a percentage of total population of any state east of the Mississippi River, as well as one of the most diverse collections of tribal groups of any state.

The Menominee have been in the region of the western Great Lakes since well before European contact. Few tribes in Wisconsin trace their origins as close to their current location as the Menominee. They likely developed from Paleo-Indian groups that had inhabited the area for several centuries.

Soon after French explorer Jean Nicolet arrived in Green Bay in 1634, the Menominee became involved in the fur trade. In the early 19th century, New York tribes such as the Oneida, Stockbridge, Munsee, Brothertown, and Mohican negotiated with the US government and the Menominee to settle in Menominee territory. Continued negotiations between the Menominee and the US government led to the establishment of the current reservation borders in the 1850s.

After the Civil War, there was a large influx of logging operations. The first lumber camp on tribal land was established in 1872. Many Menominee worked in lumber camps. Even in satellite photographs today, the boundaries of the Menominee Reservation are clearly delineated by its dense forests.

With the lumber industry came sawmills, the expansion of the railroad, and shortly thereafter tourists. The Wolf River, long an important means of transporting logs through the reservation, was transformed into a major tourist attraction by the early 20th century.

During those same decades, some well-intentioned (and not so well-intentioned) white men of influence wanted to hasten the pace of Indian assimilation. The introduction of logging, the clearing of land for farms, and the establishment of boarding schools for Indian children all created pressures to assimilate.

It was during this transitional period that A.J. Kingsbury began traveling around northern Wisconsin. His photographs show Indians who maintained much of their traditional culture, as well as many who were reaching out to the growing tourist trade.

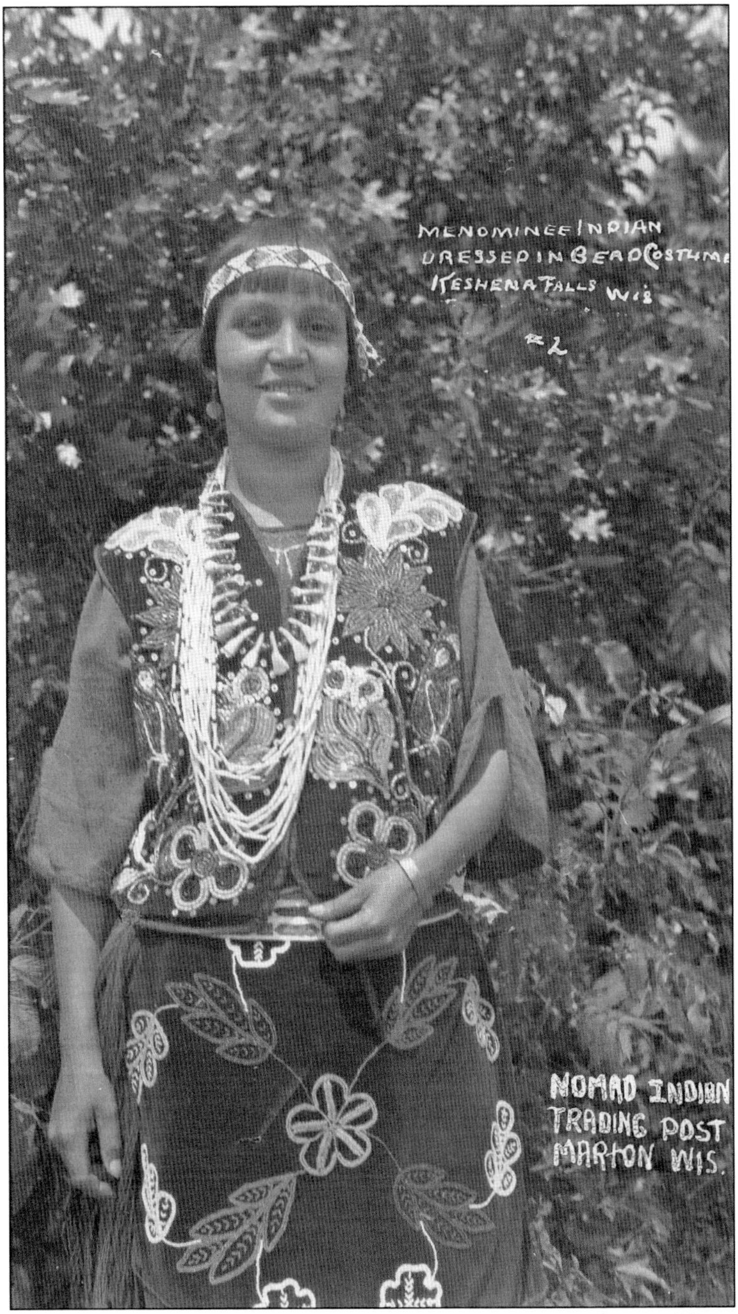

Beadwork as an art form among the Indians evolved from the uses of animal bone, antler, and shells that decorated clothing and household tools prior to contact with Europeans. Europeans introduced glass beads, and Indians throughout North America developed a sophisticated art form using beads of different sizes and colors. Venetian glass beads were the most prized. Generally, Indians of the woodland, or Great Lakes region, developed floral patterns, while plains Indians created geometric patterns, but there was considerable overlapping of influences. Decorative beadwork was used on everyday clothing, ceremonial clothing, and in the case of plains Indians, decoration on horses.

Reginald Oshkosh was a chief of the Menominee and grandson of the first chief to have been named "Chief Oshkosh." This photographic pose, along with the feathered head dress, was meant to appeal to the tourist trade, which the Menominee encouraged. Chief Oshkosh can be seen wearing traditional beadwork items. The medium of beadwork was created by Indians but later travelled back across the Atlantic, becoming a popular decorative art in Victorian England.

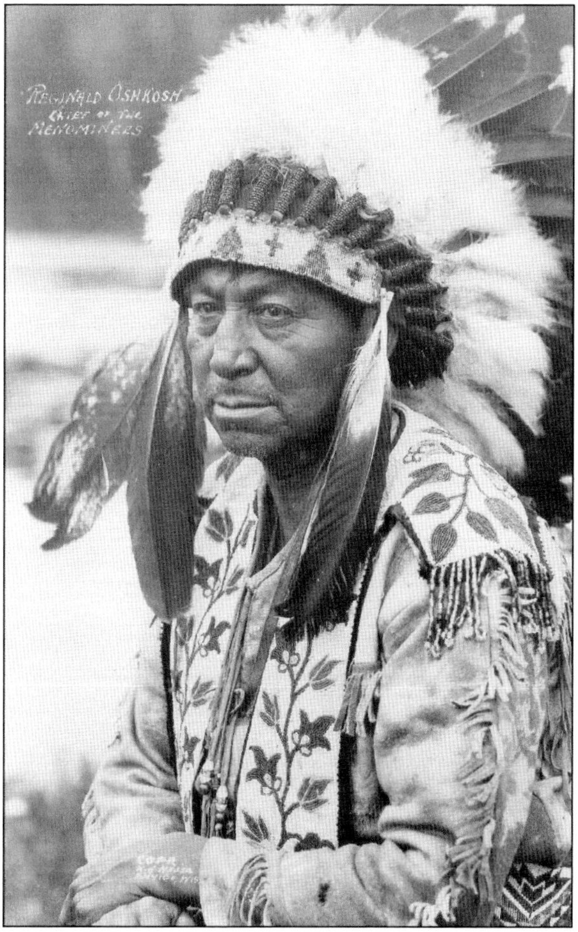

In the 1820s, the Menominee negotiated with the US government to accept Oneida, Stockbridge, Munsee, and Brothertown onto their lands. In the 1840s, there was an attempt to relocate the Menominee to Minnesota, but they resisted, continued negotiating, and in 1854 were granted land along the Wolf and Oconto Rivers as a permanent home.

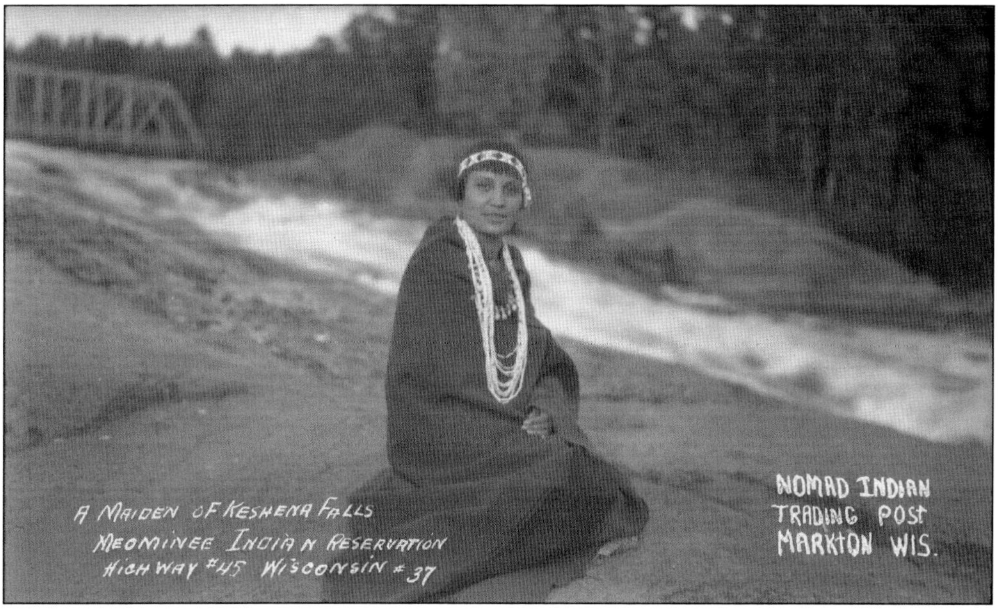

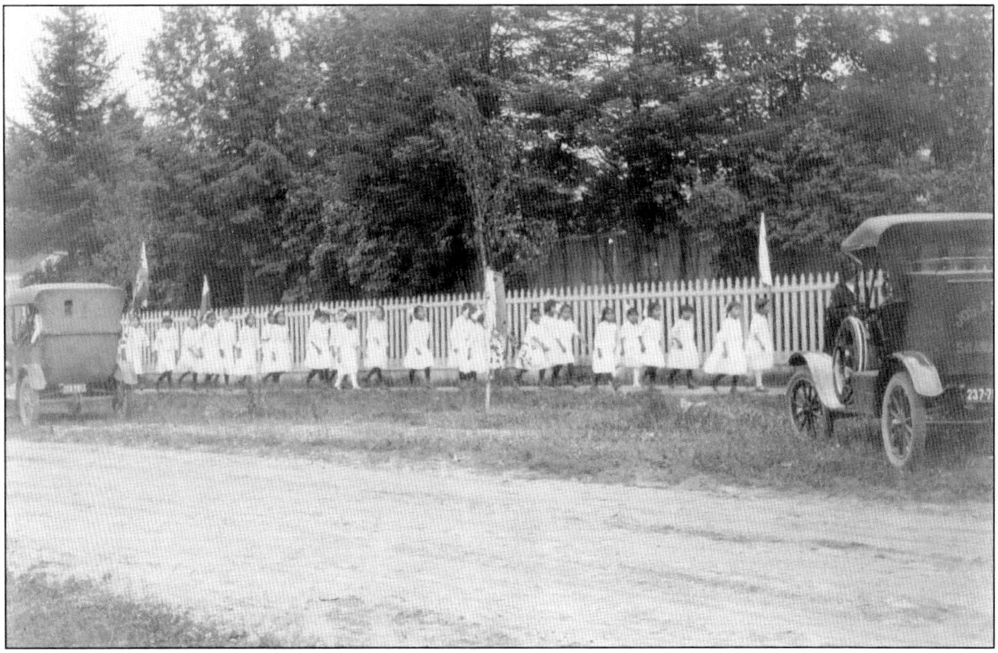

Well into the early 20th century, among the distressing policies affecting native tribes were the boarding schools for Indian children. Thousands in the United States and Canada were forced into these schools against parents' wishes. Children were made to dress, talk, and act like white children in an attempt at forced assimilation. Scenes such as these still generate sadness and regret.

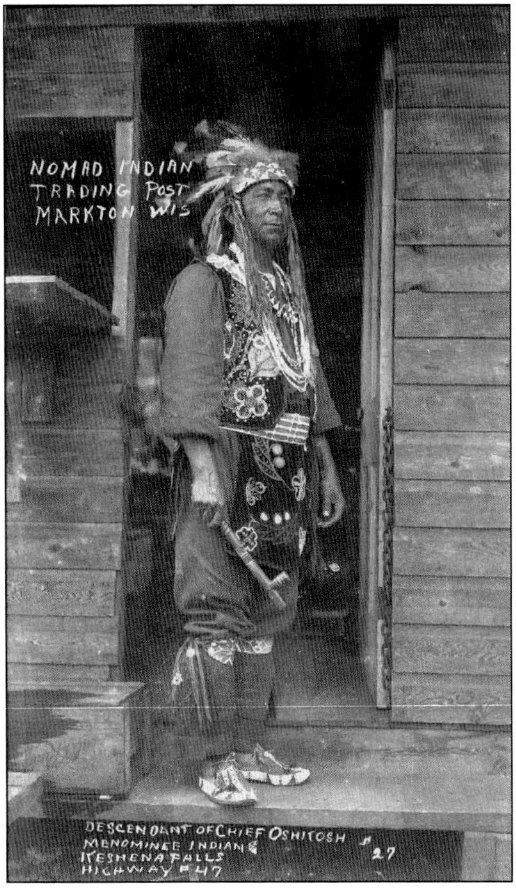

This is a descendant of Chief Oshkosh, an important figure in Menominee history. Chief Oshkosh, a protégé of Chief Tomah, negotiated terms with Washington officials that allocated space for New York tribes. This prevented the Menominee from being removed to west of the Mississippi River. This occurred in the 1830s, the crisis years following the Blackhawk Wars in northern Illinois and southern Wisconsin.

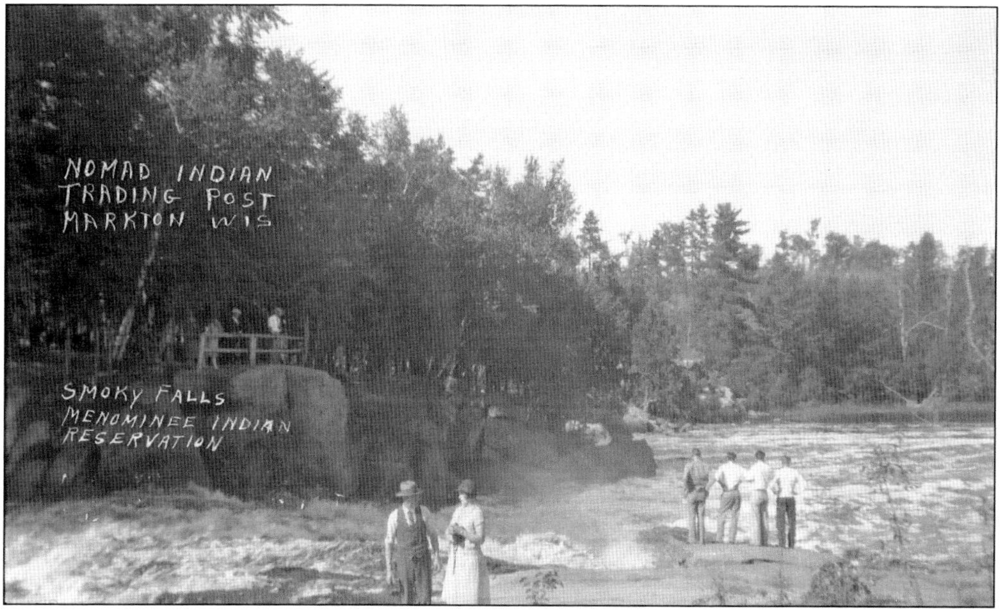

The Menominee have a long and complex history with Wisconsin and the federal government. Although not a wealthy tribe, the Menominee were moderately comfortable when, in 1953, they negotiated termination of their reservation status and became a separate county. The move created problems, and after long political and legal negotiations, often acrimonious, tribal recognition was restored.

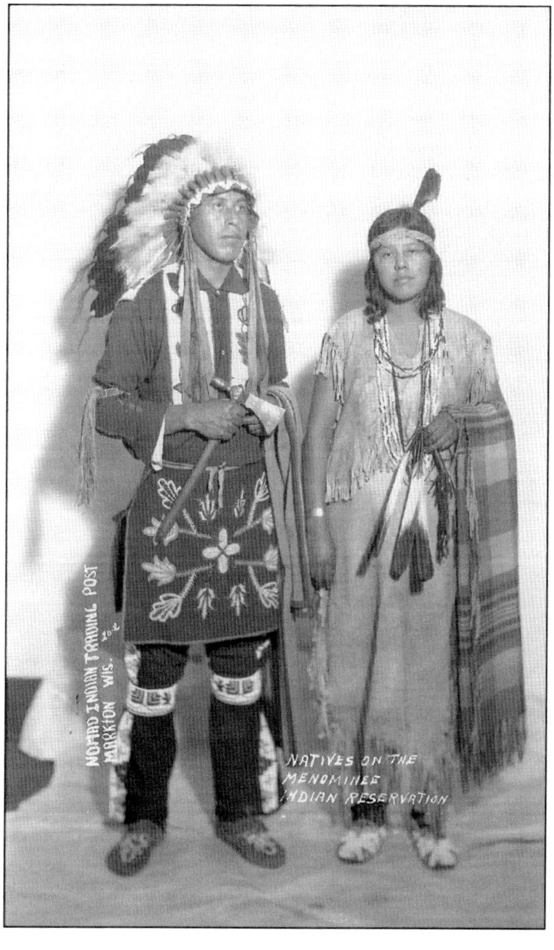

The woodland Indians can be grouped into four cultural divisions: the Central Algonkian, the Eastern Algonkian, the Subarctic Algonkian, and the Iroquois. Both the Ojibwe and Menominee, along with the Ottawa, Potawatami, and Cree, were part of the forest tribes of the Central Algonkian. It is estimated that at the time of Columbus, the Ojibwe numbered about 50,000 while the Menominee were only at 3,000.

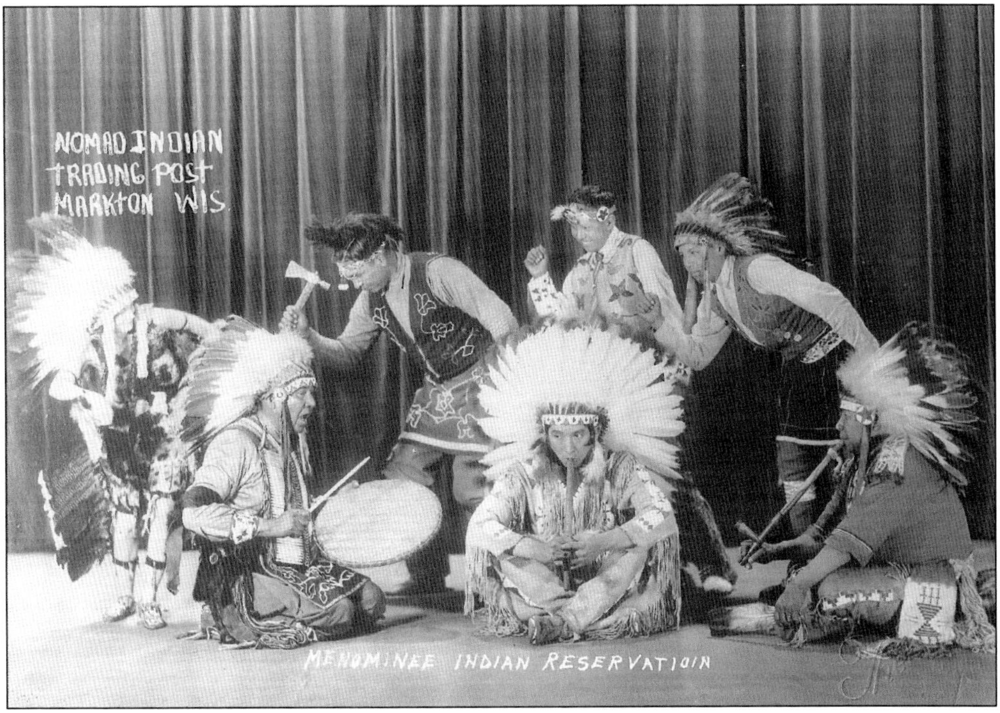

In what is an obviously posed photograph designed to appeal to tourists, one must wonder why this stereotype seemed so appealing to whites and why the Menominee would be willing to pose this way. There are accounts that suggest they liked Kingsbury and trusted him. The feathered bonnets they are wearing here are not those typically worn by the Menominee.

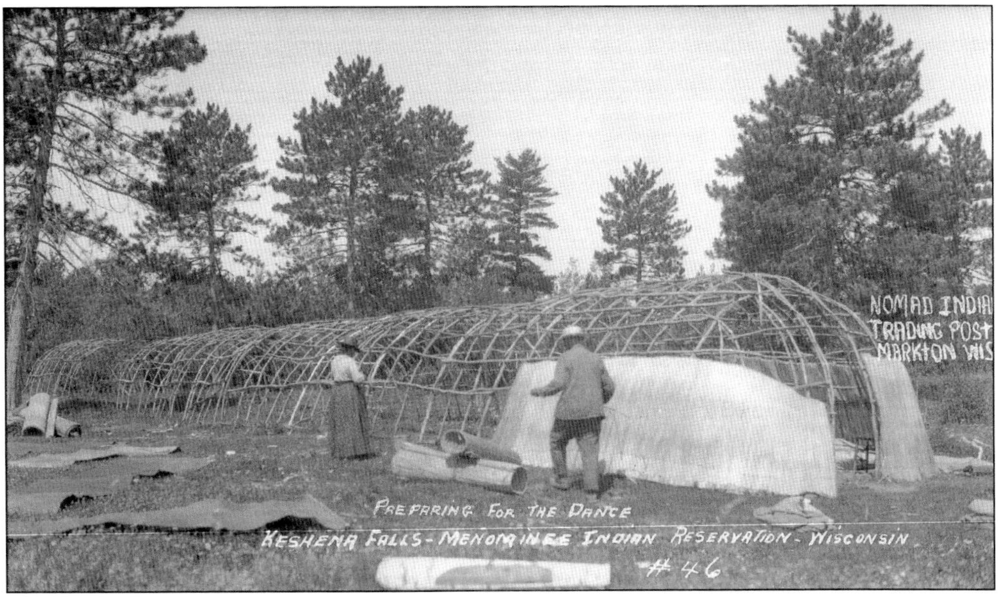

Many Indians initially welcomed outsiders to witness their ceremonial dances, but when they saw how they were stereotyped, they closed some dances to the public; however, by the early 20th century, they were willing to perform some dances for tourists. This photograph may depict the preparations for a public show open to tourists.

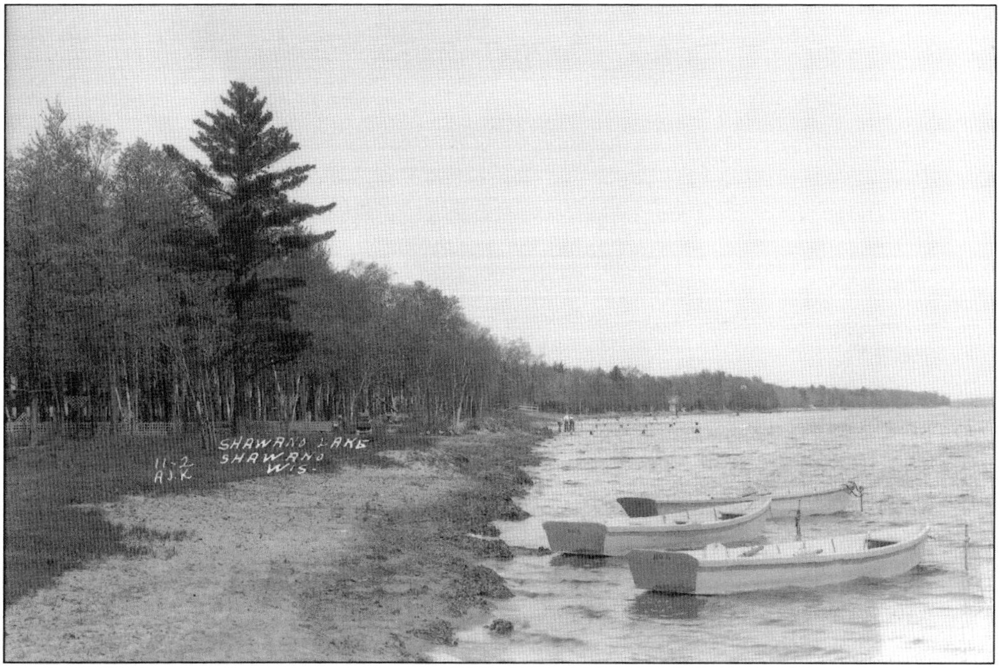

Shawano Lake is connected to the Wolf River at the city of Shawano. Industrial and urban development there created problems. In 1892, a paper mill dam prevented sturgeon from reaching their spring spawning grounds at Keshena Falls. In 1900, Menominee were denied access to camp sites on Shawano Lake, from where they would harvest wild rice in the fall. These problems have since been resolved.

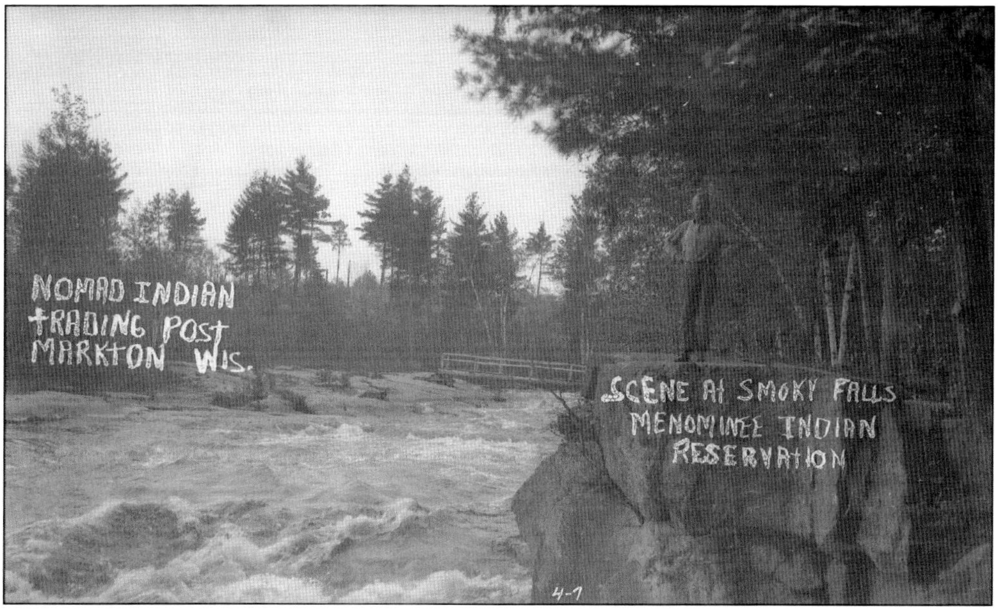

The Wolf River today is one of the few unspoiled rivers in the nation and is a federally designated wild river. Much of the upper Wolf River runs through the Menominee reservation. The many rapids such as these at Smoky Falls are a favorite destination for kayakers and rafters. The river is a source of tourism revenue for the Menominee.

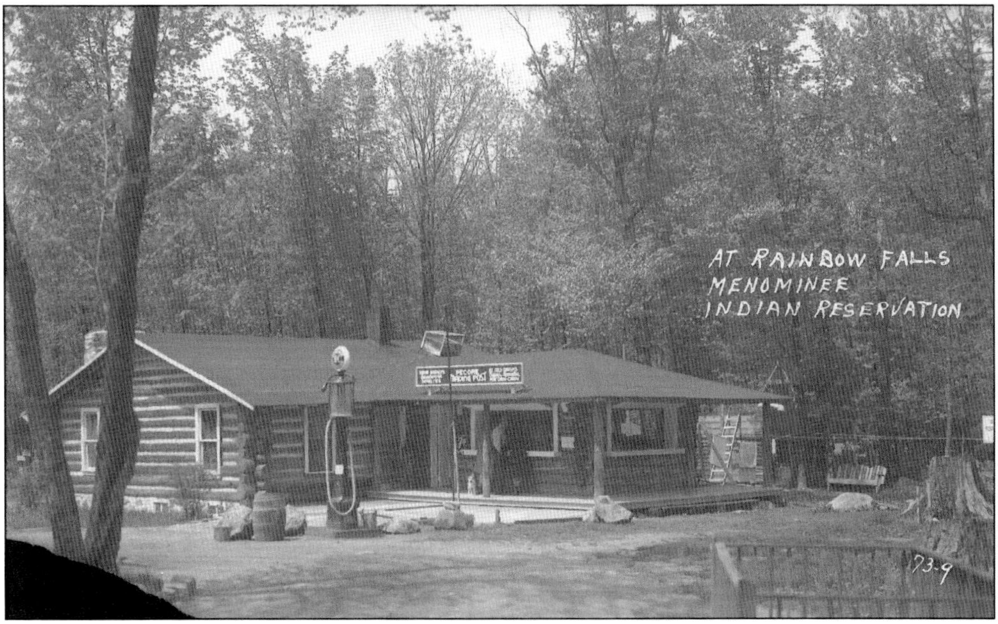

A number of locations along the Wolf River became tourist attractions. These were generally located at falls or rapids. At sites such as this at Rainbow Falls, there were trading posts selling food, gas, and souvenirs.

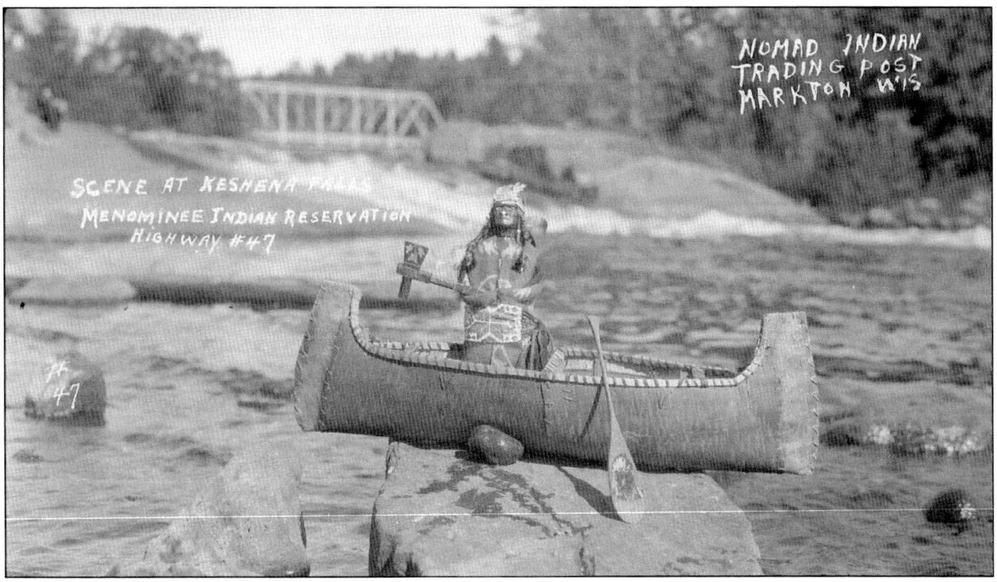

Shown here are examples of some of the items prepared by the Menominee for sale to visiting tourists. The birch bark canoe, invented by Indians, is ideal for transportation in the region's rivers and lakes where portages are necessary. The birch bark canoe has long been associated with woodland Indians. Replicas were likely a very popular souvenir.

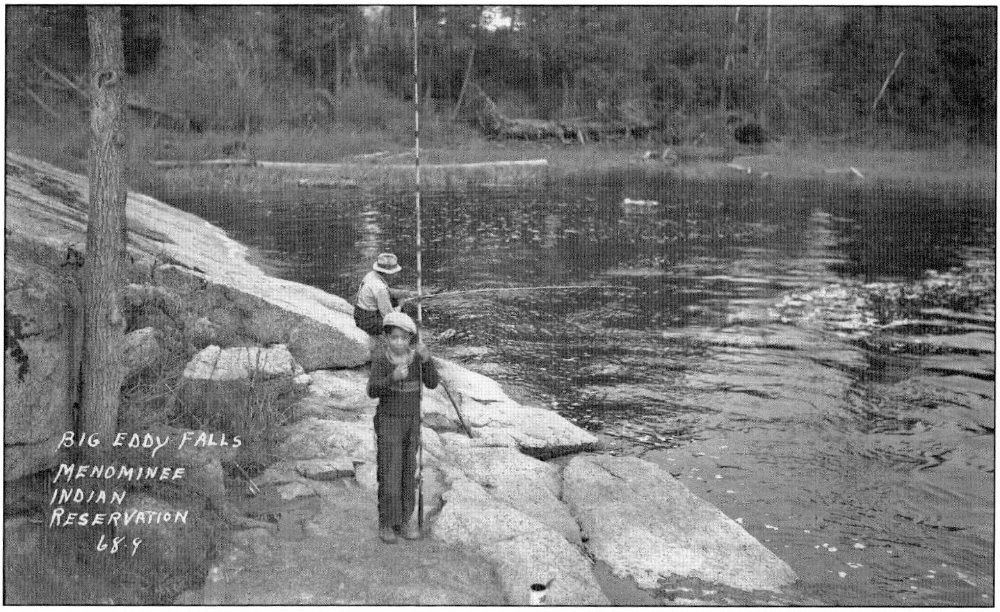

Fishing on the Wolf River provides a mainstay of the Menominee diet. Sturgeon spawn in the Wolf in the spring. Populations of these large, ancient fish had been declining but are now rebounding thanks to conservation efforts. White bass, or sand bass, also spawn in the Wolf in late May and are a popular fish, averaging 8 to 12 inches and sometimes 19 inches in length.

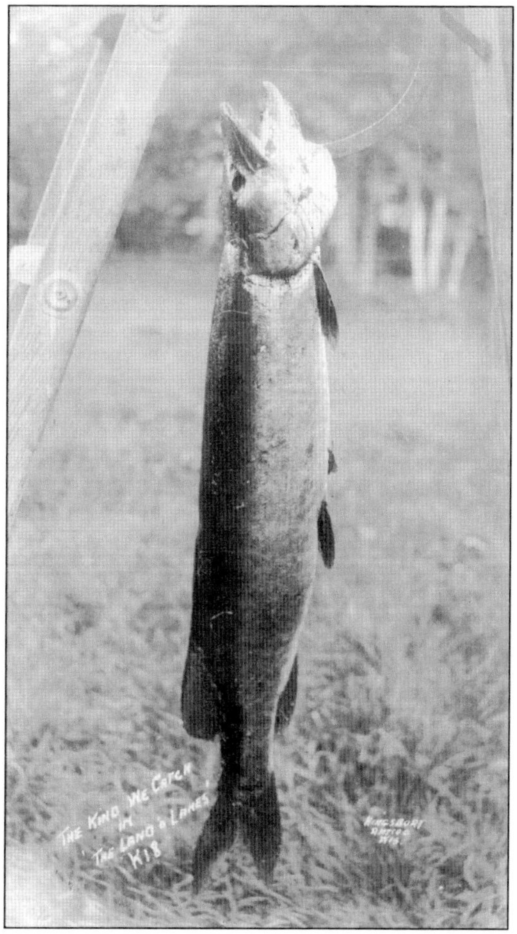

The word *muskellunge* (or *muskie*) is one of many Algonquian words incorporated into English. Algonquian was the basis of some 30 different Indian languages spoken in this region, including Menominee and Ojibwe. Other Algonkian words include moose, succotash, hominy, and squash. Several state names and cities in Wisconsin, including Antigo, are derived from Algonkian words. (Courtesy of Prestor Pictures.)

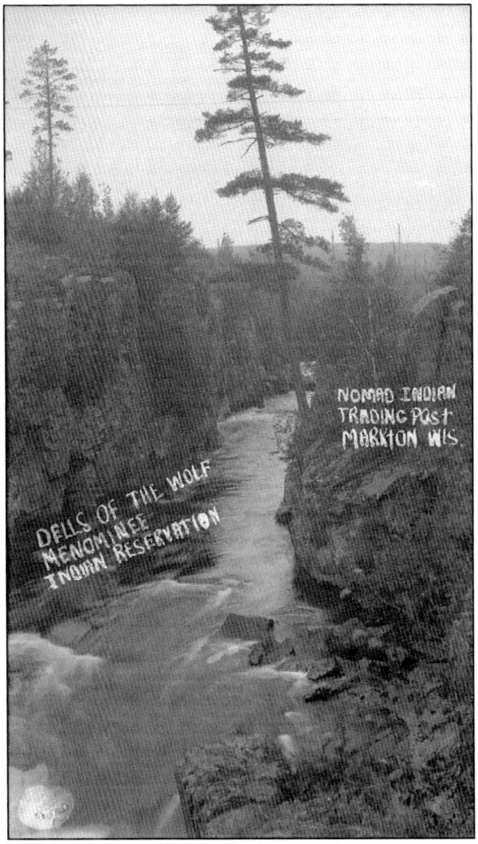

The Wolf River's headwaters are in Forest County. It flows through Langlade, Menominee, and Shawano Counties. The pristine quality of the Wolf was threatened by a proposed zinc mine in Crandon, Forest County, in the 1970s, but a coalition of Indian groups, environmentalists, and rural citizens resisted development. The purchase of the mine site by the Sokaogan Mole Lake Chippewa preserved this natural waterway so vital to the Menominee.

Even to this day, roads through the reservation pass through tall stands of trees. The Menominee have long used sustainable logging as opposed to clear-cutting. These procedures are only now recognized as good logging practice. The thick forests form a tree canopy and an outline of the Menominee reservation that is obvious in satellite images of the area.

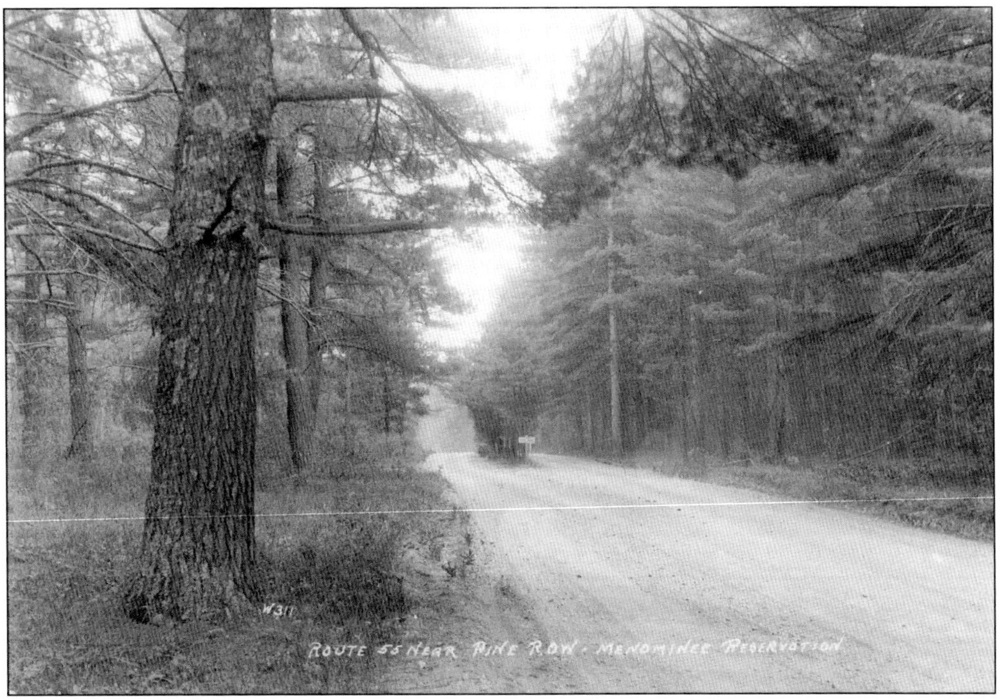

Five

Ojibwe Tribe

The Ojibwe were given that name by other Indians. The word *Ojibwe* means "puckered moccasin people" after their style of sewing the seams of their moccasins. French traders, on hearing "Ojibwe," thought they heard "Chippewa," and that became another name used by some people. The Ojibwe refer to themselves as Anishinabe. They originally came from the eastern seaboard and didn't settle in the area that was to become Wisconsin until the late 18th and early 19th centuries.

Oral histories of the Ojibwe tell of their living on the North Atlantic coast. Prophets told the tribes that they should move to where the food grew on water. During their migrations, the discovery of other tribes harvesting wild rice suggested that they had arrived at their destination.

Together with their allies, the Ottawa and Potawatomi, the Ojibwe had moved westward through Canada. In the United States, they settled primarily in what are now Michigan, Wisconsin, and Minnesota. By the late 17th century, Ojibwe had established trade relationships with French fur traders and had moved into northern Wisconsin. There they encountered the Dakota Sioux, with whom they fought for control of the land. Conflict between the two tribes continued until a treaty in 1825.

Wisconsin became a territory in 1836 and a state in 1848. In 1852, the Ojibwe were able to convince the US government that they should remain in Wisconsin. By 1854, many of their reservations had been officially established. The Indians' isolation in 1870s northern Wisconsin was rapidly coming to an end. The last decades of the 19th century were largely defined by the growth of the lumber industry, railroad expansion, and the first incursions of tourists.

By 1908, A.J. Kingsbury was taking pictures of it all. Over a few years, he developed a good working relationship with the Indians, many of whom had inner conflicts over the extent to which they should cooperate in the development of their reservations and surrounding areas.

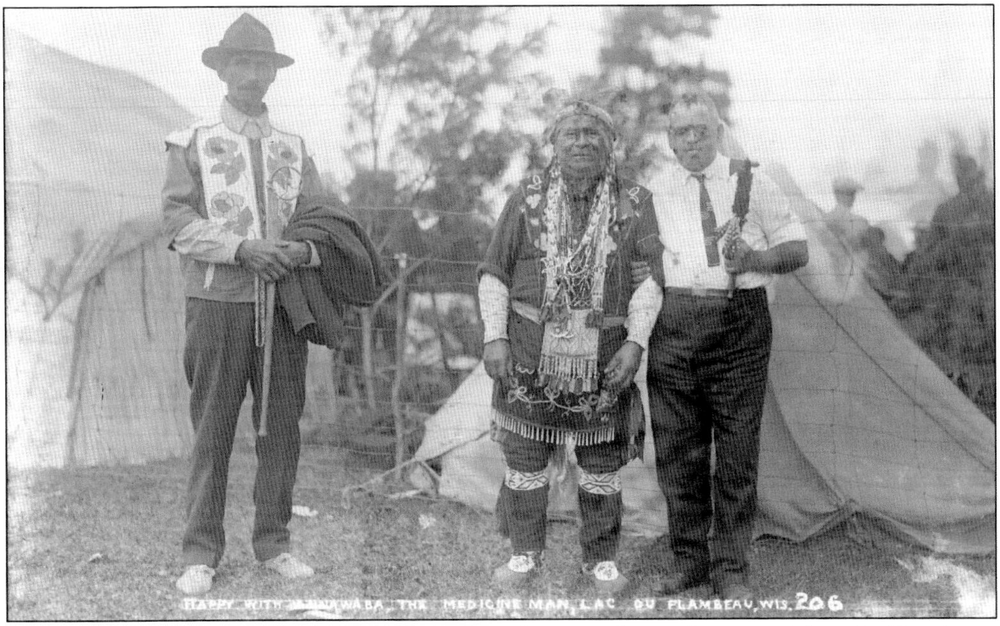

Kingsbury was very popular among the many photographers who visited Lac du Flambeau, probably because he was willing to pay the Indians to pose. He is shown holding a tomahawk, standing next to two Ojibwe men who are wearing a mix of traditional and Whites' clothing. Although the original negative has been damaged, the photograph is revealing in how the Ojibwe interacted with Kingsbury.

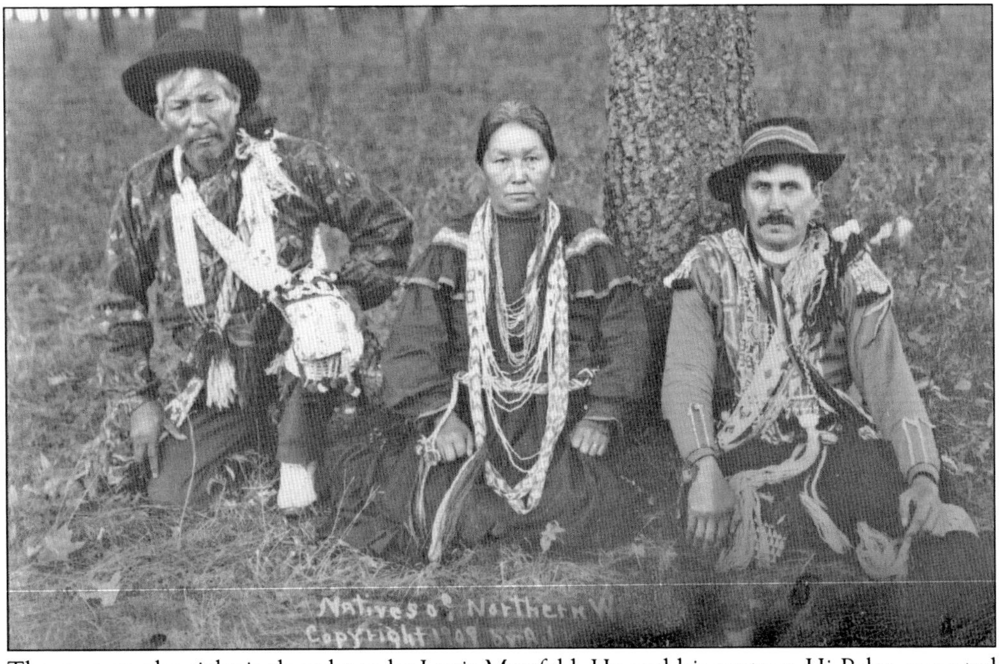

The man on the right is thought to be Louis Motzfeld. He and his partner, Hi Polar, operated a way station and trading post in the 1870s, along the military trail from Shawano County to Michigan's Upper Peninsula. Both Motzfeld and Polar married Ojibwe women and were among the first Anglo settlers in the area.

An-Ni-Wa-Bi was a medicine man at Lac du Flambeau. While being tribal chief was a hereditary position, it was largely ceremonial in what was a decentralized Ojibwe culture. Chiefs were involved in negotiations with other tribes or whites. Much tribal influence in daily affairs rested in the hands of the shaman, or medicine man. He was arguably the most important man in the day-to-day life of the tribe.

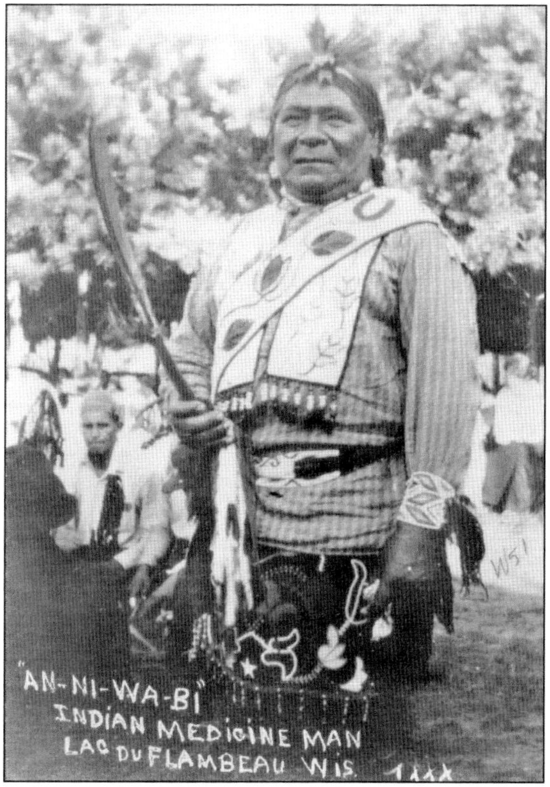

Mebi-Ma-ga-ha-Wi-Kwe, or Tillie Catfish Besoni, was a bead worker with the Lac du Flambeau Ojibwe. With expansion of white tourism into northern Wisconsin, there was also a market for beadwork items for the tourist trade. This photograph was likely made for a postcard so that Tillie Catfish could make her work known to tourists.

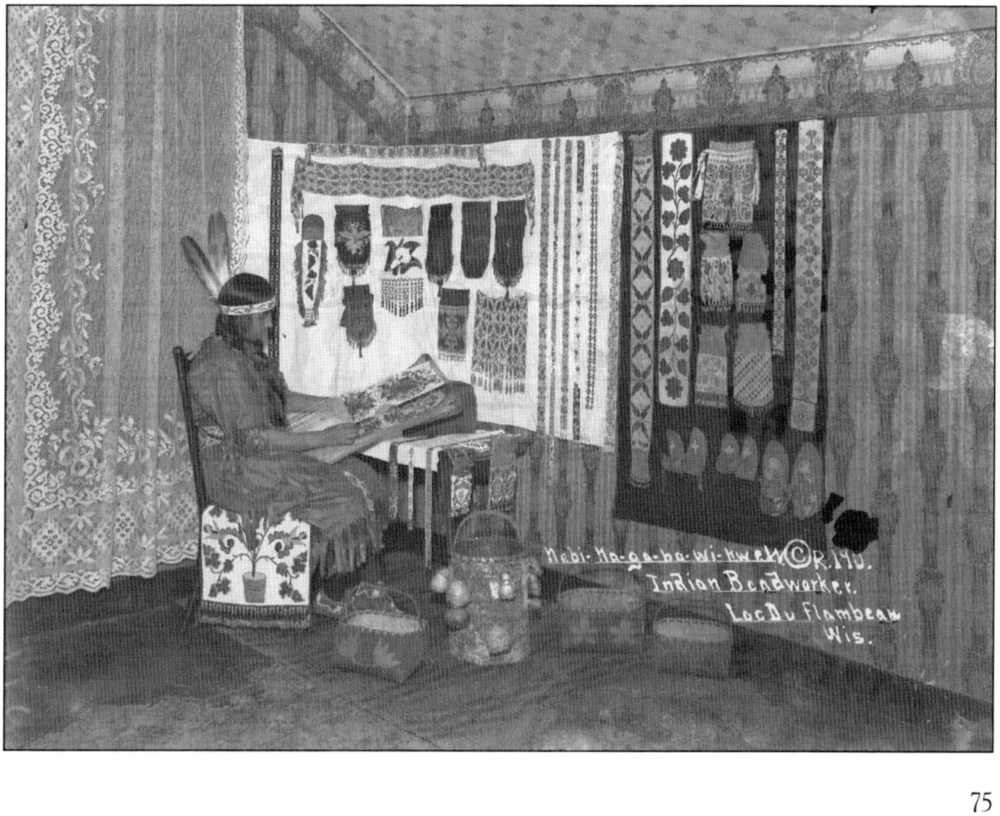

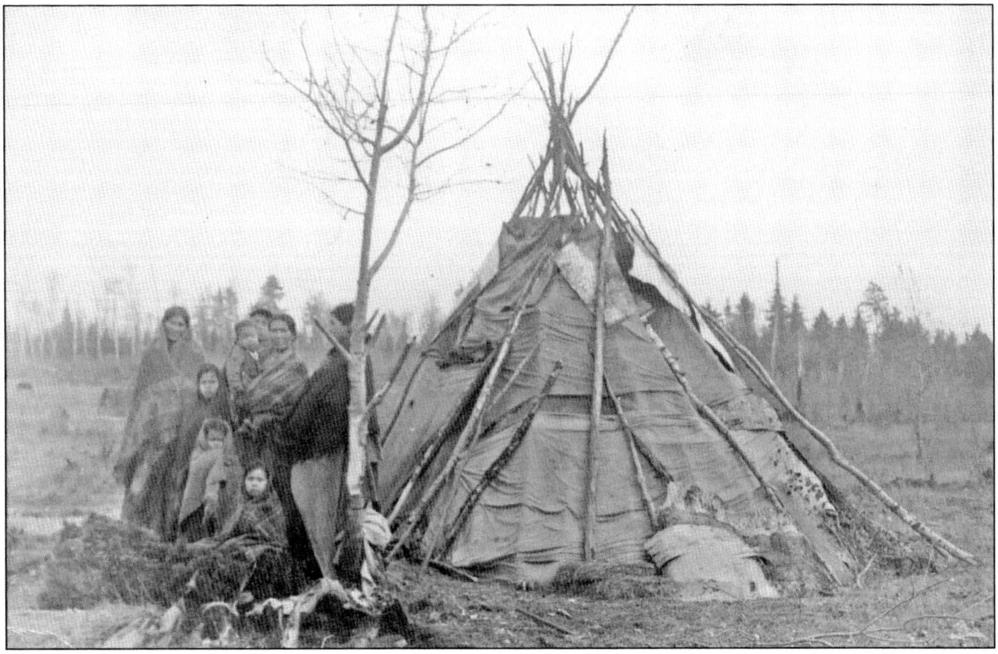

The teepee structure was used by the Ojibwe as a temporary shelter in their seasonal migrations. Its materials were easily transported, and it could quickly be assembled. People moved from place to place depending on the season to hunt and fish, gather fruits, and harvest wild rice, and the teepee provide overnight shelter.

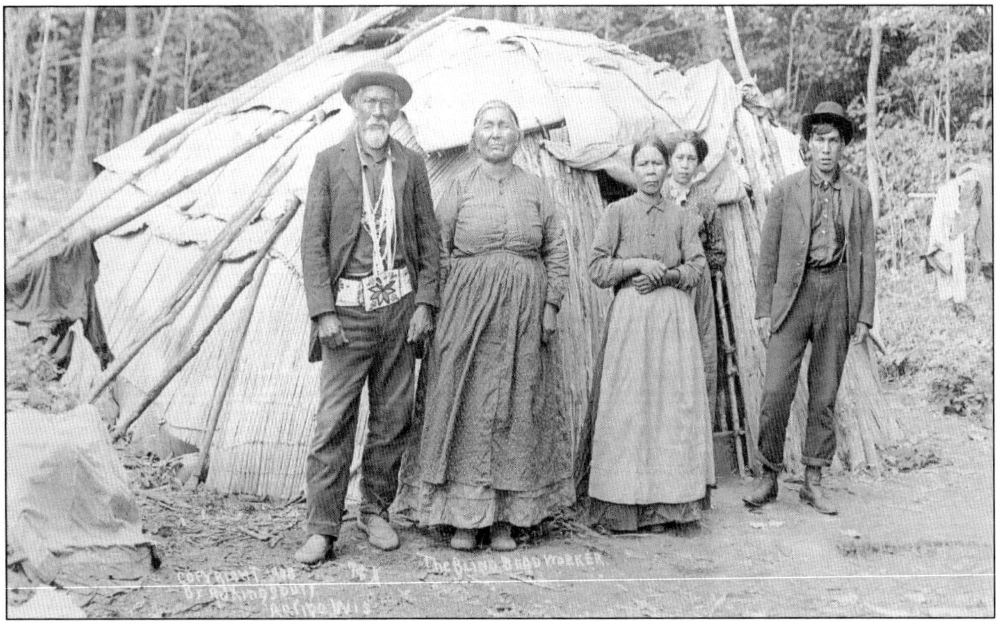

This wigwam was a more permanent, typical Ojibwe home. These dwellings were easily constructed but were used for longer periods of time. A framework of saplings would be covered by panels of birch bark and/or animal hides, depending on the season. A cattail mat would be unrolled around the circumference of the wigwam. The units of the wigwam could be disassembled and packed up when the tribe moved. (Courtesy of Prestor Pictures.)

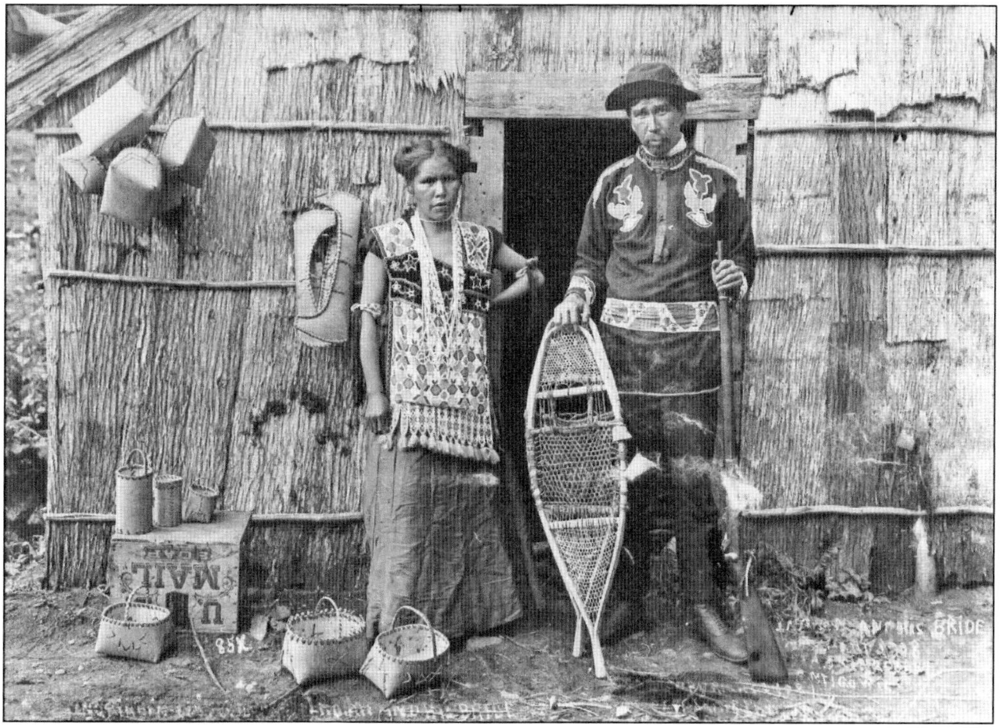

This c. 1908 photograph shows Maggie Bearskin Skye and George St. Germaine posing with some handcrafted items, including birch bark items and beadwork, as a form of advertising to tourists. Both people were favorite subjects of Kingsbury and are seen in many photographs. George St. Germaine was also a fishing guide.

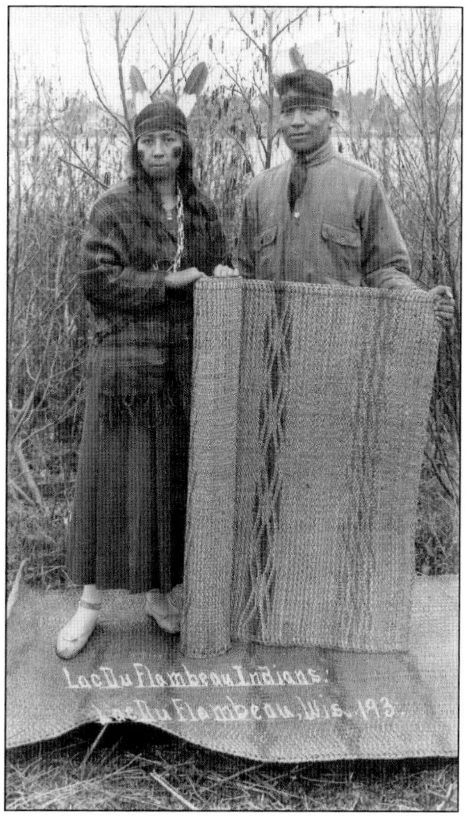

Woven mats served many purposes. The most common material used was bulrushes, but when these were scarce, the inner bark of the red cedar was a common substitute. Mats could serve as floor coverings in the wigwam, as well as dwelling partitions, and may be laid on the ground or floor for serving food on ceremonial occasions.

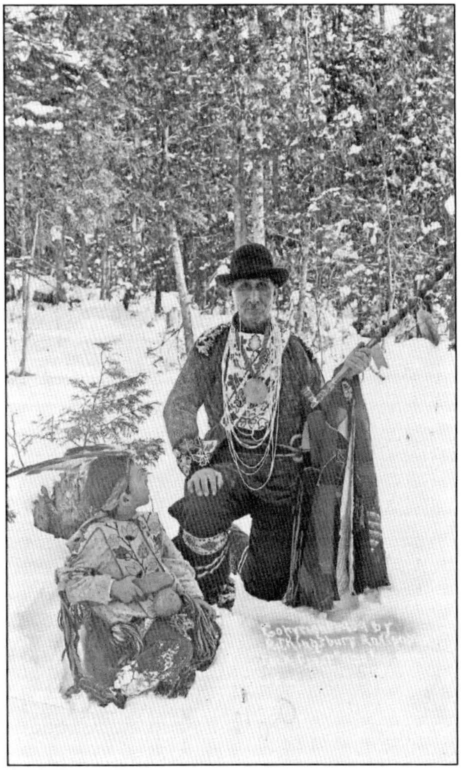

A few Ojibwe were likely along the southern shore of Lake Superior before the time of Columbus, but major numbers did not arrive until the 18th century. Once their winter trapping possibilities dwindled, they moved inland, bringing them into conflict with the Dakota. By the mid-19th century, those conflicts and treaties with the US government forced them to cede nearly two-thirds of what is now northern Wisconsin.

The Wayman family poses in front of their wigwam home with some crafts to be marketed to tourists. The man on the right is John "45" Wayman. He is holding his rifle, which may signify that he is also a hunting guide.

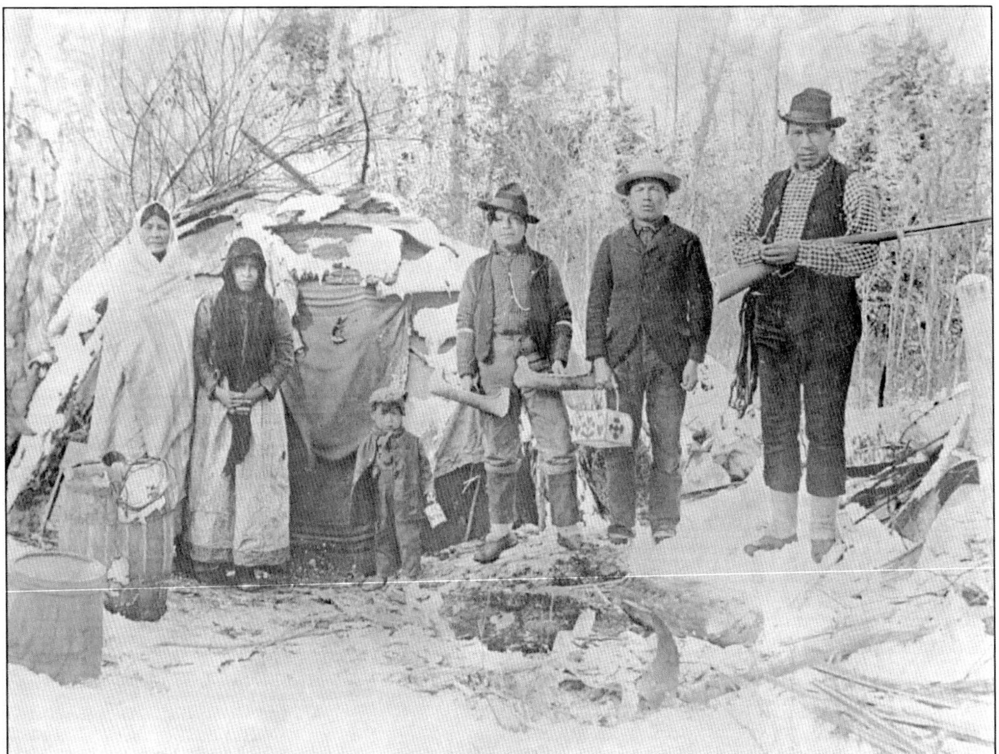

Prior to contact with European explorers and fur traders, basic women's clothing consisted of a deerskin dress worn over an undershirt of woven nettle fiber. In post-contact times, broadcloth replaced deerskin as the prime material for the basic dress. Often a second piece of appliquéd or beaded broadcloth was worn over the basic dress.

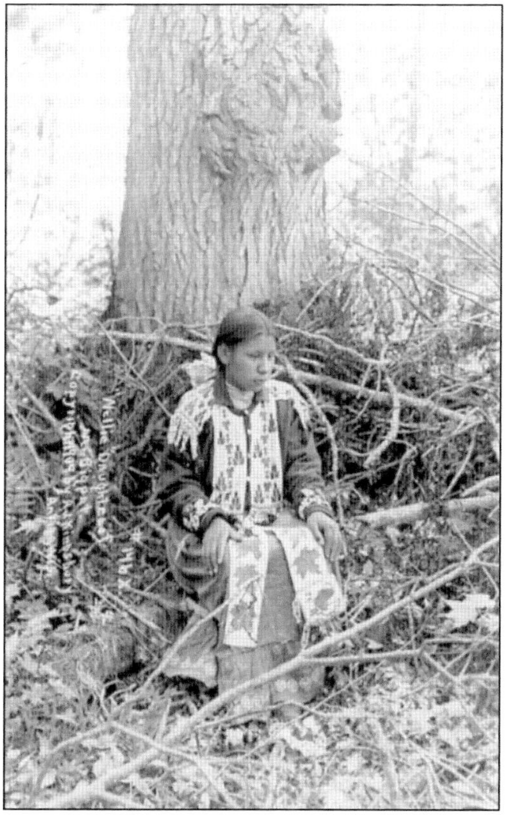

This picture of an extended family in the town of Three Lakes is one of many photographs by Kingsbury that show day-to-day activities at a time when the Ojibwe were moving into more urban or small-town environments, leaving behind many of their woodland traditions.

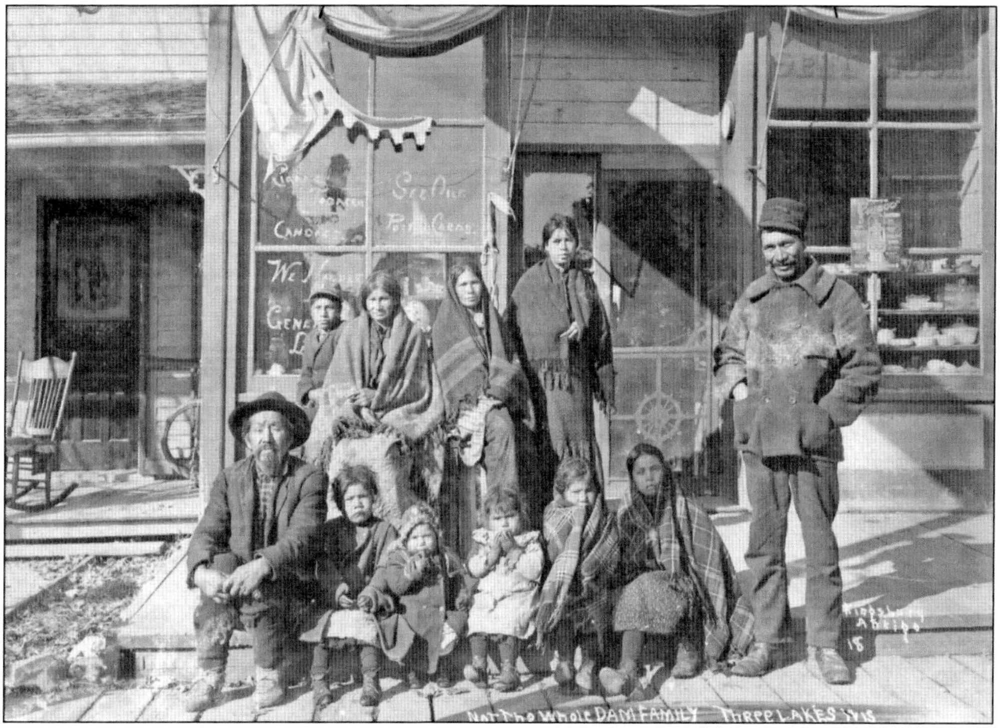

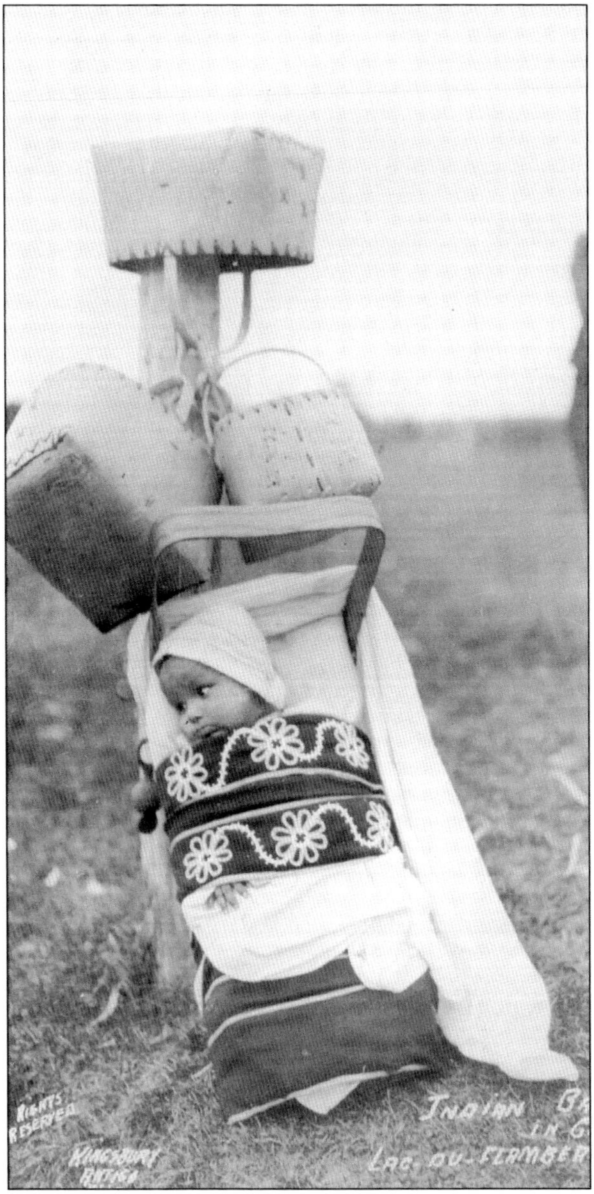

Most Americans probably think "papoose" when they see this image. Generally, they think a papoose is a Native American baby, but papoose also has a long history as the word for the apparatus holding the baby. It is also commonly called a cradleboard. Cradleboards were used for babies before they could walk. The board helped keep the baby's back straight, it was secure and comfortable, and it allowed the mother freedom of movement during the day. A cradleboard could be leaned against something so the baby could see the mother as she worked, or the mother could strap the board to her back as she moved about. Cradleboards wrapped a baby in natural materials. The back, a flat board or a framework of flexible twigs, was covered with cushioning and absorbent materials that kept the baby warm and relatively dry. Moss, shredded tree bark, and rabbit pelts were often used. Cradleboards frequently had a covered framework protruding over the baby's head. These provided shade and protection should the cradleboard fall forward. (Courtesy of Prestor Pictures.)

Doris Dowd was another favorite subject of Kingsbury's. She is shown here with an infant in a cradleboard that is typical of the Ojibwe. She and the infant are wearing excellent examples of beadwork. Interestingly, she is wearing a bandolier bag. These were usually made to be worn by men.

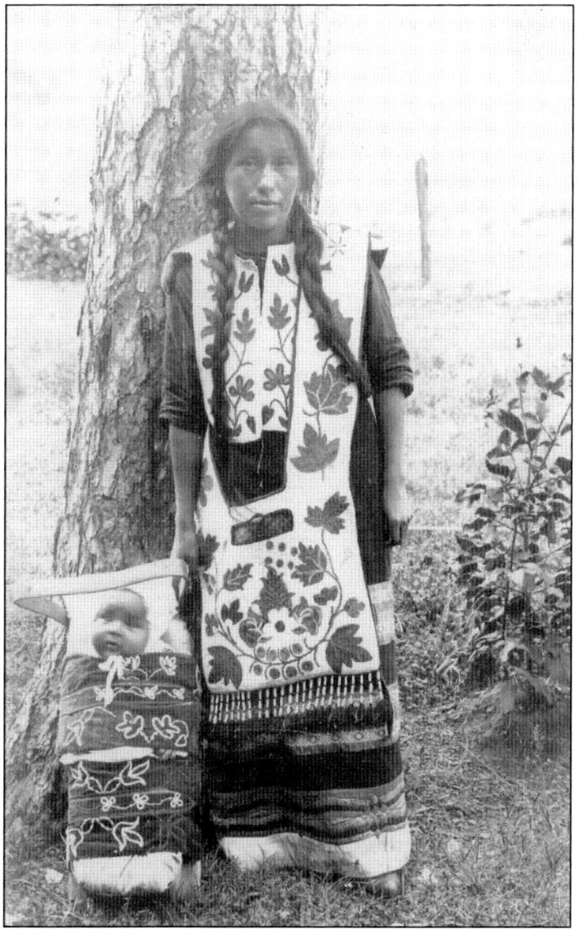

Ojibwe life centered around the seasons and the quest for food. Spring was a time for spearfishing and processing maple syrup. Summer days were spent fishing, carrying out minimal hunting, and growing corn, beans, and squash. Fall was spent harvesting wild rice; women generally harvested the rice. In winter, the activities included hunting deer and trapping fur-bearing animals. (Courtesy of Prestor Pictures.)

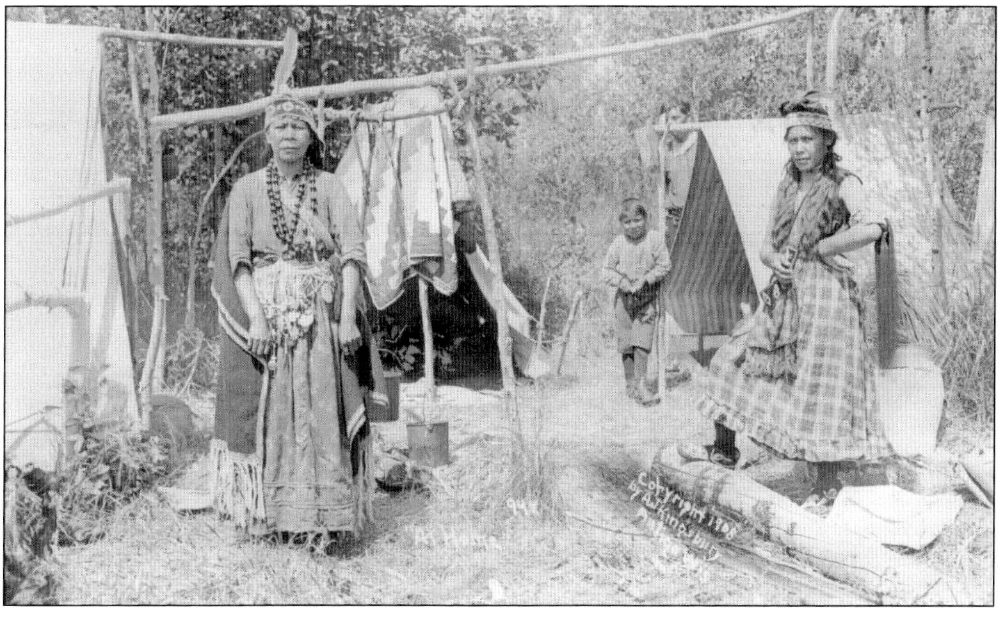

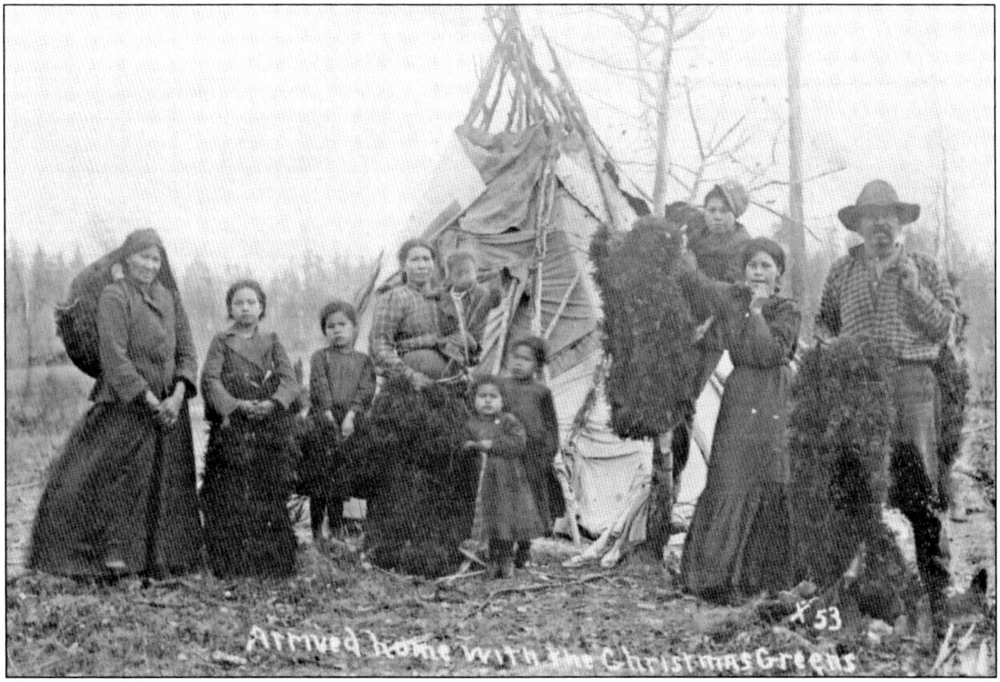

Ojibwe families would travel throughout the North Woods, staying in temporary teepee shelters. They would collect evergreen boughs to be woven into wreaths that were sold to white settlers and tourists as Christmas decorations.

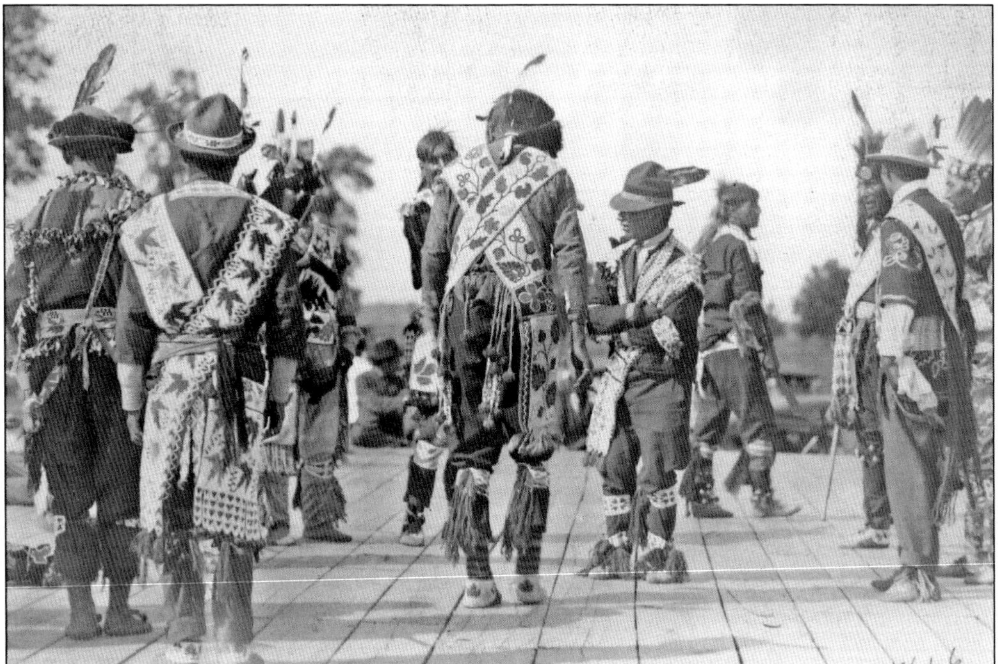

Dressed in ceremonial attire and standing on a prepared wooden platform, these Ojibwe men are likely preparing to dance for visiting tourists. Tourists, photographers, and whites were not welcome to participate in or view a number of dances.

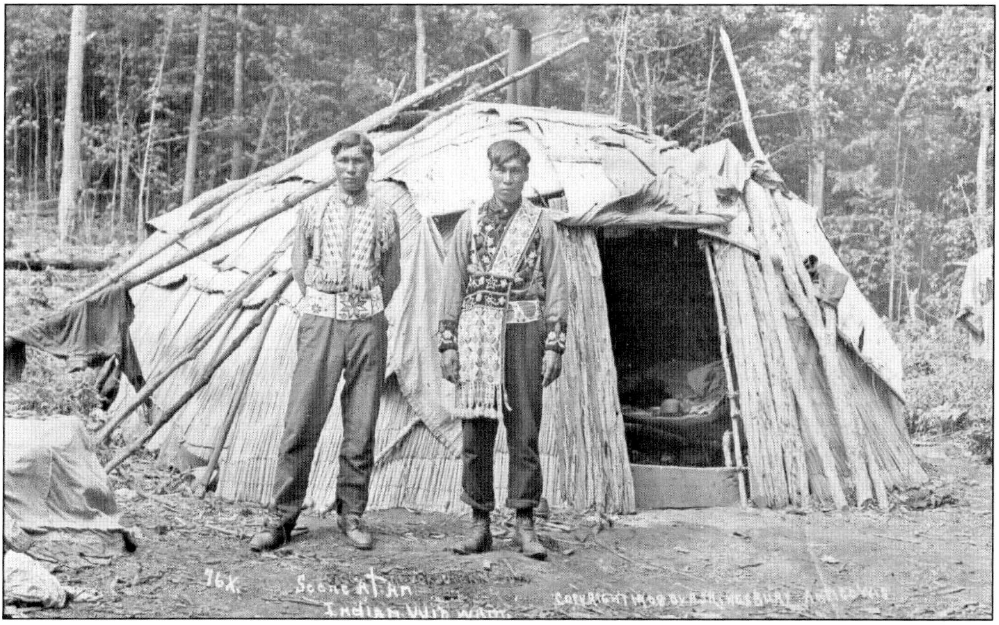

The man on the right is wearing a bandolier bag. These are arguably the epitome of Indian beadwork, and each bag took about a year to create. They were made by women and said to be for men to wear at special events; however, there are many photographs of women wearing bandolier bags. Perhaps they wore them in honor of a male family member.

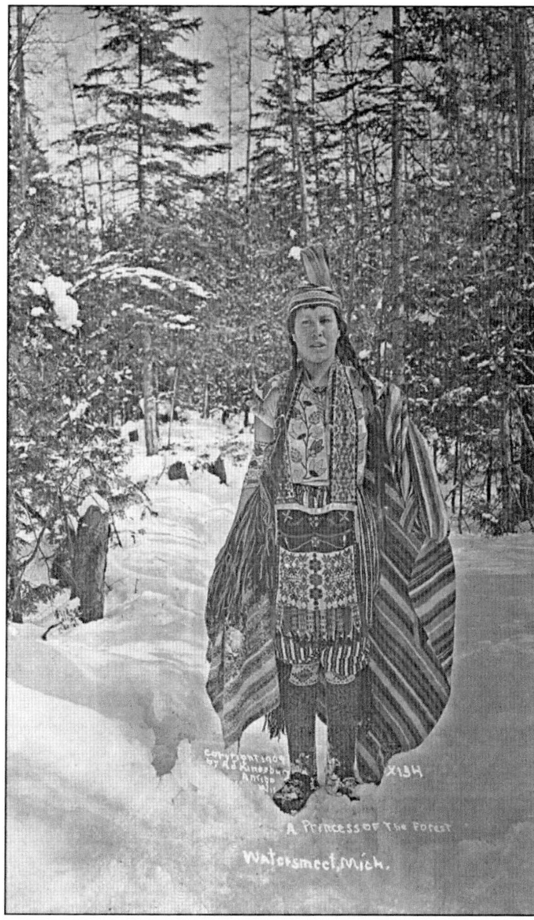

The woman here wears a bandolier bag over a floral-patterned vest. The floral pattern is typical of the Ojibwe, as well as other woodland Indians, and although the symmetry of the pattern is atypical, it is not unique.

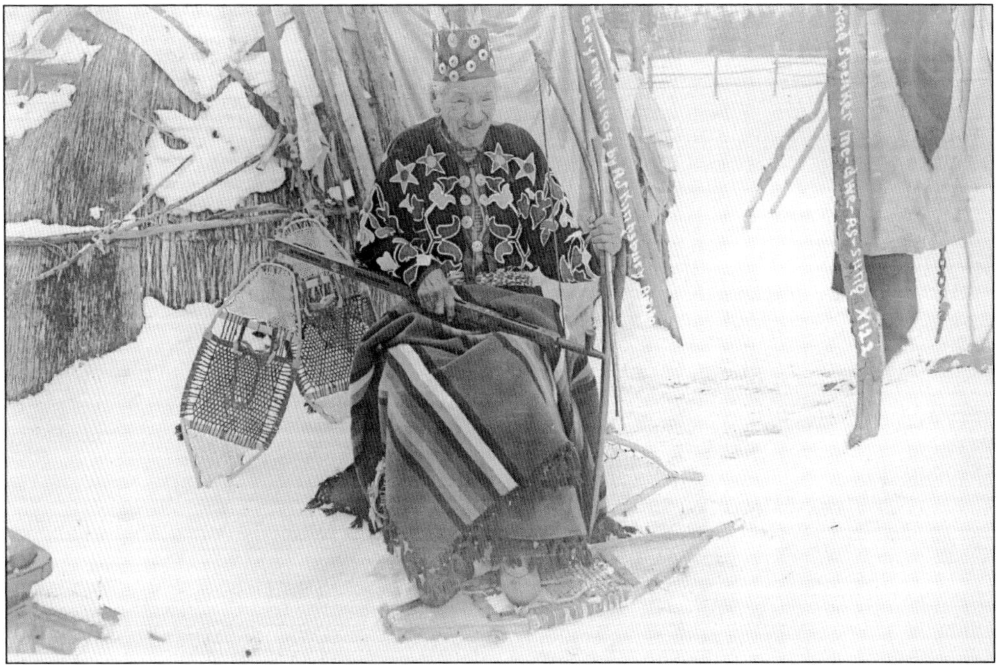

Pictured here is Me-dwe-as-sung, the head speaker of the Lac du Flambeau band. His beaded vest is typical of the decorative arts tradition of the woodland Indians in the Great Lakes region. He holds a long pipe across his lap and a bow and arrow in his left hand. (Courtesy of Prestor Pictures.)

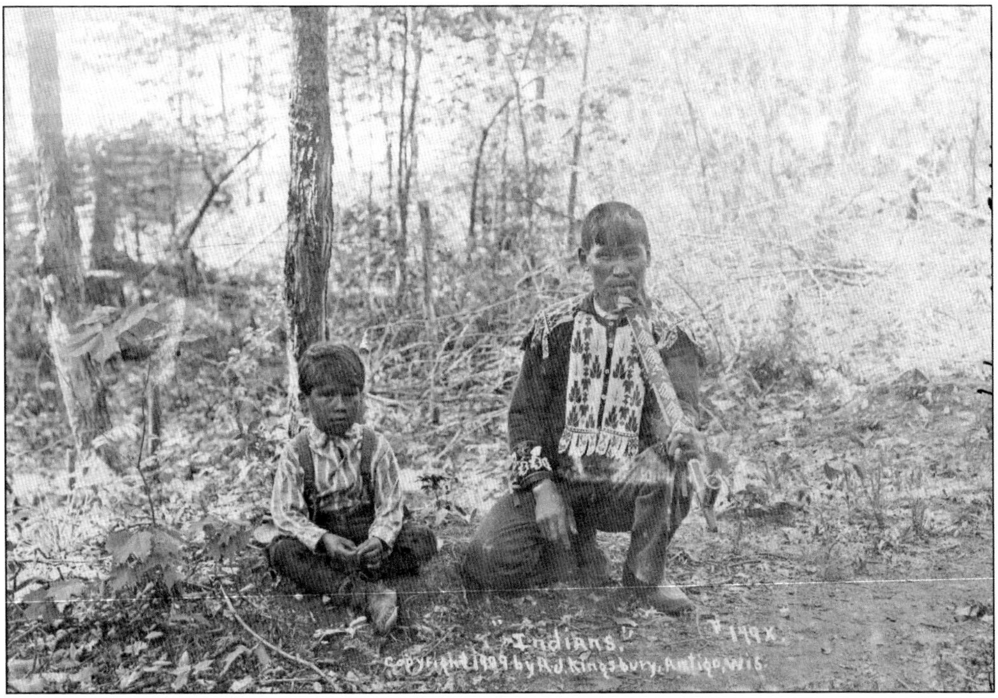

Kingsbury posed this interesting scene of a man and boy. The boy is wearing traditional white man's clothing, while the man is wearing beautiful Indian beadwork items and holding an elaborately decorated pipe.

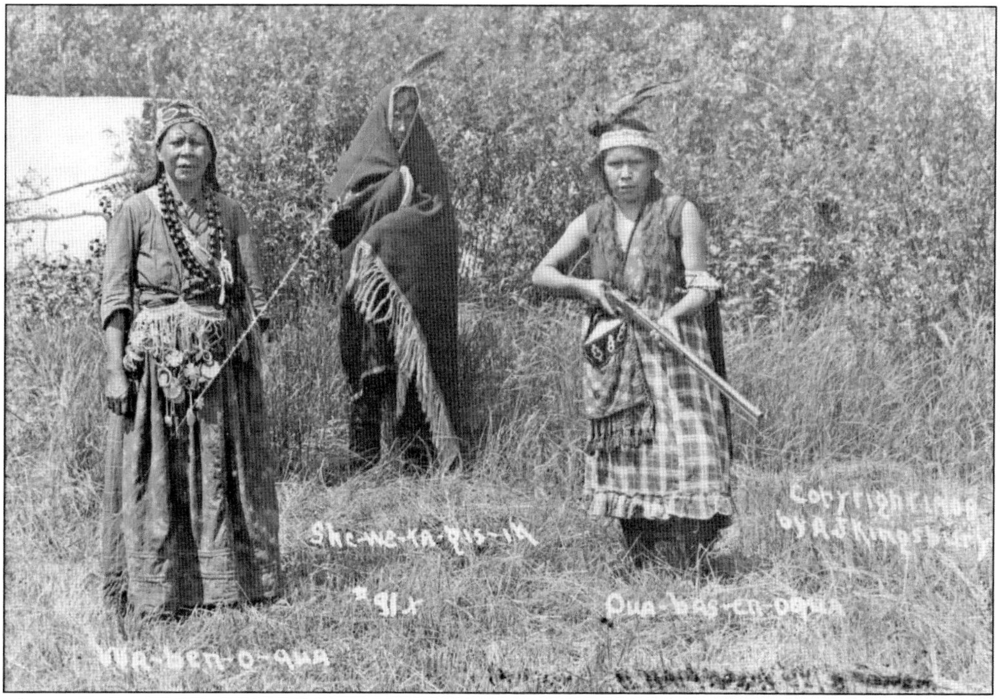

The woman on the right, at Lac du Flambeau, is shown with a rifle. Men were usually the hunters but not exclusively so. Ojibwe women also hunted and acted as guides along with the men.

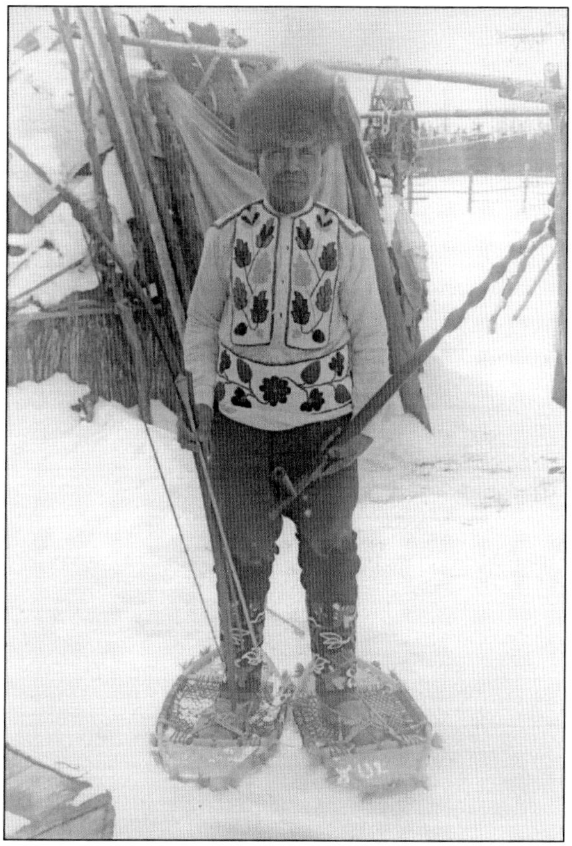

Snowshoes were invented by either the woodland Indians or those in the Canadian subarctic. They were indispensible to men during their long winter hunts. Strips of green ash were bent over a fire or in hot water. Rawhide thongs, woven in a hexagonal pattern, formed the center, and a leather strap held the foot in place.

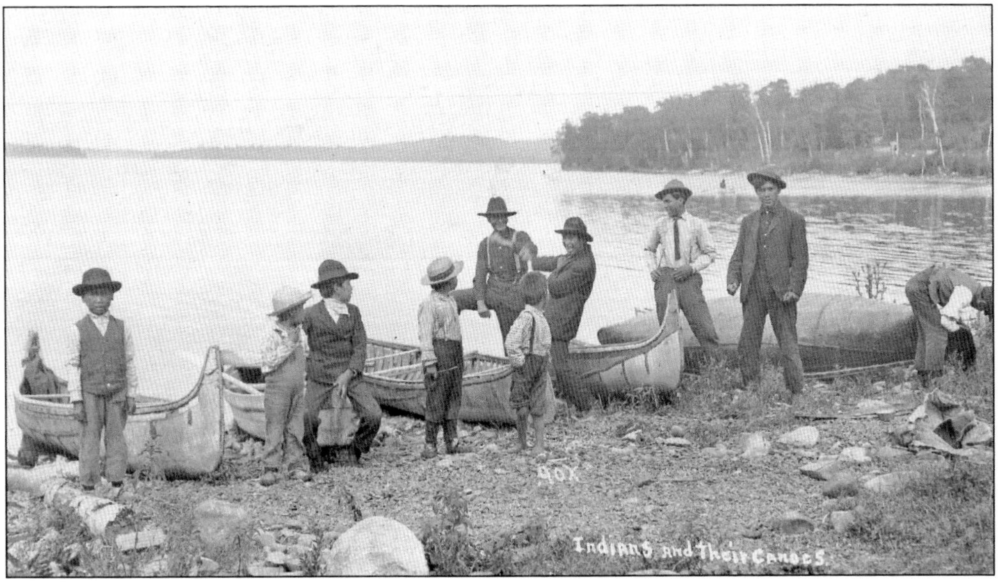

At Lac du Flambeau, the Indians operated resorts and took visitors canoeing and fishing. Birch bark was used in many ways, including usage as storage containers, cooking containers (they could be heated over a fire if used properly), and wigwam coverings, as well as in traditional canoe construction.

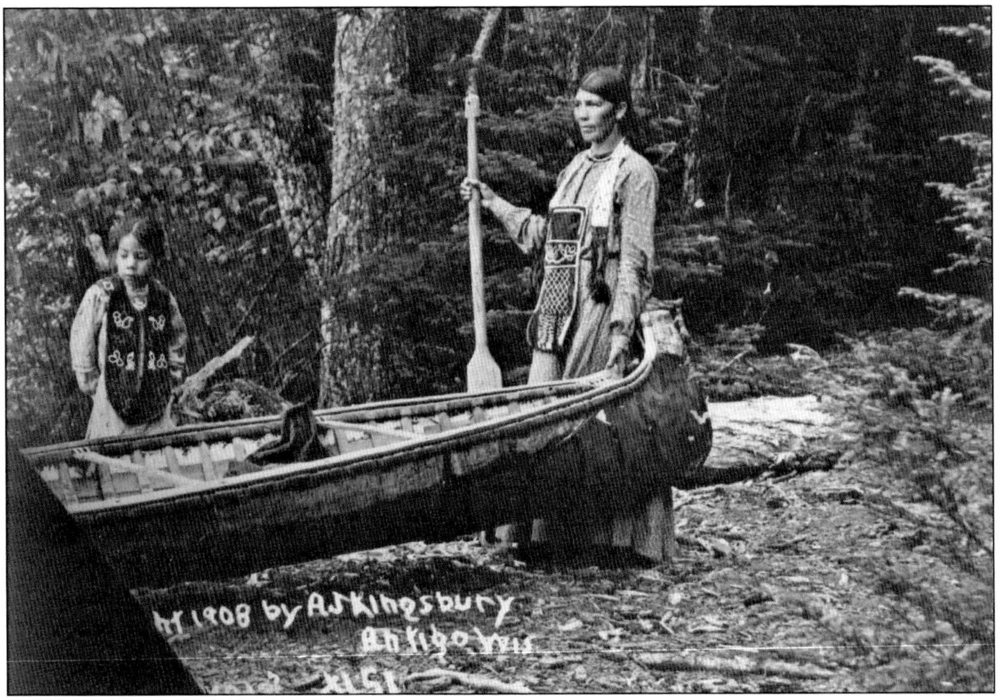

Bark used for canoes was peeled in the spring and was sturdier than bark in other seasons. The large sheets required felling the tree. For a portion of a canoe that was to be decorated, sections of bark were peeled later in the season. The bark peeled in summer would hold dyes better and was used for baskets because it was lighter.. Peeling bark for containers required smaller sections and did not harm the tree.

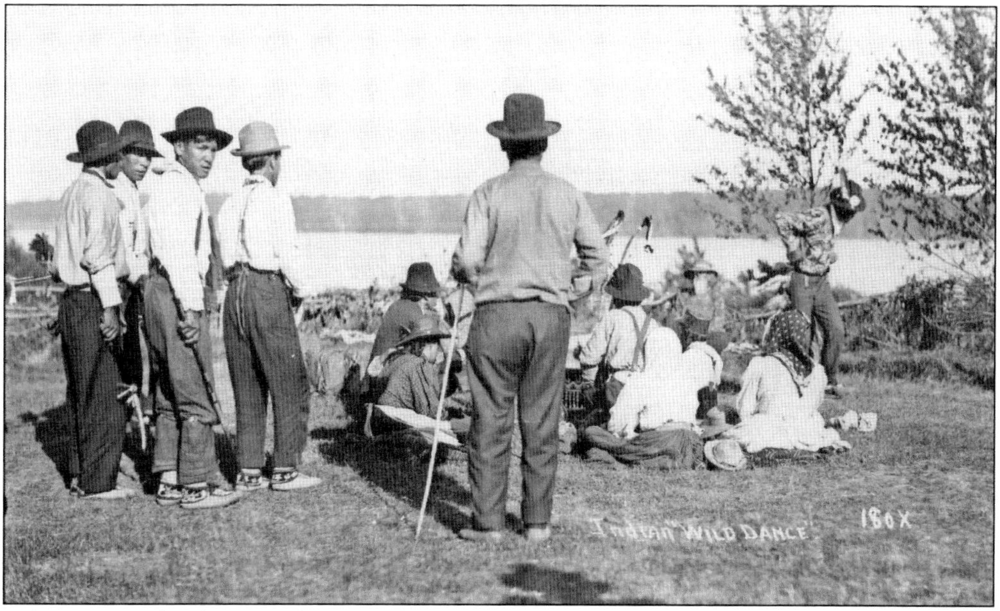

"The time . . . for the annual get-together of the Chippewa tribe and Indian Pageant which will be held in the old Indian village at Lac du Flambeau from August 7th to the 15th. There will be war dances, canoe races, Indian games, and sports. Visitors will be able to see Indians making birch bark canoes, beadwork and rugs, and will be able to hear them singing the old Indian love songs," reported the *Minocqua Times* on August 6, 1937.

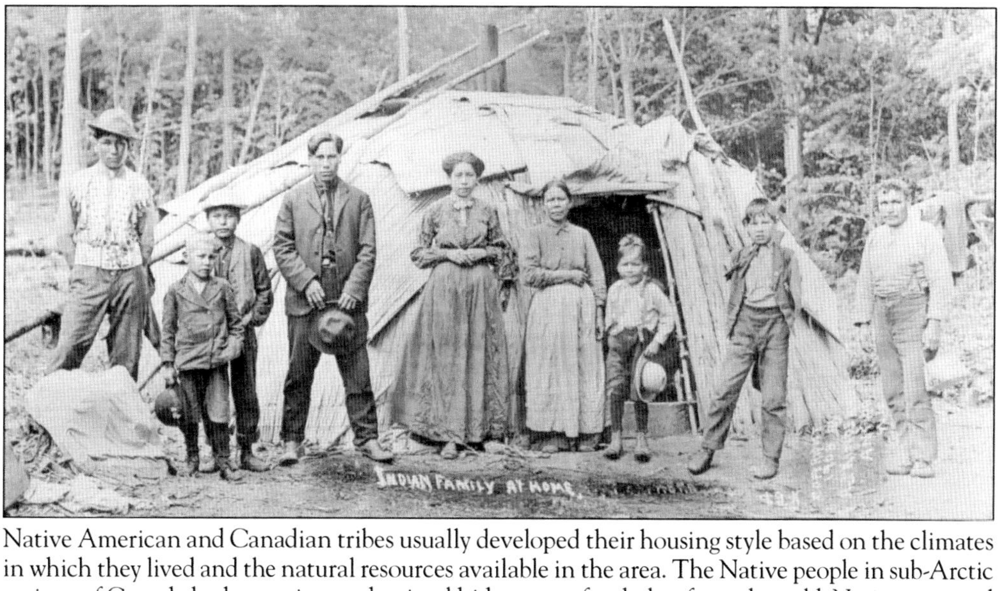

Native American and Canadian tribes usually developed their housing style based on the climates in which they lived and the natural resources available in the area. The Native people in sub-Arctic regions of Canada had snow, ice, and animal hides to use for shelter from the cold. Natives situated in the western deserts of what became the United States and Mexico lived in high temperatures and could not farm where water was scarce, which affected their housing needs. The woodland Indians living around the Great Lakes area developed sturdy and fairly long lasting wigwams, like the one seen here. Birch bark, sticks, animal hides, and grass mats, used for the construction of the wigwams, were easily available. When properly built, wigwams provided good protection against the elements. (Courtesy of Prestor Pictures.)

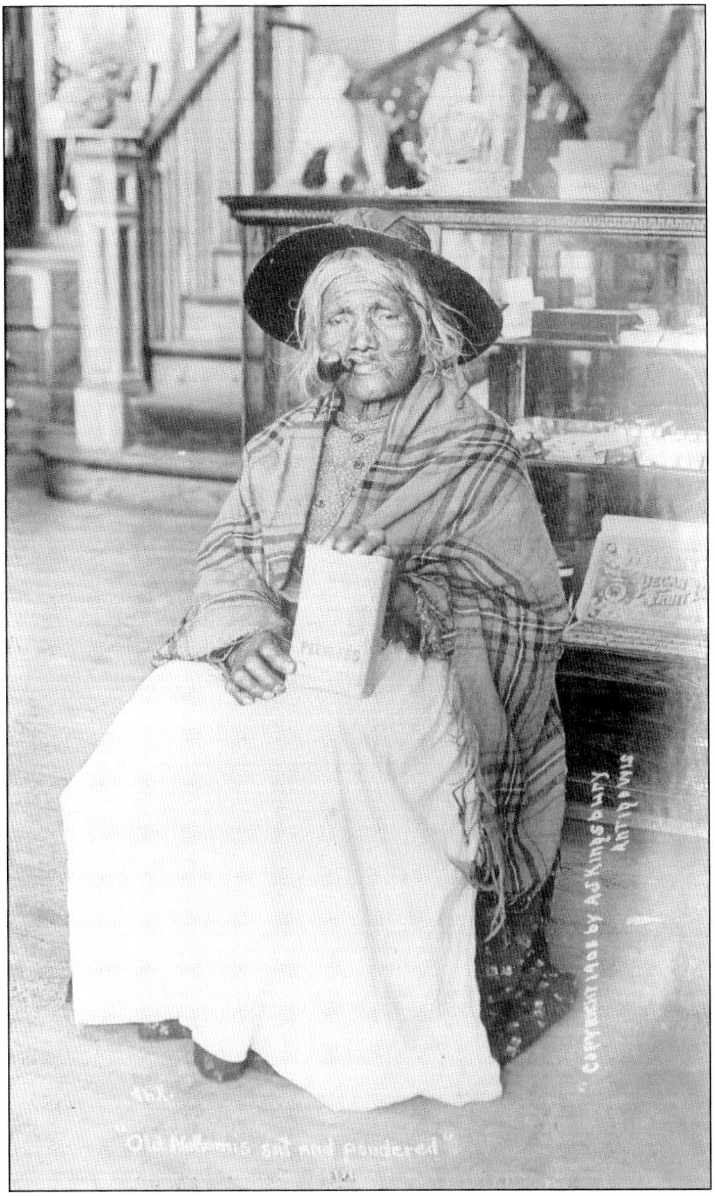

The caption to this image reads, "Old Nakomis sat and pondered." This woman, named Gingwashnokwe, displays a package of Peerless Tobacco. Kingsbury probably asked her to pose like this to make a saleable postcard image. One might ponder whether he was intentionally implying the image of cigar-store wooden Indians. By 1900, few wooden Indians were still in use, but it is interesting to note their history. Native Americans introduced tobacco to early European sailors. The sailors carried it home, and tobacco use spread. In the 1600s, though, most Europeans were illiterate. It was the custom for many merchants to display a three-dimensional trade symbol in front of their stores, so the passing citizens would know what was sold inside. Scissors indicated a tailor, a pocket watch for a jeweler, a tooth for a dentist, and a shoe, a gun, and a red and white striped pole all advertised the business inside. So too did the wooden Indian represent the tobacconist. These trade symbols continued to prove useful in 19th-century America due to the variety of non-English speaking immigrants. (Courtesy of Prestor Pictures.)

Six

Logging Industry

Wisconsin's extensive northern forests were a powerful magnet for lumbermen interested in supplying a growing nation's recovery from a devastating Civil War. At first, logging camps were situated along major waterways, since rivers were the highways transporting logs from the forests to sawmills and markets. The Wolf River was such a thoroughfare, with many small lumber camps and towns, such as Langlade and Lily, springing up. It was also in the camps along the Wolf that many Menominee Indians found employment.

With the later expansion of rail lines into northern Wisconsin, logging became feasible in areas away from the major rivers. This made the growth of towns such as Antigo and Elcho possible. Langlade County was covered by a spider-web network of short rail lines leading to lumber camps and sawmills. While some of these camp lines lasted decades, others were in place for only a few years. Once the nearby forest had been clear-cut, tracks were taken up and laid into well-forested areas.

Life in a logging camp was not for the faint of heart. The diary of a woman who worked as a cook described how cabins were so poorly built, she would wake up to find herself covered in a layer of snow that had blown in through the gaps between the walls' logs during the night. Cooks needed to awaken at 4:00 a.m. in order to prepare breakfast for the crew.

Logging was difficult and dangerous work, particularly during river drives when logs could pile up and dams might give way. Much of the tree cutting took place in winter when logs could be skidded out on paths layered by a horse-drawn ice wagon in what might be thought of as an early form of a Zamboni. At first, oxen were used, but they were soon replaced by horses and, eventually, by motorized haulers. By the 1930s, many forests had been clear-cut, creating serious environmental problems and loss of logging revenues. The Civilian Conservation Corps of the New Deal replenished the forest lands by implementing a program of organized replanting.

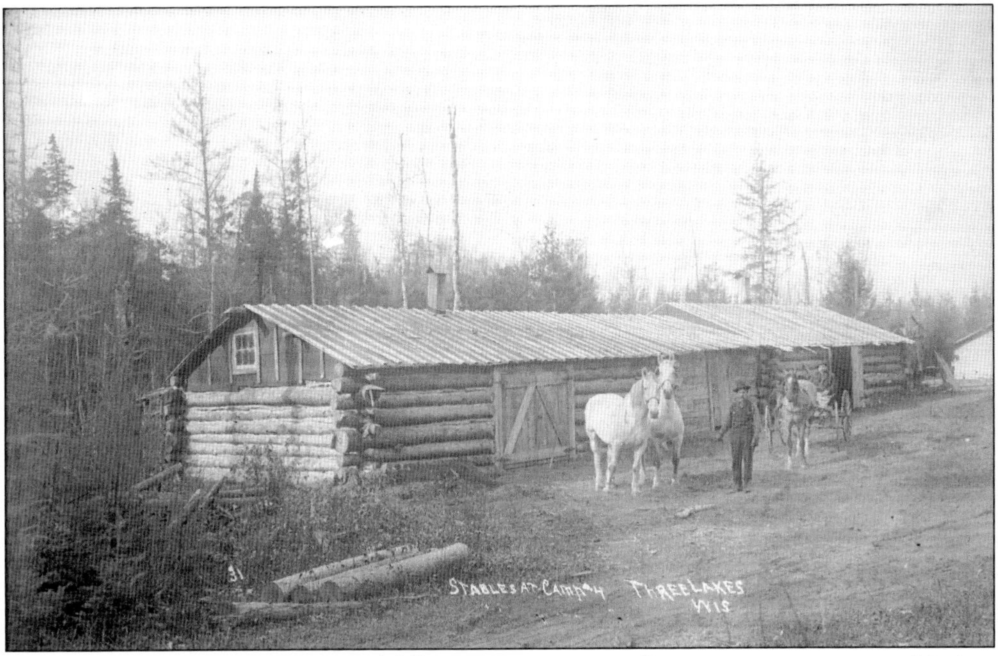

Establishing a lumber camp required following a set routine. Once an area was surveyed in late summer or early fall, some of the crew cut logs for the buildings, including bunkhouses, cooking and dining halls, a blacksmith shop, and stables. Other men cut paths from the camp to the river landing or railroad siding. Then, by early winter, the work began of harvesting timber.

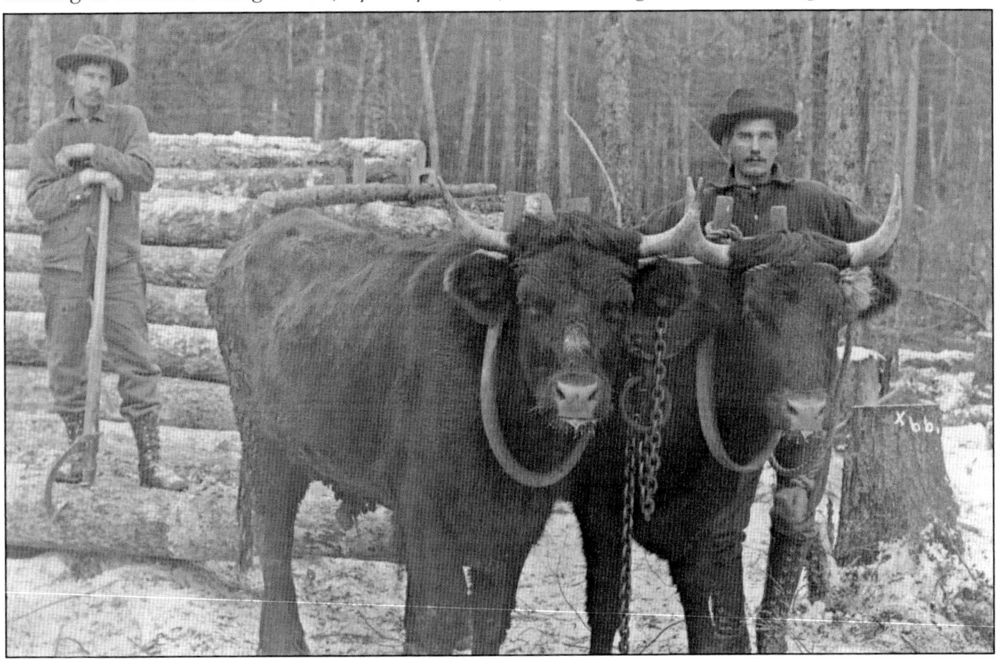

When northern Wisconsin first opened up to logging shortly after the Civil War, the loggers relied mainly on oxen to haul the cut trees out of the woods, as they were more sure-footed than horses. Using oxen provided a large advantage, since much of the work was done in winter and on icy paths.

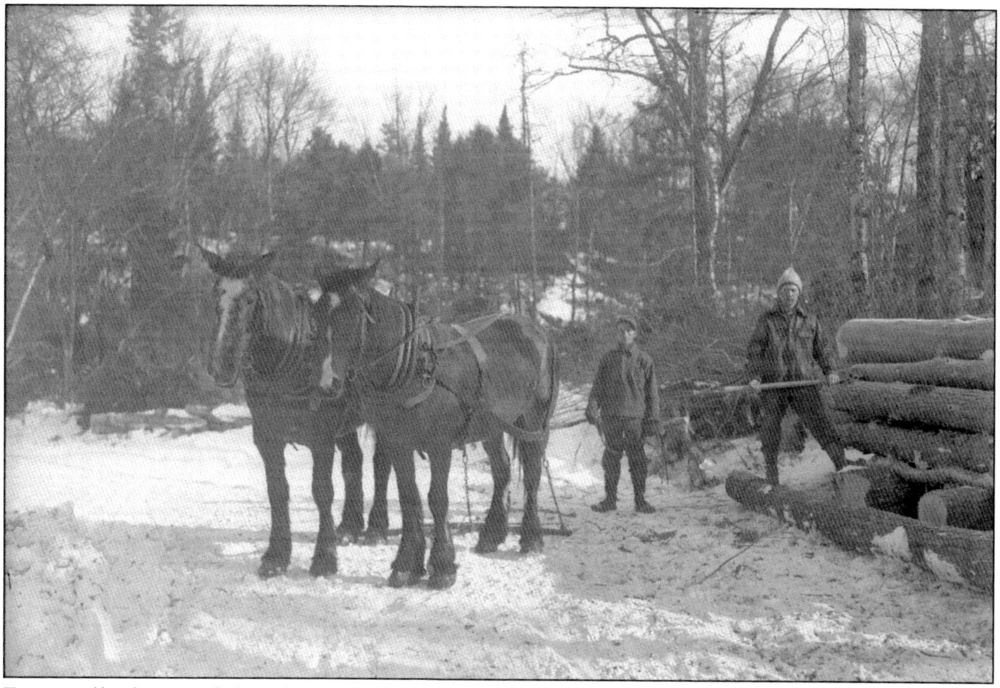

Eventually, horses did replace oxen as a means of skidding logs out of the woods. A major disadvantage of the switch to horses was the loss of beef for the table from oxen no longer fit to work.

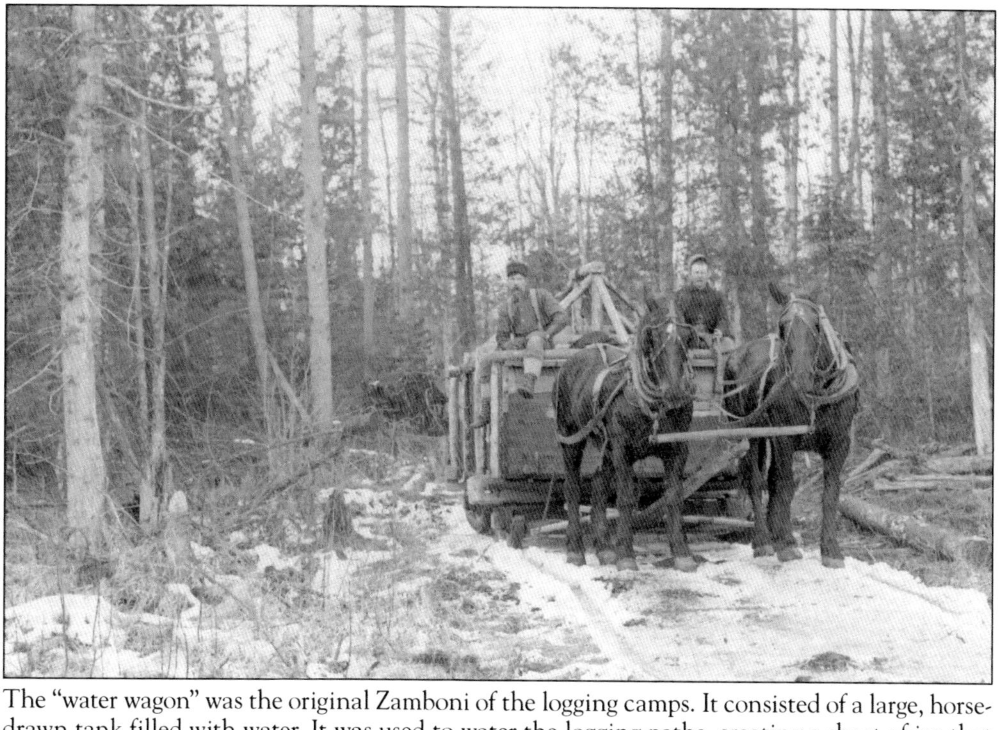

The "water wagon" was the original Zamboni of the logging camps. It consisted of a large, horse-drawn tank filled with water. It was used to water the logging paths, creating a sheet of ice that reduced friction and made hauling logs out of the woods easier.

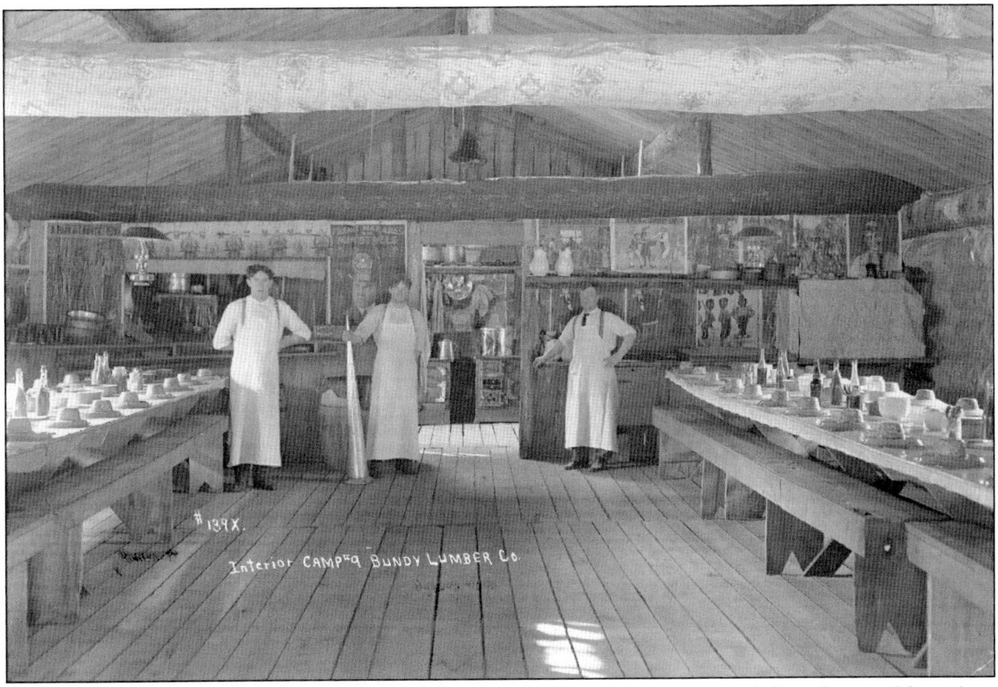

Women often worked in the camps as cooks. In her diary, Ada Moran noted that she would awaken at 4:00 a.m. to start cooking. Often, when she awoke, she first had to dust off a two- or three-inch layer of snow that had blown in through the gaps between the cabin walls' logs.

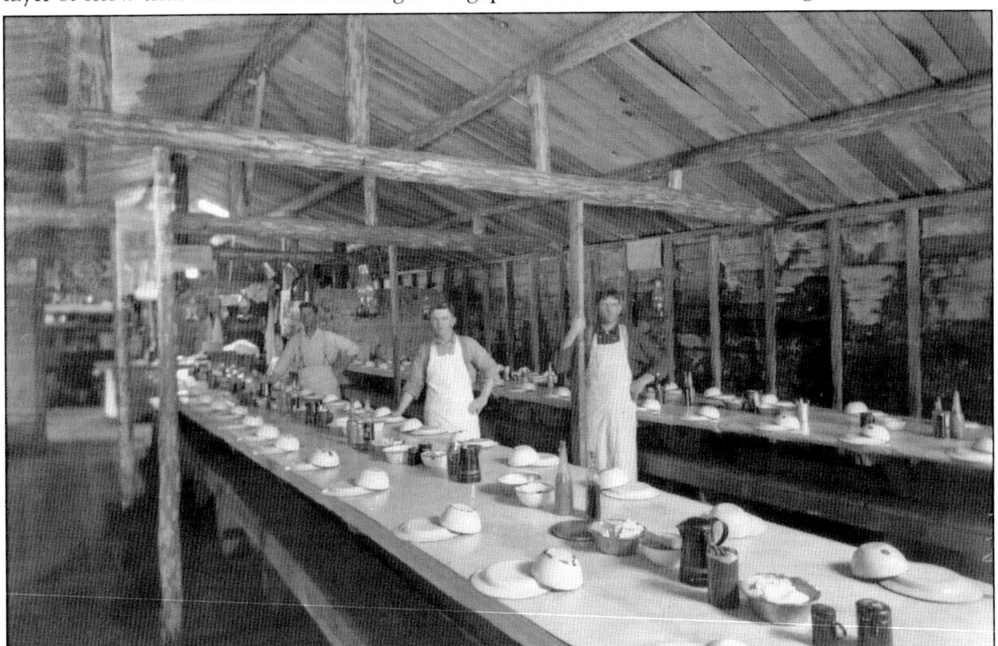

Ada Moran's description of her work states, "For breakfast we had pork, beefsteak or sausages, griddle cakes, fried spuds, doughnuts, and coffee. For dinner we had beef stew or pot roast, potatoes, onions or rutabagas, good brown gravy, and pie. For supper there was provided fried potatoes, cold meat or fish, batter cake, prunes, coffee or tea, mince, apple or prune pie."

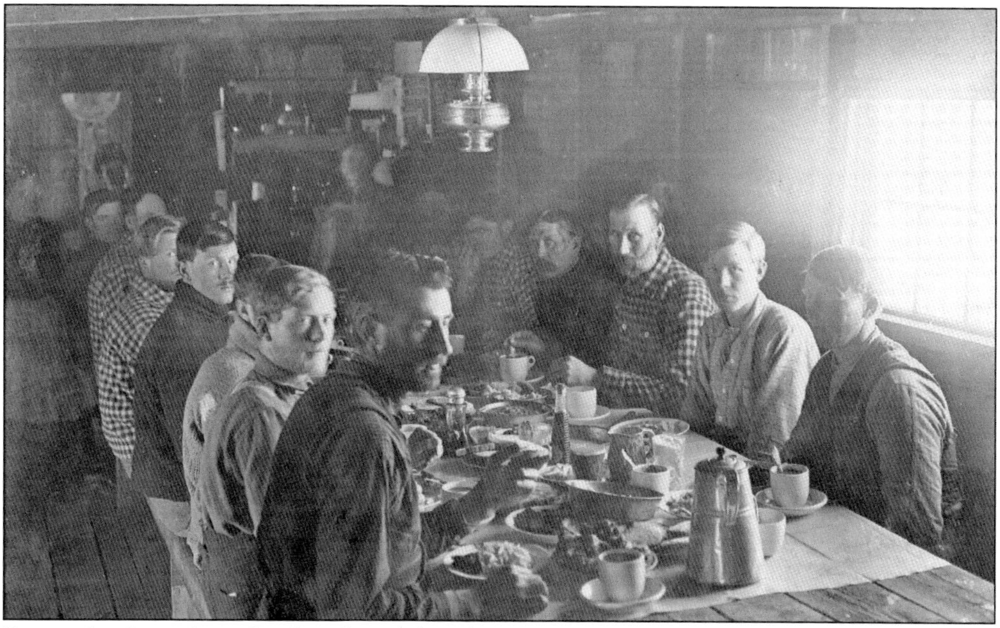

Being a lumberjack was hard work with long hours in winter cold and snow for poor pay. But the food? It has been said that the camps with the best food got the best lumberjacks. And some men would quit a camp with a bad cook. Each meal provided a large selection of foods, and the men ate as much as they wanted. (Courtesy of Prestor Pictures.)

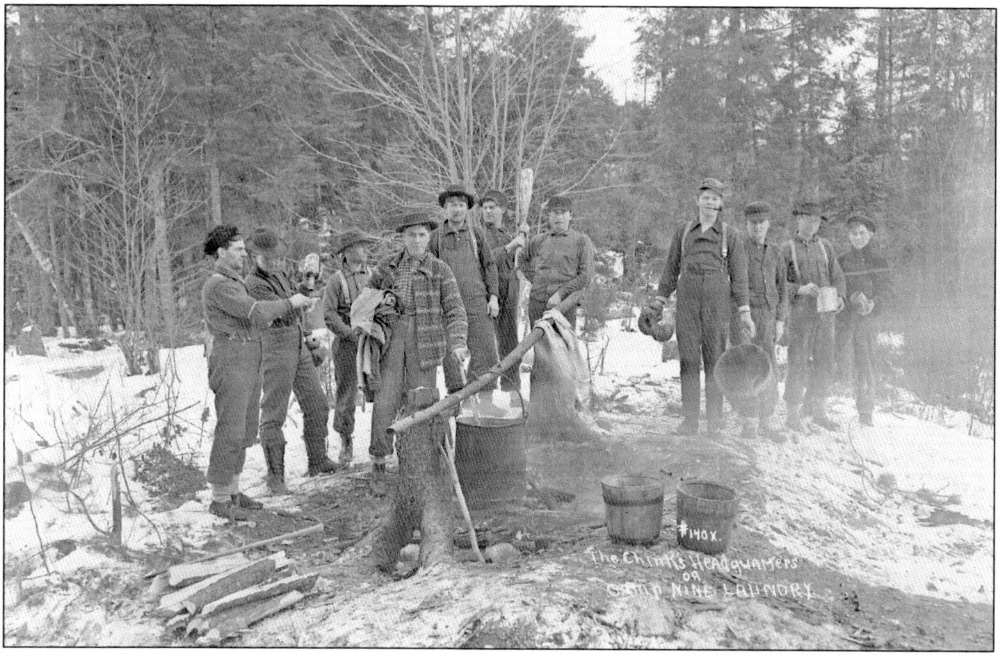

Many lumberjacks had to live far from home, even far from the closest small town. Laundry facilities in the forest consisted of two tree trunks with a strong branch between them, supporting a large metal pot of boiling water. Here, the men of Camp Nine are waiting their turn with the hot water. One man is stirring his laundry in the pot, and the man holding a wood bucket is also carrying boxing gloves.

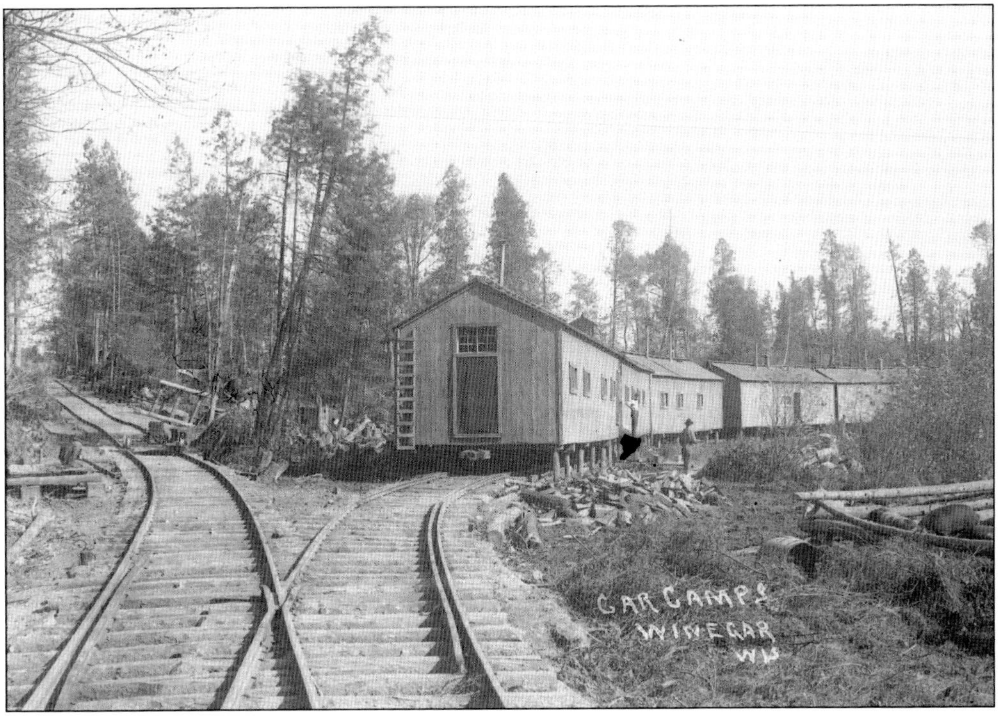

Logging camps' barracks and bunkhouses were sometimes placed on railcars so that they might more easily be moved to a new site once the immediate area was clear-cut.

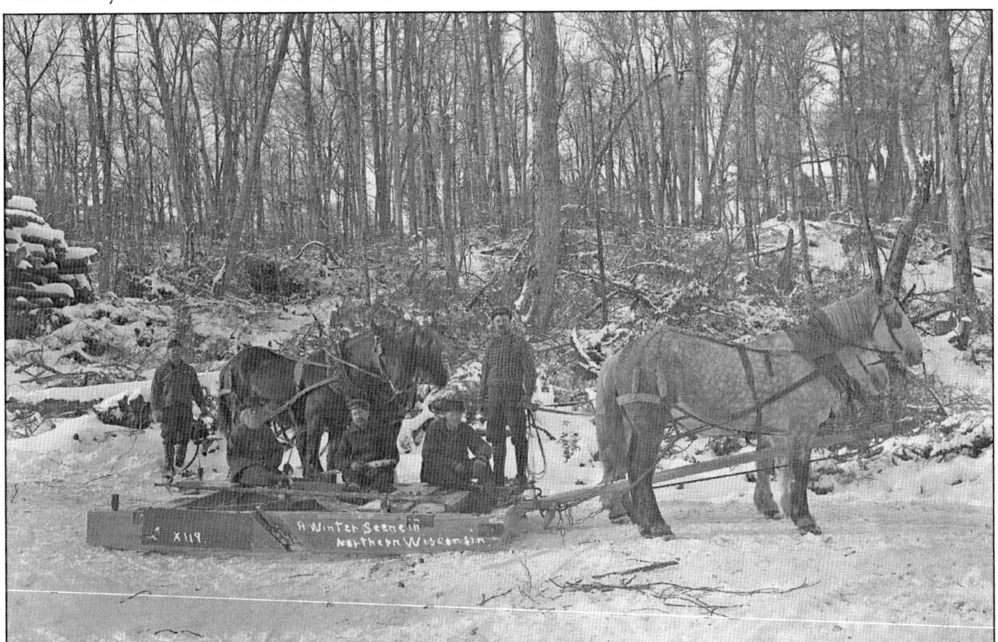

The use of sleighs to haul logs was not initially an obvious choice. In the very early years, a travois was used. Two wooden runners, turned up at the ends and bolted across the center, were hitched to a pair of oxen. Logs were rolled onto this device using other oxen, and then the team hitched to the travois pulled the load to a nearby river.

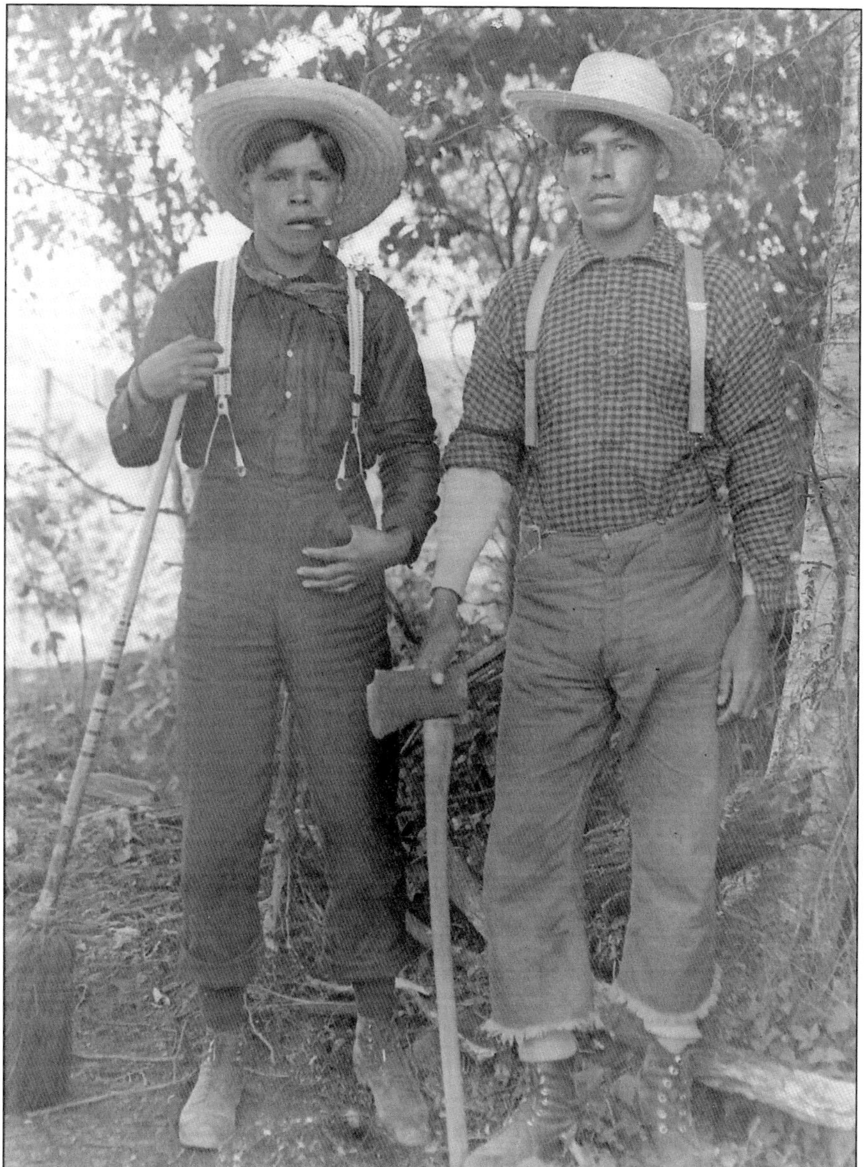

The Menominee proved to be far better stewards of their forests than most early loggers by practicing sustainable logging. They did selective cutting from the time that their tribal boundaries became established in 1854. In 1871, the US government approved a plan to expand commercial logging, and the Menominee sold timber to sawmills off the reservation. Indians from the Menominee reservation often found employment in the lumber camps outside their reservation, where they faced less discrimination than in other employment. By 1905, at an annual rate of 20 million board feet, they had harvested 300 million board feet of timber. In 1905, a major tornado blew down 40 million board feet. Much of it was hardwood, which could not be floated on the Wolf to mills. The loss had a major impact on the community. Sen. Robert M. LaFollette introduced legislation directing the US Forest Service and the Department of Interior to organize logging on a sustainable basis consistent with the Menominees' vision. Lumber is still a major industry in the area.

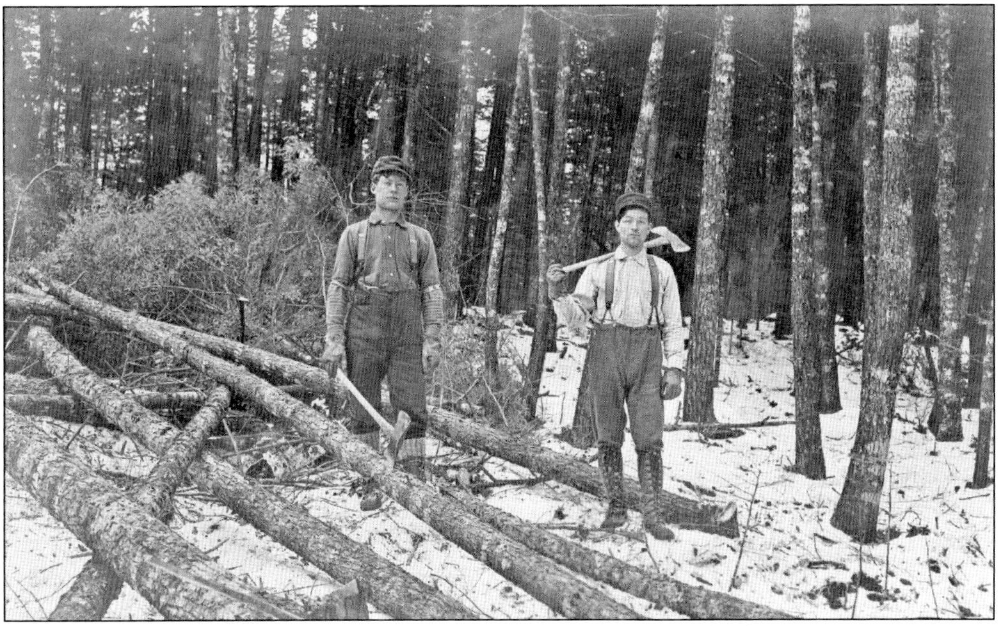

On November 24, 1922, the *Minocqua Times* documented that for the first time in many years, the lumber companies operating in neighboring counties were reporting shortages of men for the woods, "Early this fall they started in by paying from $30 a month and up, including board and lodging and they have now raised the wages to $40 per month and up." In 1921, lumbermen were paid about $25 per month. (Courtesy of Prestor Pictures.)

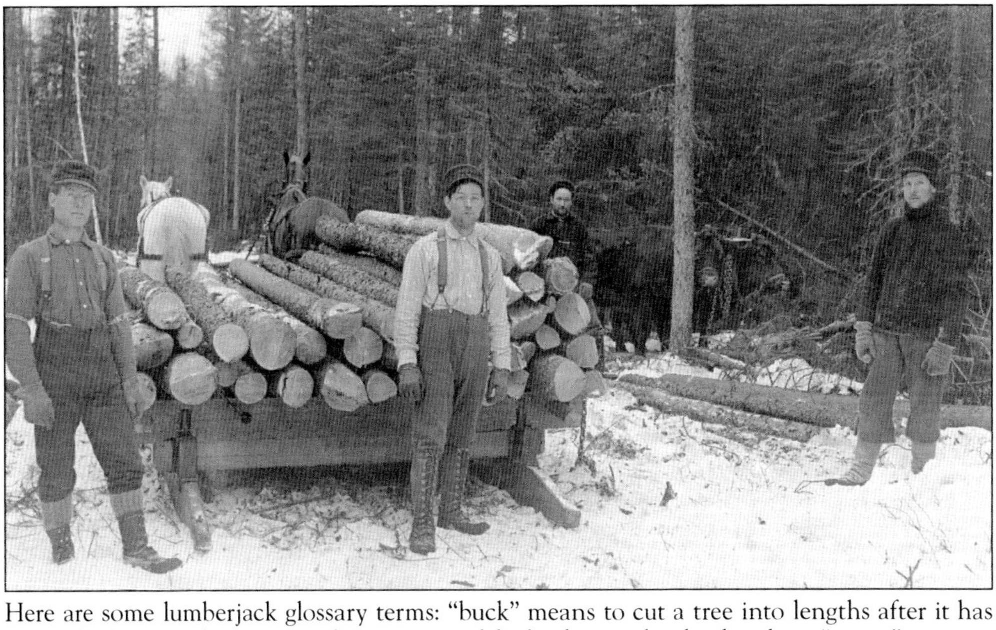

Here are some lumberjack glossary terms: "buck" means to cut a tree into lengths after it has been felled; "gin pole" means a short spar, used for loading and unloading logs; "gyppo" means a contract worker; "iron burner" is the camp blacksmith; "macaroni" is sawdust; "Swedish fiddle" is a crosscut saw; "snoose" is damp snuff; "pulaski" is a thick-handled tool with oval eye used as a combination axe and hoe; and "king snipe" is the boss of a track-laying crew. (Courtesy of Prestor Pictures.)

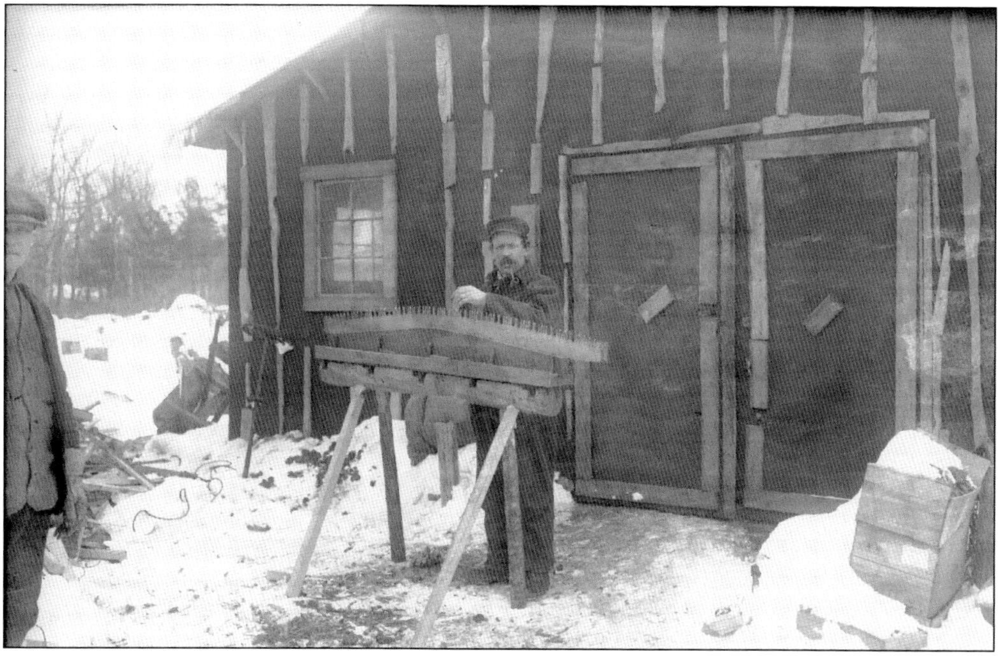

The task of sharpening saw blades at the lumber camps was one requiring great skill, and the person in charge of blade sharpening was paid more than most loggers. Men who cut down trees in the bush were called sawyers. Most sawyers had two saws. He (lumberjacks were always men) would use one saw working each day, while his second saw was being sharpened.

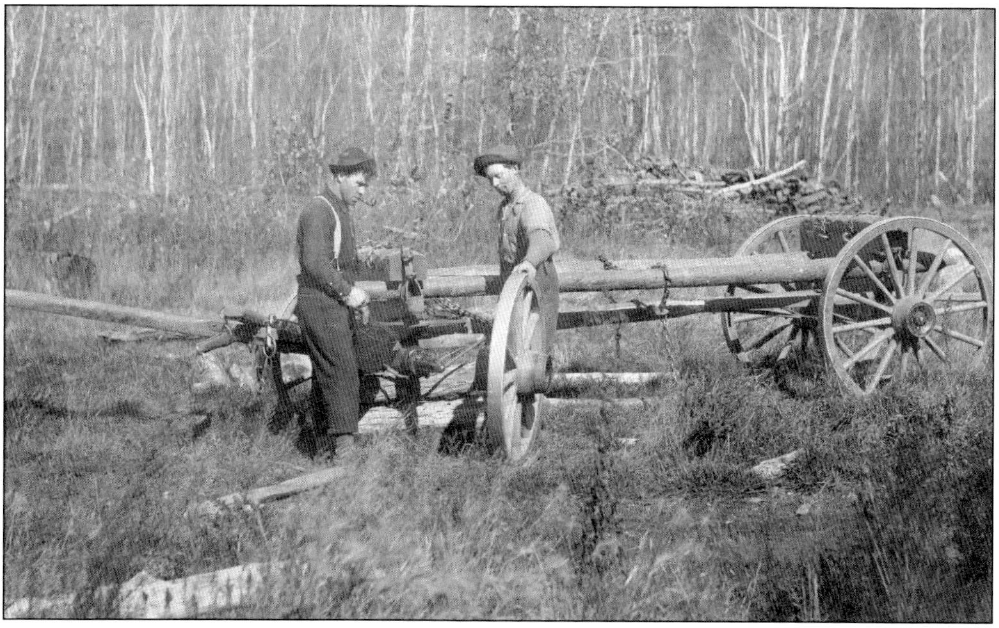

These loggers are doing basic maintenance to one of their wagon wheels. They are simply re-greasing what will be the inside of the hub. These are wood hub wheels with approximately two-inch-wide steel tires around them. Considering the consistently heavy loads of trees this wagon would carry, combined with the natural unevenness of the ground they must traverse, it is mighty important to keep everything in proper working order. (Courtesy of Prestor Pictures.)

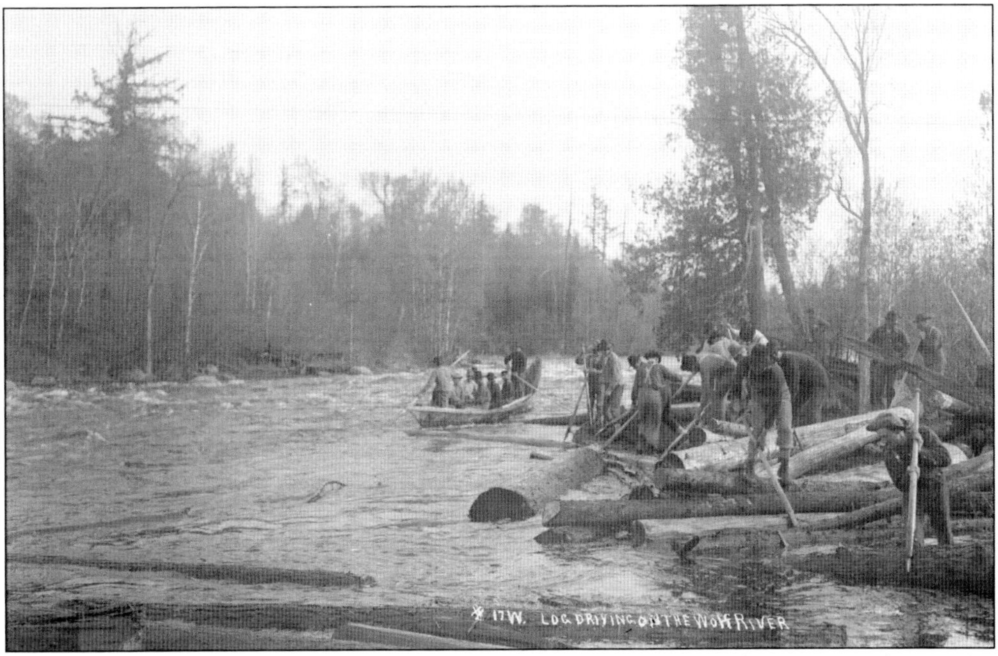

The end of the heyday of the pine logging along the Wolf River was forecast as early as 1886. The December 9, 1886, *Forest Republican* noted, "The Upper Wolf is stripped clean of Pine. The Lower Wolf is bare." The newspaper predicted the eventual demise of major mills in Oshkosh, the ultimate destination of logs harvested along the Wolf.

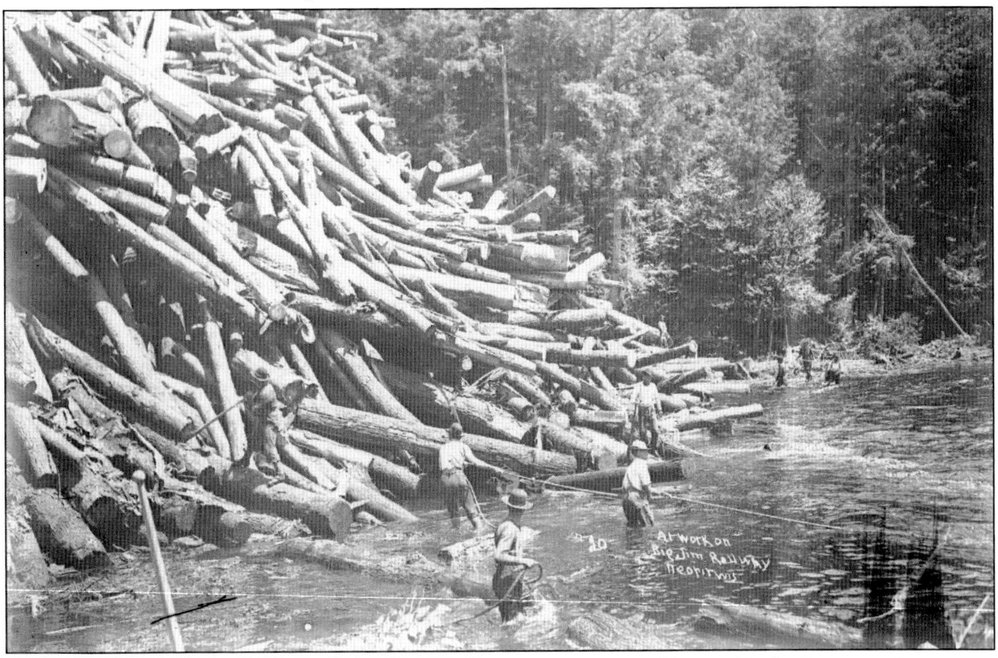

Controlling the entry of logs and the flow to downstream sawmills was likely the most dangerous of the loggers' tasks. For breaking apart log jams, loggers used cant hooks. These were long wooden poles with a large metal hook near the end. (A peavey is a cant hook with a sharp spike added to its end.) When cant hooks did not work, the lumbermen occasionally resorted to dynamite.

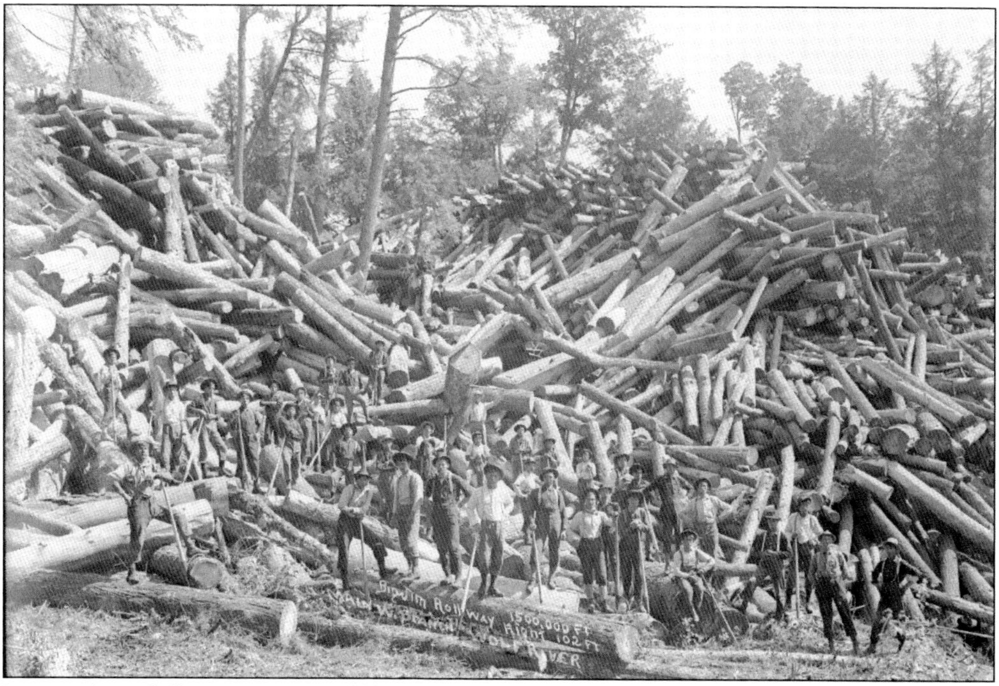

Loggers from different camps would brand the ends of logs with different symbols, much like how cowboys brand cattle. This was necessary to distinguish their logs from those of others once they were pooled for transport downstream to the sawmill.

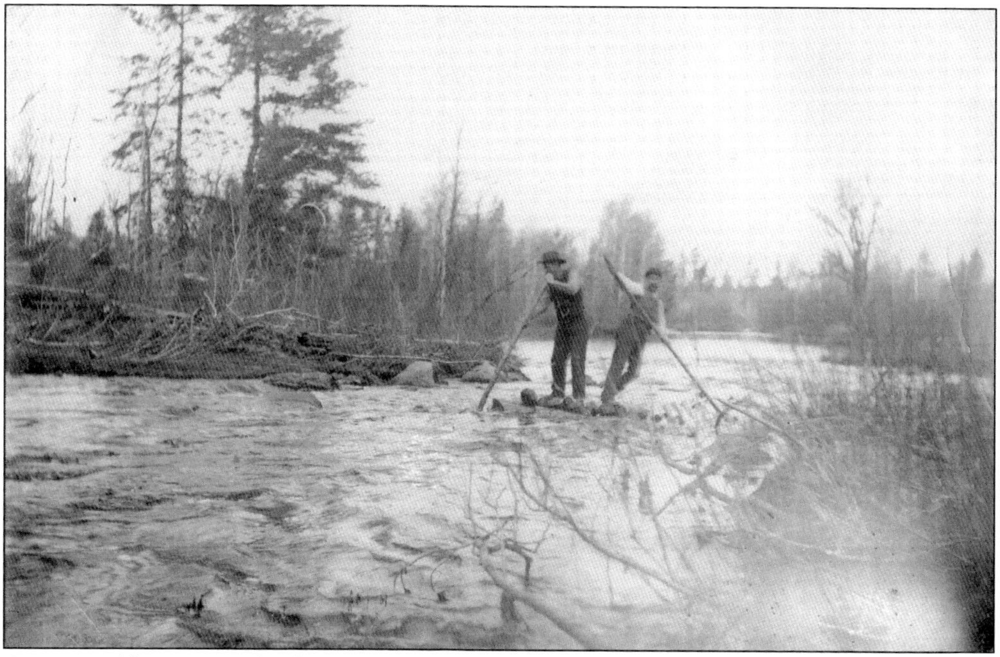

Crews would maintain the flow of logs while on rafts. A major river route in eastern Langlade County was the Wolf River. Millions of feet of logs would move down the Wolf each year. Many logging camps were located along this river. Towns such as Langlade, Lily, and Hollister were quite prominent when Antigo was a mere cluster of cabins.

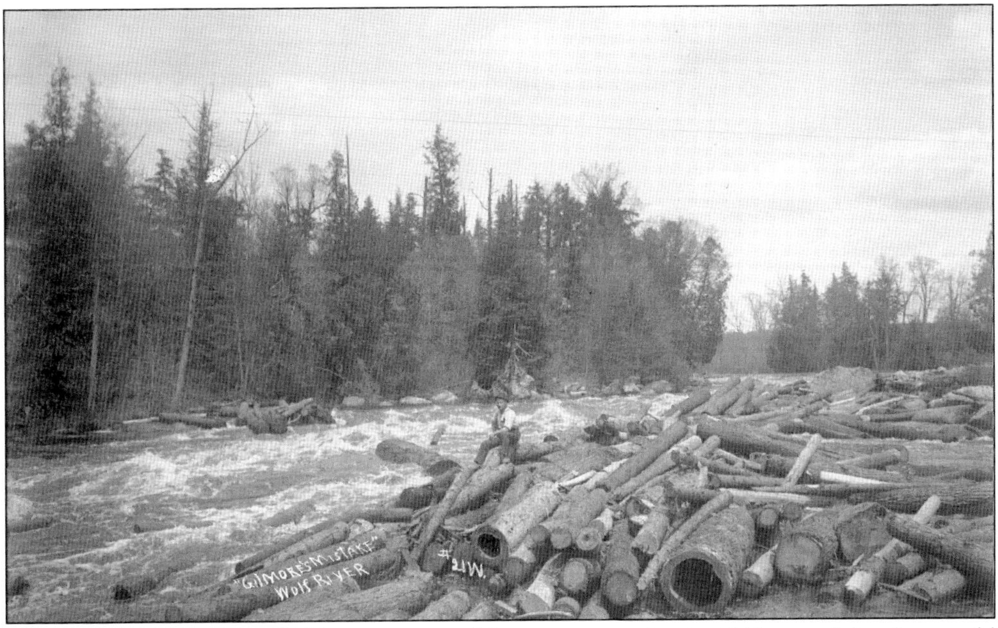

Gilmore's Mistake on the Wolf River is named for a surveyor who, in 1868, stated that logs could not be floated down the Wolf since it went underground at some point. The Wolf was covered at that site by a thick mat of cedar that formed a dense canopy over the river. Today, much of the Wolf River is undeveloped, and the rapids at Gilmore's Mistake are a favorite of white-water kayakers and rafters.

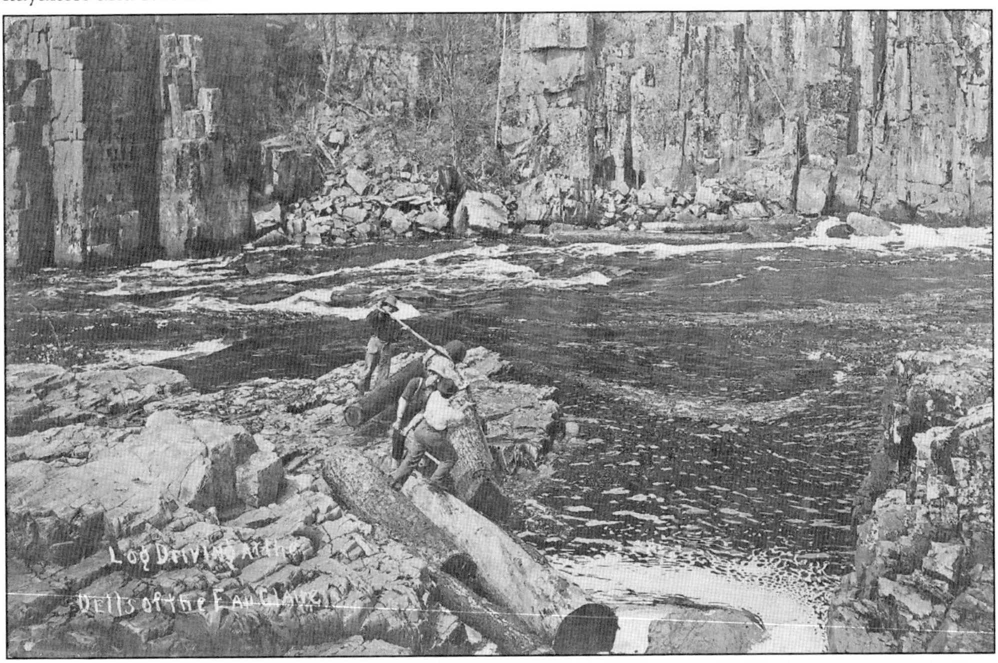

The first successful river log drive in Langlade County took place in 1865, fourteen years before Antigo was founded. The Eau Claire River was used to deliver logs downstream. An earlier drive resulted in the loss of all logs when they became lodged in the Eau Claire dells. They were not freed for several years, and by the time high water finally carried them out, they were worthless.

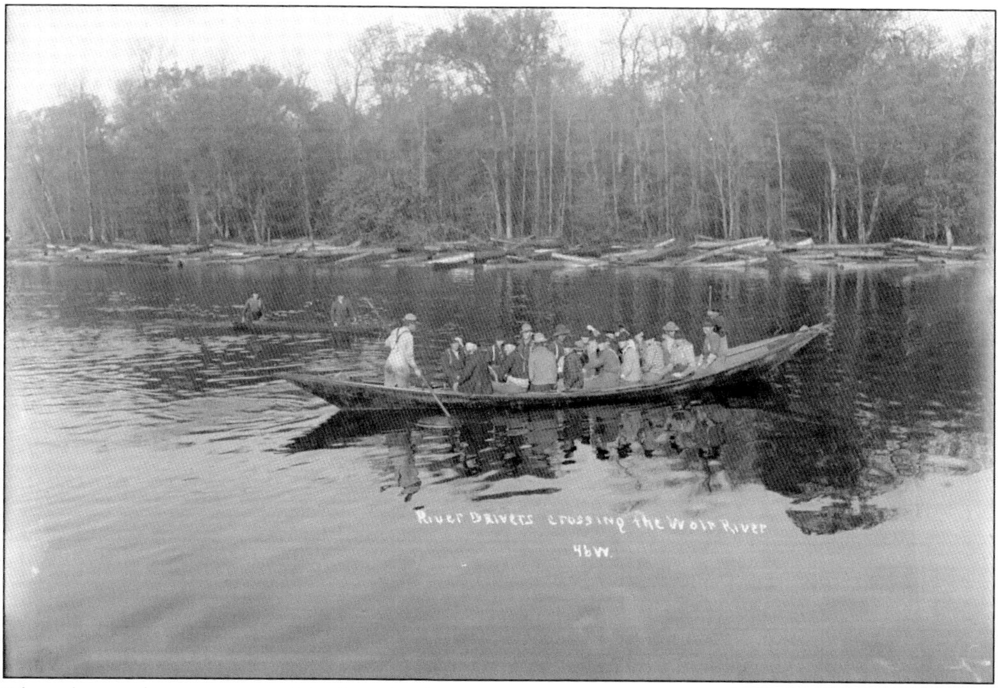

These bateau boats were used for ferrying loggers across rivers, as well as herding logs during drives. Flat bottomed, rugged, and with a shallow draft, the bateau would slide up onto logs rather than be crushed when floating logs crashed together.

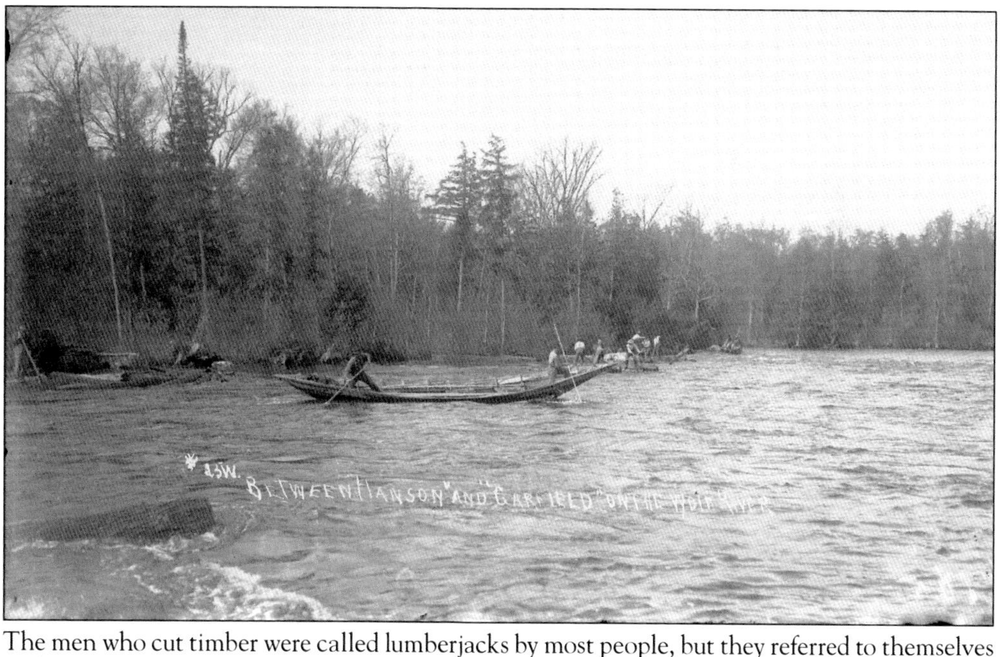

The men who cut timber were called lumberjacks by most people, but they referred to themselves as shanty boys. In the early days of logging, many were from Ireland, by way of Canada, or were French Canadians. As a result, their songs had a strong tinge of Ireland in their melodies, and French words frequently crept into their logging terms. Sometimes, fights broke out between rival crews for rights of the river.

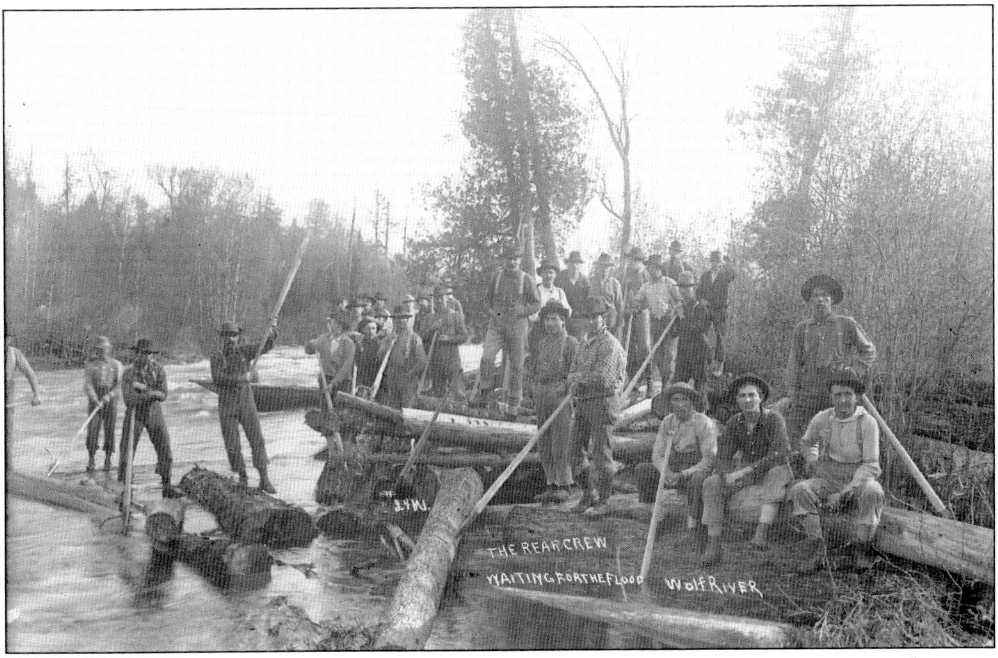

It was the large stands of pines that first attracted the timber cruisers and loggers to the area, starting in the mid-19th century. Logging increased greatly after the Civil War. Prior to the railroad's arrival, logging occurred near rivers, and the pine was floated downstream to mills. The harvesting of hardwood only occurred later.

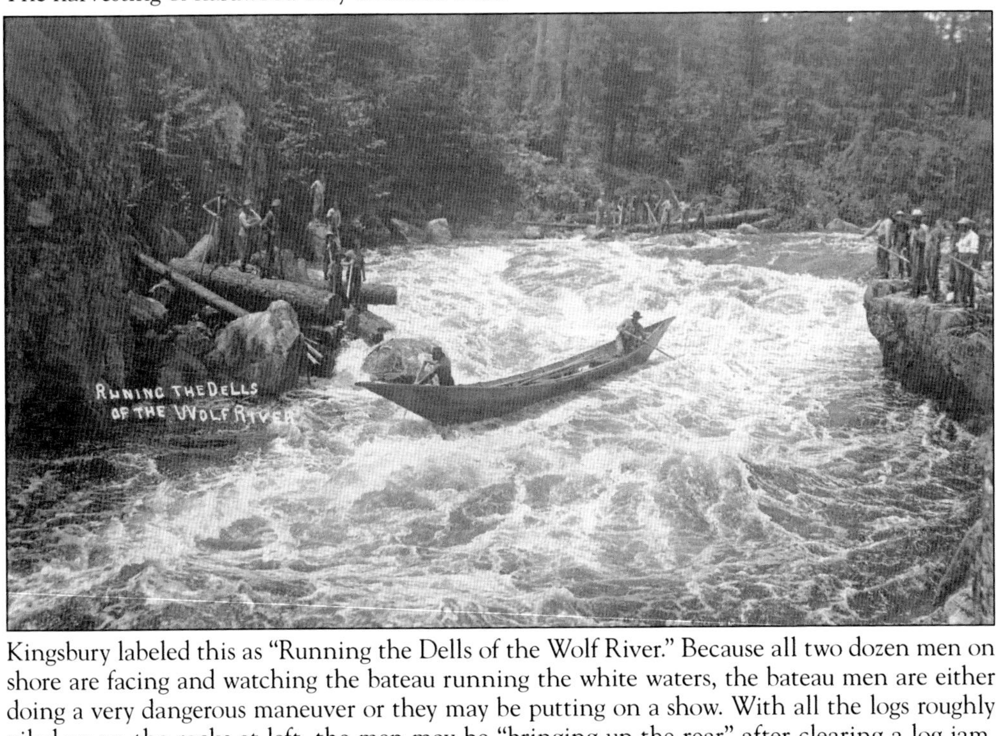

Kingsbury labeled this as "Running the Dells of the Wolf River." Because all two dozen men on shore are facing and watching the bateau running the white waters, the bateau men are either doing a very dangerous maneuver or they may be putting on a show. With all the logs roughly piled up on the rocks at left, the men may be "bringing up the rear" after clearing a log jam. (Courtesy of Prestor Pictures.)

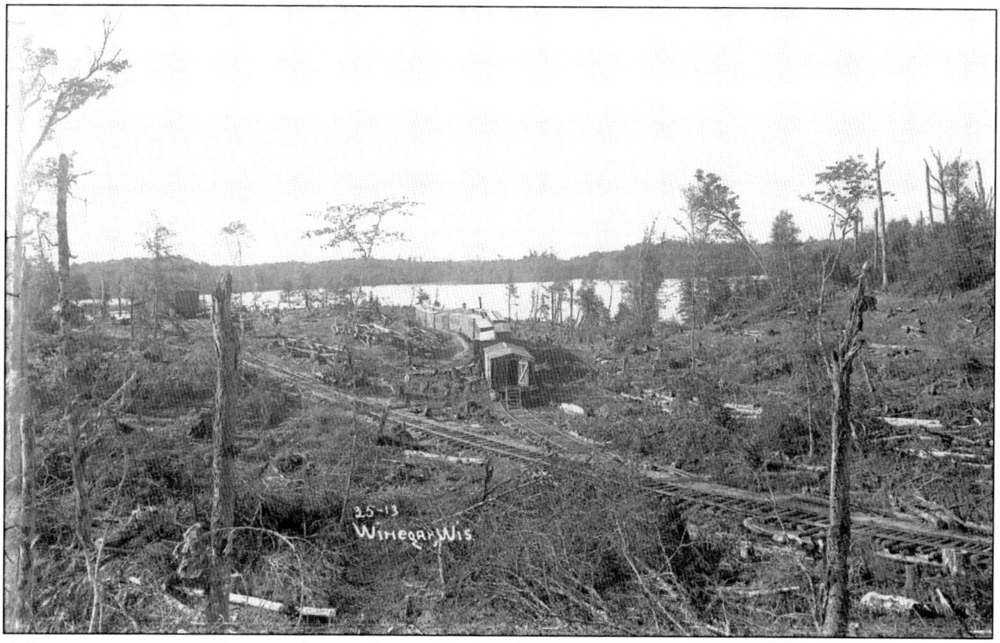

A logging camp at Winegar, located near the border of Michigan's Upper Peninsula, shows how areas were cleared of all large trees. Towns such as Winegar often altered names, changing to whatever logging company was currently in the area.

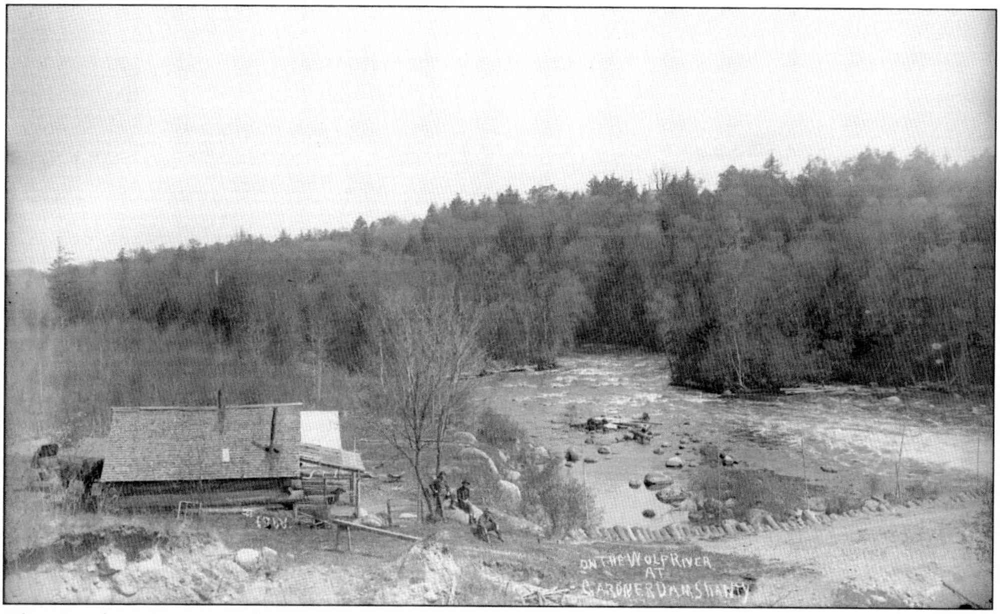

The Gardner Dam on the Wolf River was one of many that controlled water flow. On a May night in 1874, high water forced its way over the dam. Nine dam tenders awoke to the roar and rushed to open the gates, but the dam gave way. According to John Satterlee, a Menominee Indian logger who survived the incident, in the *Shawano County Journal* on January 12, 1922, it sounded like "a barrel full of fire crackers shooting in rapid succession." Four of the nine men were lost in the raging torrent of water and logs. Satterlee went on to write extensively on Menominee tribal lore and customs.

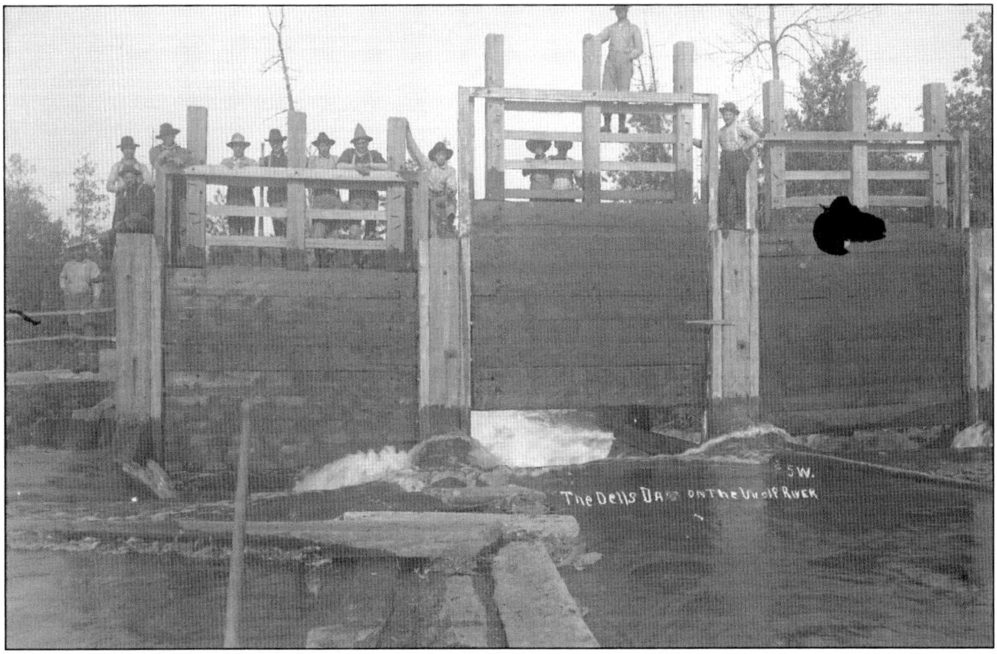

When logging companies first investigated using the Wolf River to float logs to sawmills, they found that most of the river was too shallow and had lots of big boulders in the way. They blasted the boulders to pieces, but the shallow river could only work if dams were built. They would accumulate water into reservoirs that logs could be floated on. Then, as needed, the water was released, causing deep and fast-moving torrents that carried the logs downstream. The image above is a close-up of the dam's front side, showing its three gates opened to different heights. The photograph below shows the dam's front from farther back, so one can see the men positioning the logs. The men walk on man-made walkways called booms. The booms help to funnel the logs into the proper gate as the men push and position the wood to avoid logjams.

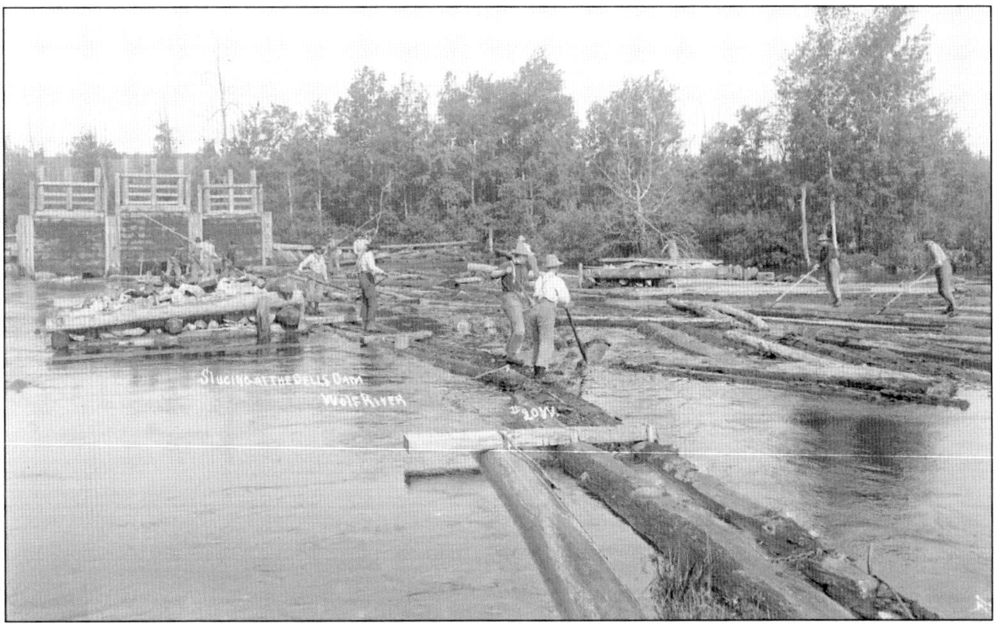

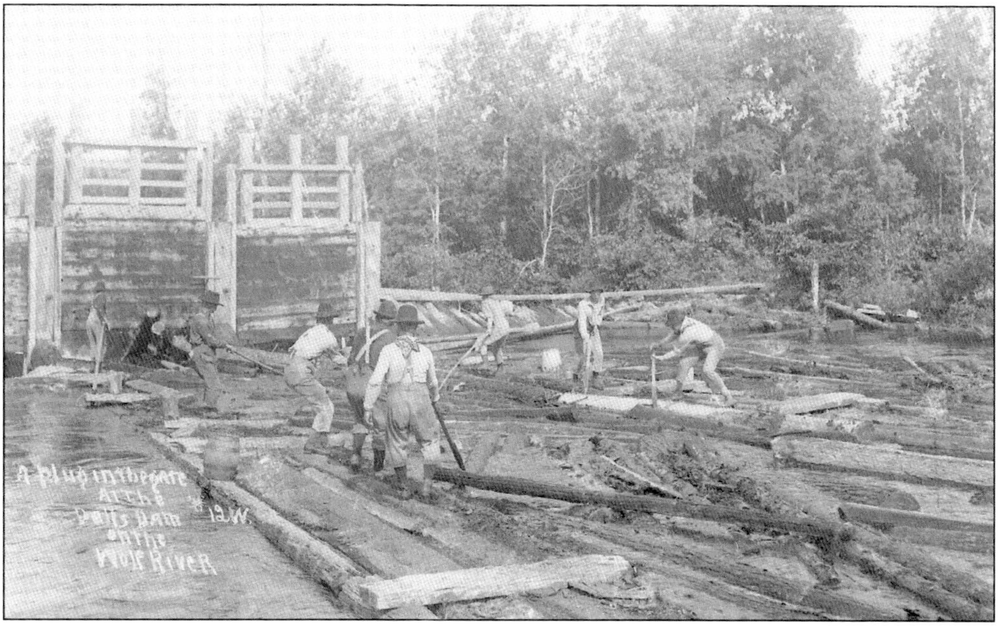

The booms also serve as a funnel, forcing logs into the center gate. Unfortunately, logs usually do not float in an orderly fashion. Kingsbury calls this "a plug in the gate at the Dells Dam on the Wolf River." One can see upended logs under the center gate and that the jumble of logs between the drivers' walkways has gotten messy and troublesome to straighten out. Driving logs was very hard and hazardous work.

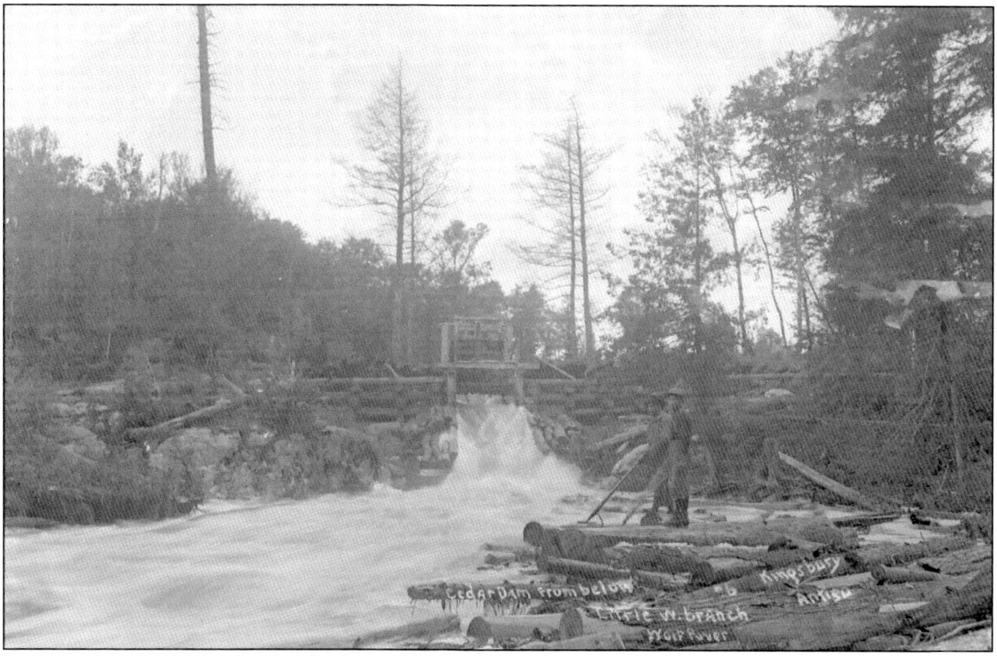

Pictured here is the backside of a dam. This is the "Cedar Dam from Below, Little W. branch, Wolf River." This dam has only one gate. One can see the force of white water rushing down and away from the gate. The two men seem to have briefly posed for the camera. It looks like their work is to keep forcing the bunched-up logs, one at a time, back out into the racing stream.

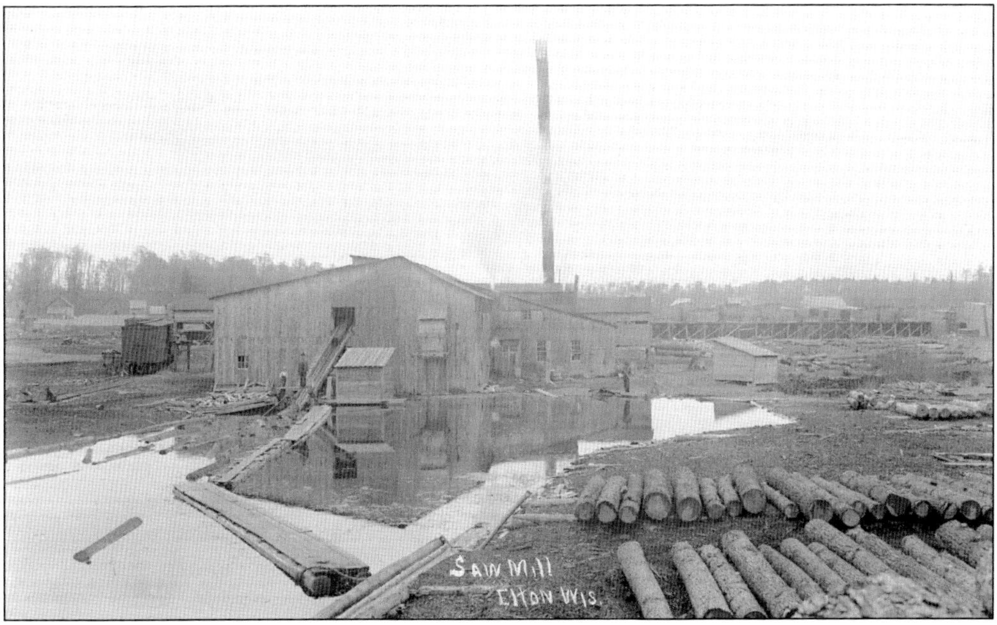

Both photographs on this page are of a sawmill in Elton, Wisconsin. This one shows the mill from the river, as though the viewer is approaching the mill. Notice that the three-section boom floating from land at lower center and angling toward the mill is funneling logs to the intake ramp. That ramp is called the jack ladder, and a conveyor belt of spiked steel links is an endless-flat-link chain.

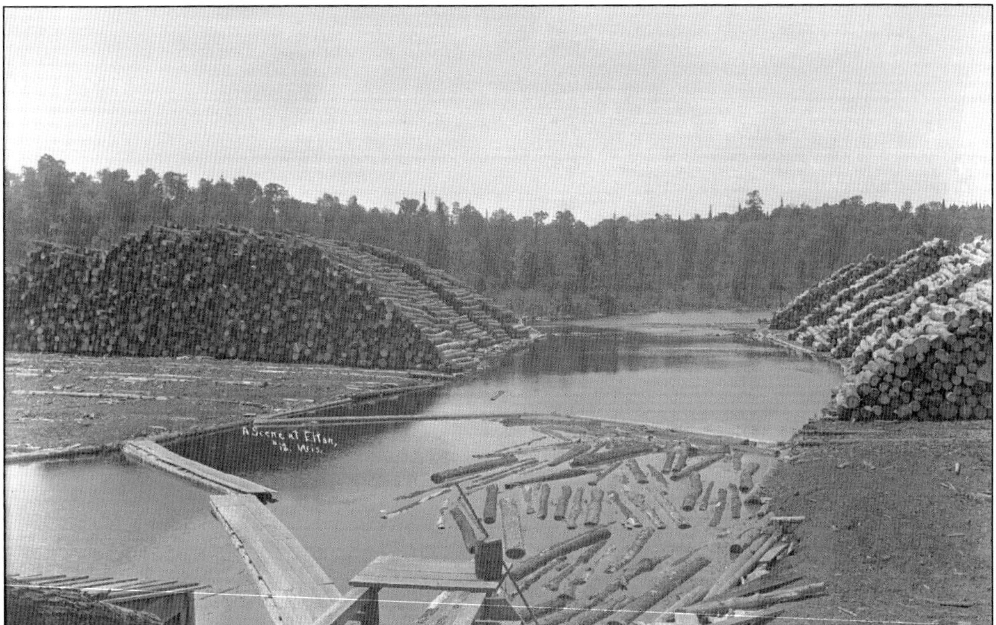

Compared to the photograph above, this image was captured from the opposite direction. Men working in the mill would see this view as thy looked out at the river. The obvious high point of this view is that it shows the immense piles of logs waiting to be fed to the sawmill. Piling logs this way is known as "decking."

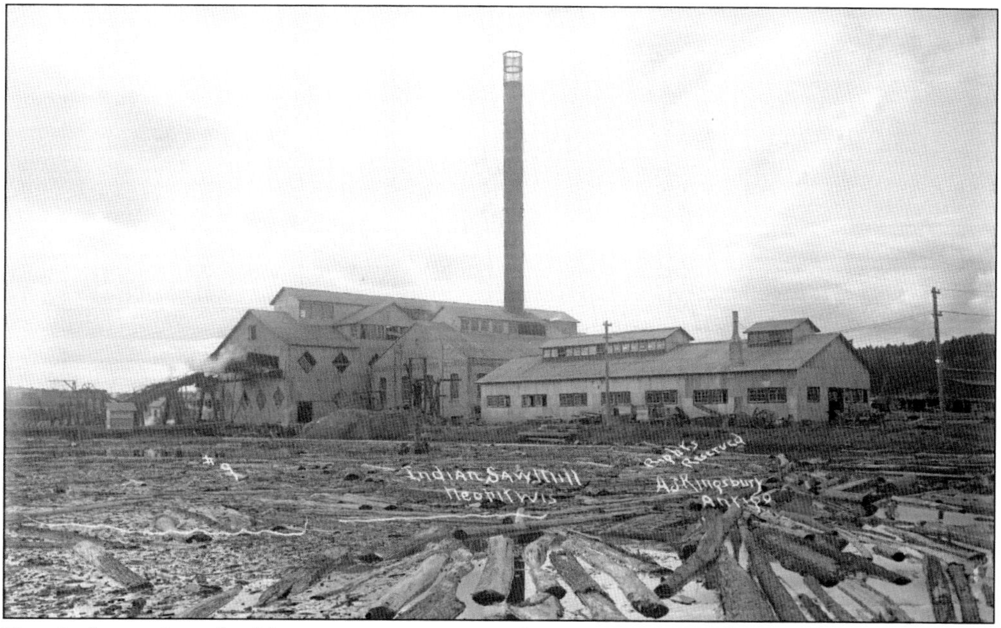

Neopit, located on the Menominee reservation, has a major sawmill. Initially, timber barons wanted to log in Menominee territory, but the Menominee organized their own tribal lumber camp in 1872. Years of dispute about who had timber rights was finally resolved in 1906, when Sen. Robert LaFollette Sr. sponsored legislation granting the Menominee funds to operate their own sawmill at Neopit.

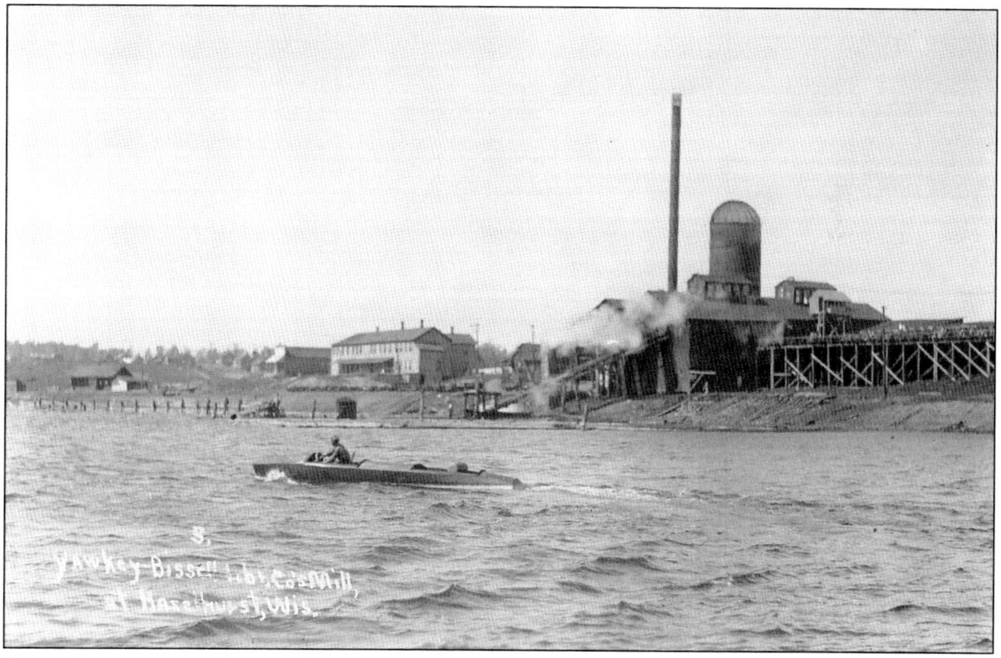

Cyrus Carpenter Yawkey was born in Chicago in 1862. At the age of 27, he settled in Hazelhurst, Wisconsin, where he helped found the Yawkey and Lee Lumber Company, the first of his many enterprises. In 1899, he moved to Wausau, where he became involved in several additional businesses, including the Yawkey and Bissel Lumber Company. This is the company's sawmill.

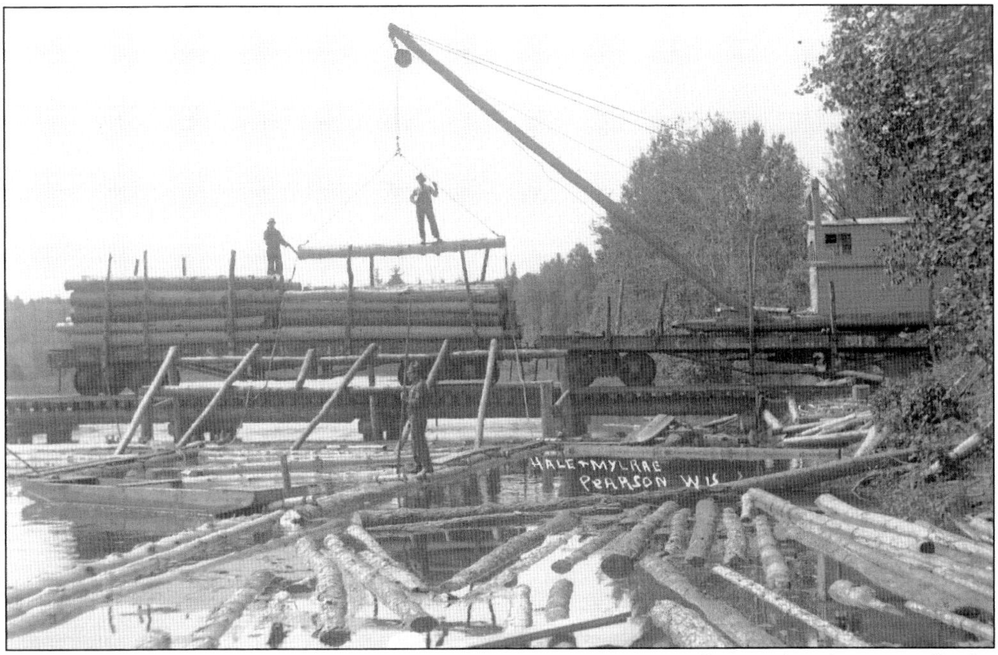

At Pearson, Wisconsin, the river log drive does not end at a sawmill. A railroad crane pulls the logs up skid poles from the river. These skid poles lessen the amount of dead weight the crane has to lift and prevents logs from swinging as they rise from the water. Often, only a couple of men would be needed on the river, and one man, the top loader, would position the logs.

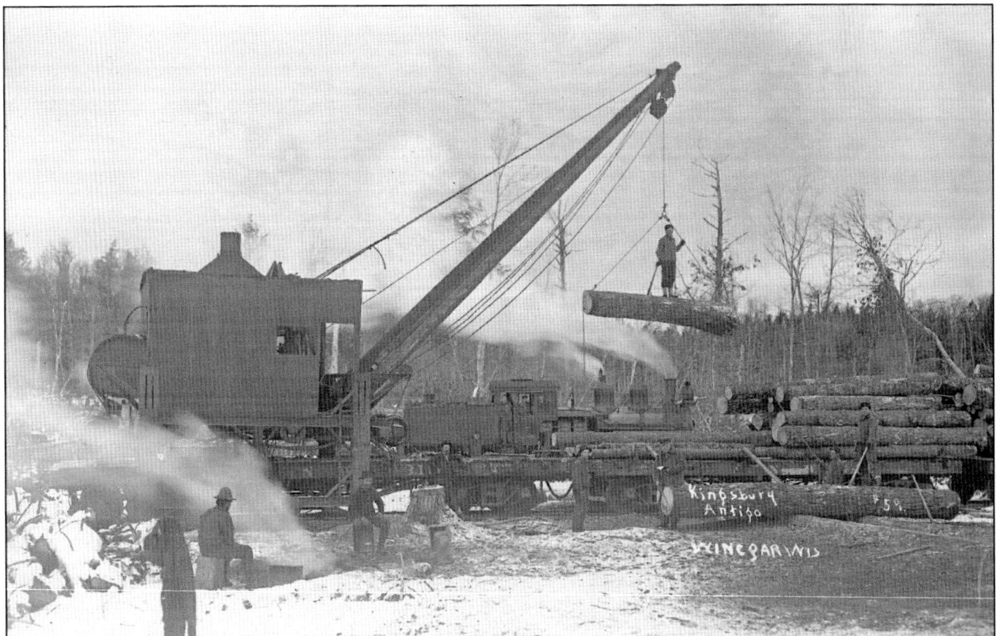

Seen here at Winegar, Wisconsin, the steam crane needs shorter skid poles to load the railroad flatcar. The man behind the "K" in Kingsbury is reading from a notebook, and he is holding a squared stick with a small hook on the end. He is likely the scaler, a man who measures every log to calculate its volume and value. His tool is probably his scaling stick.

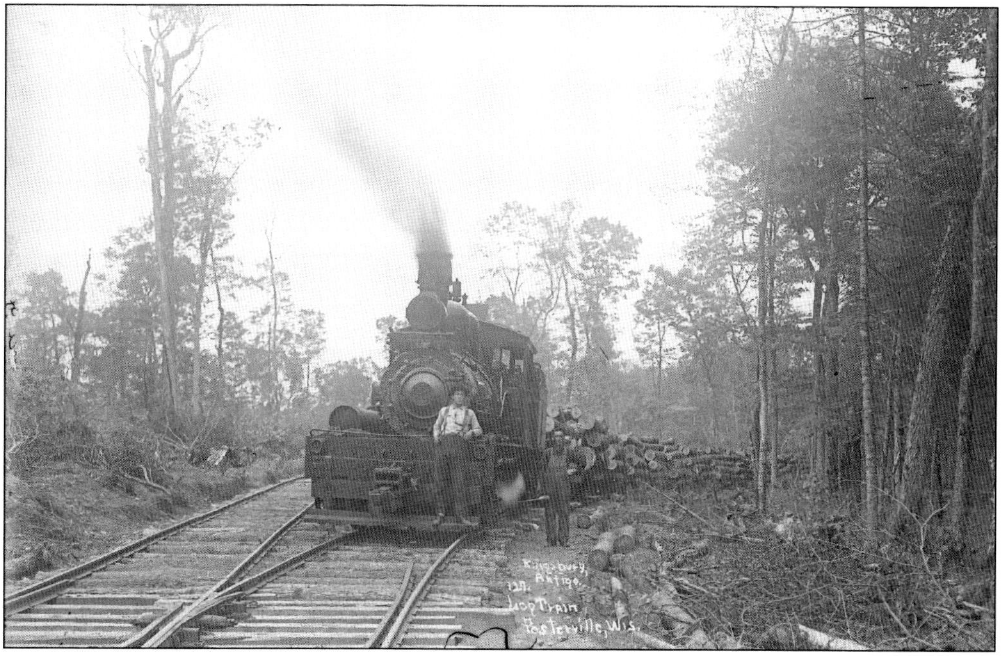

This train near Fosterville was pulling a line of log-laden cars to a mill. Fosterville, in Vilas County near the Michigan Upper Peninsula/Wisconsin border, was named after J.J. Foster. The lumber camp was owned by the Vilas County Lumber Company, which went out of business in 1910. William S. Winegar was the next owner, and he changed the name of the town from Fosterville to Winegar.

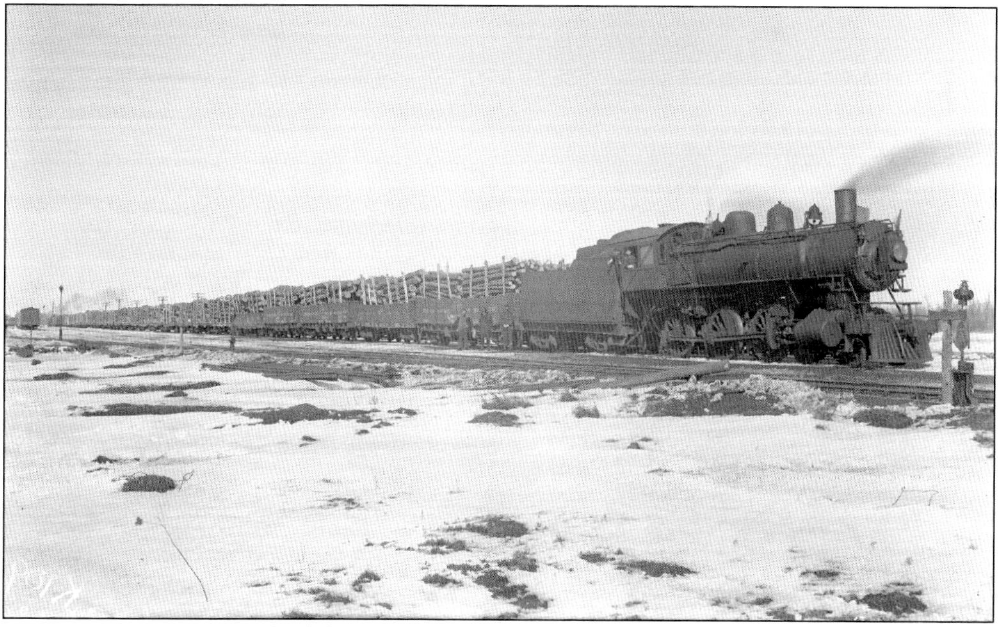

Logging companies often had their own short spur rail lines connecting to the main line. They may have been as short as a few miles to over 20 miles in length. Once their usefulness was over, the tracks were pulled up, and the settlement towns became ghost towns. People today still hike the woods looking for railroad souvenirs and mapping the logging train routes.

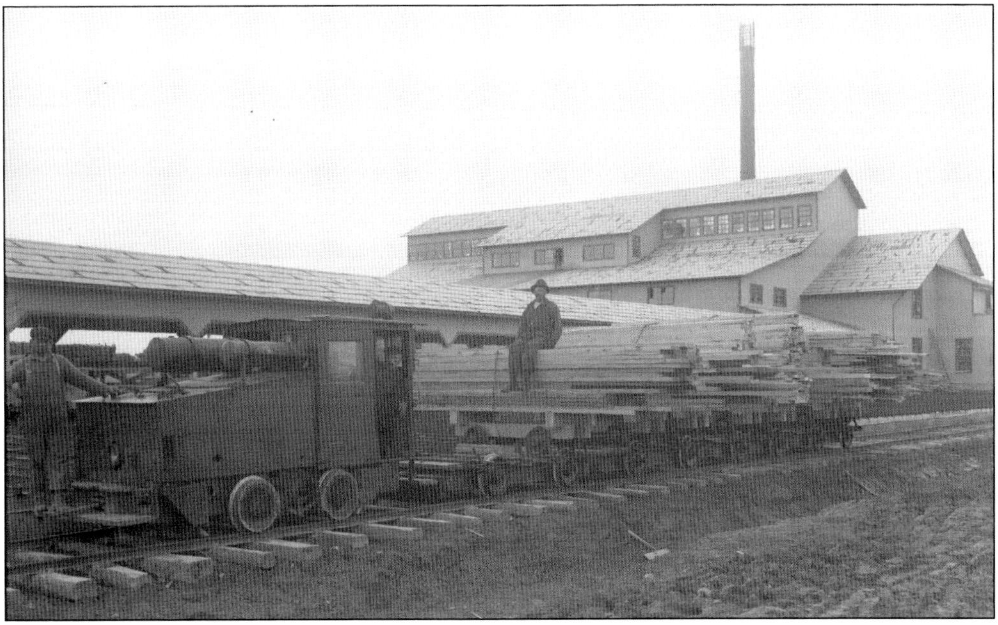

Changes came about once the pine forests were depleted. Hardwoods were not harvested at first, because they could not be floated on rivers. More sawmills were needed. An expanding network of rails could deliver the hardwoods to the sawmills. So, sawmills erupted in many small towns all over northeastern Wisconsin. Some of these towns became ghost towns once the sawmills shut down.

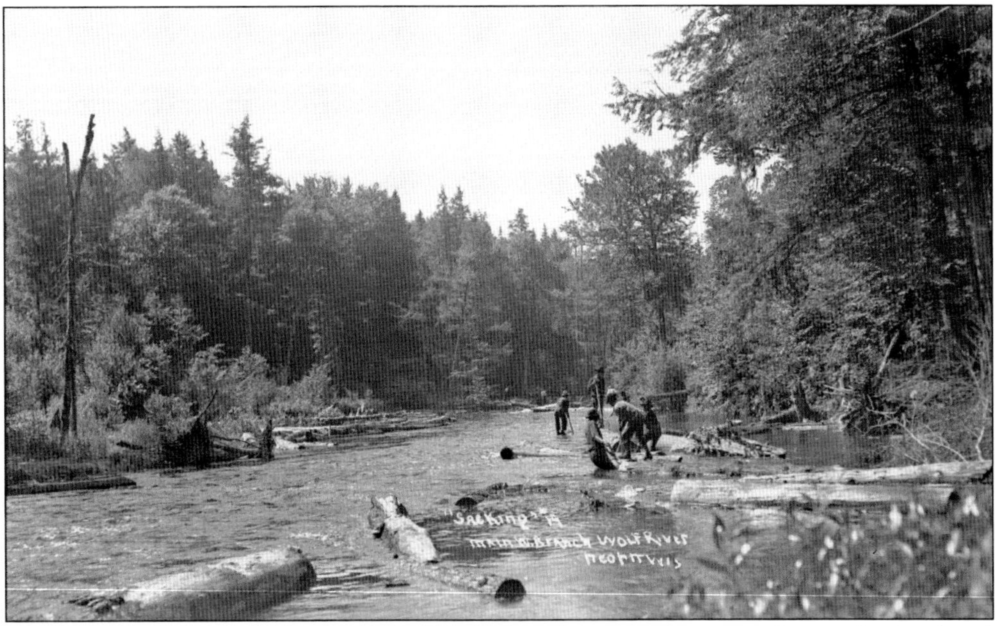

The *Minocqua Times* reported on December 1, 1922, "A new pine crop is about to be developed in northern Wisconsin. Several million feet of logs at the bottom of the Wisconsin River and tributary streams . . . are to be salvaged by the Lower Michigan Log Salvage Co. Some of the 'deadhead' logs have been at the bottom of the streams for 35 years and are of the best white logs obtainable at the early days."

Seven

Railroads

The Milwaukee, Lake Shore & Western Railroad established the first rail line in Langlade County in 1881, when it laid 23 miles of track from Aniwa to Summit Lake. Francis Deleglise's offers of free land persuaded rail officials to run the new line through his nascent city. The first train rolled into Antigo on August 15, 1881. The growth of Antigo and that of the Chicago & North Western Railway, which took over the MLS&W, were thoroughly intertwined. In 1907, the C&NW named Antigo headquarters of their Ashland division.

During 1917, the peak year of railroad travel in northern Wisconsin, it is estimated that 77 percent of all freight and 98 percent of all passengers travelled by rail. Train travel continued to be of major importance well into the 1950s. During those decades, the C&NW had more miles of track than any other Wisconsin railroad. In 1913, the C&NW owned about 25,000 acres of land in Langlade County alone.

The railroad played a prominent developmental role in the area, being involved in logging, hauling sawmill products to the main line, and servicing manufacturers. Frequently, camp lines were built and operated by the lumber companies themselves. Once their usefulness was over, the rails were removed and used for a spur line to another camp or sawmill.

Of growing importance in the early 1900s was the railroad's ability to transport large quantities of agricultural goods to market. During its peak years, the Antigo rail depot saw 10,000 railcars of potatoes pass through during the harvest season.

For several decades, railroad passenger service was secondary to the moving of timber. By World War I, however, passenger traffic reached significant numbers. People increased their rail travelling in order to visit seldom-seen relatives, enjoy a picnic outing, or even to shop in the big cities of Milwaukee and Chicago. In addition to the regular passenger trade, during summers from 1917 to 1950, the railroad operated fish runs. Special cars carried fishermen on trips to resorts in northern Wisconsin or Michigan's Upper Peninsula.

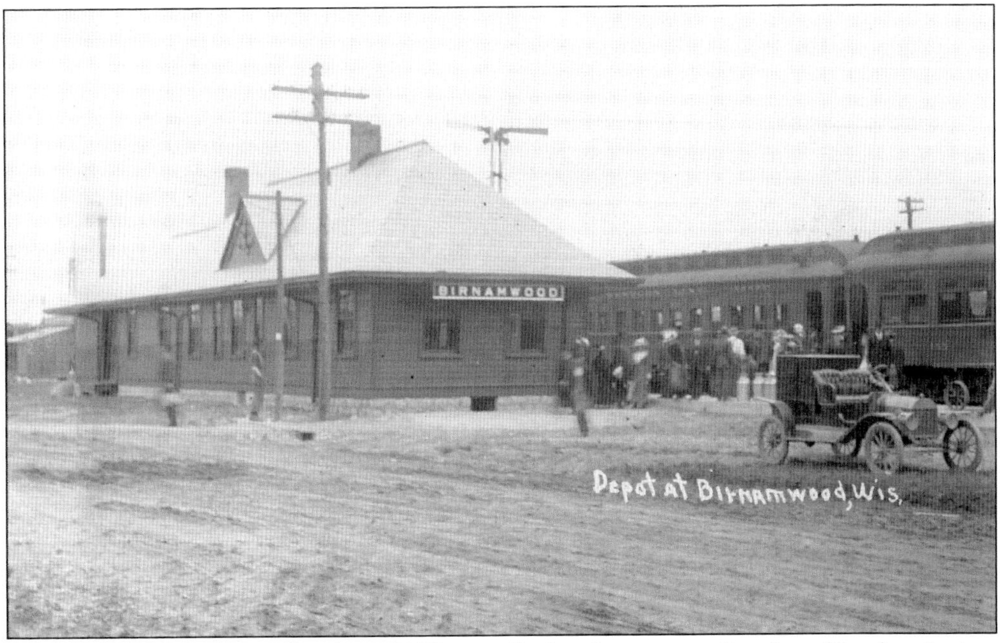

In 1880, the Milwaukee, Lake Shore & Western Railroad was expanding from Eland to Aniwa. A small community of houses and stores was established to serve the workers clearing the land. This eventually became the town of Birnamwood in Shawano County. The automobile on the right is most likely Kingsbury's. He had the rear seat removed and a large box installed to protect his photographic equipment and supplies.

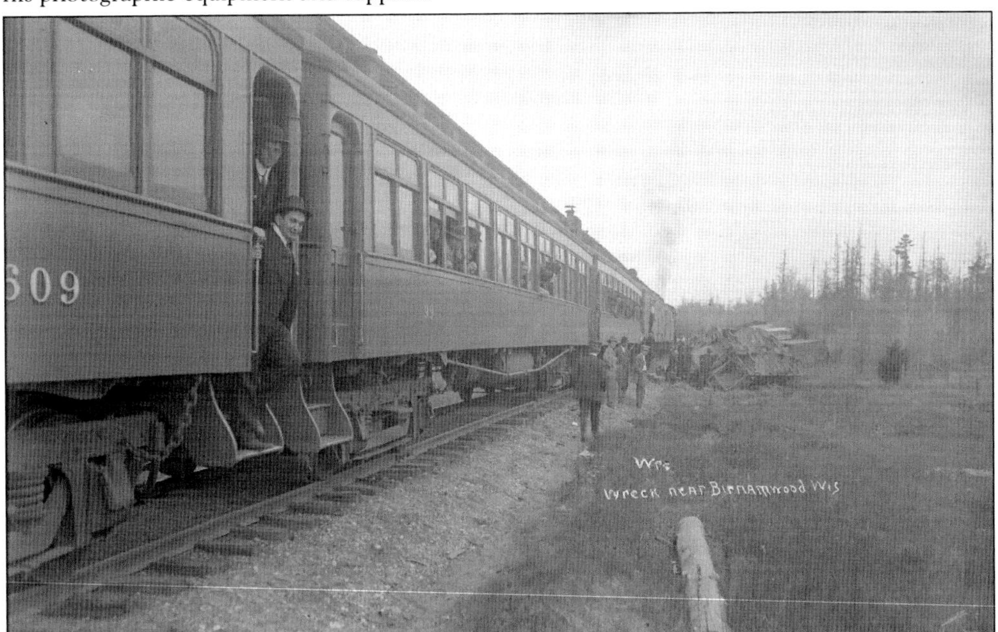

A.J. Kingsbury must have been travelling to or from Birnamwood, between Eland and Antigo, when this accident occurred. He was right on the scene with his camera to capture the looks of passengers and crew surveying the damage.

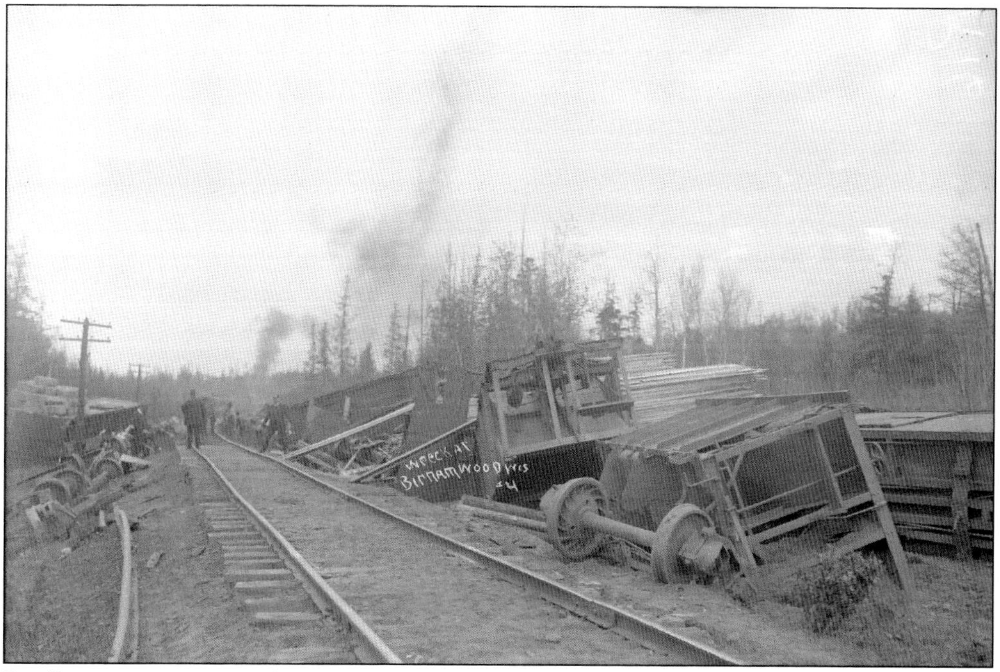

By all accounts, train wrecks were not uncommon and many were documented by photographers. Scenes such as this, captured near Birnamwood, Wisconsin, likely in the 1920s, must have attracted a great deal of interest.

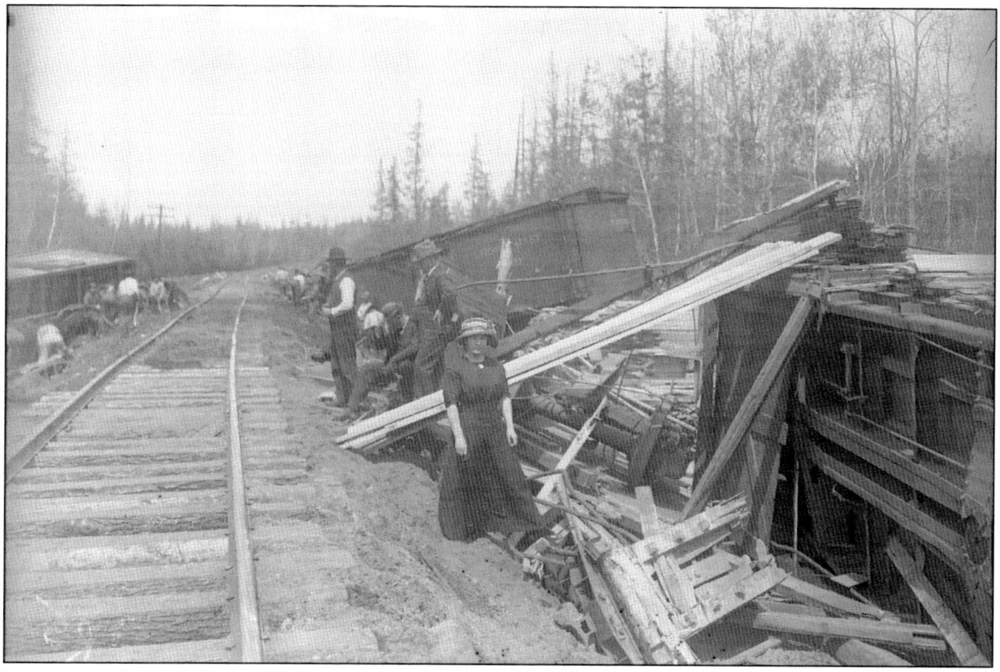

Minor wrecks and close calls were common enough in the early days of train travel that they were not memorable. However, one engineer recalled a remarkable accident when he was pulling his train into the Antigo depot. He saw a tornado approach. It detached his caboose and pushed it down the main line, where it hit another engine and killed the switchman.

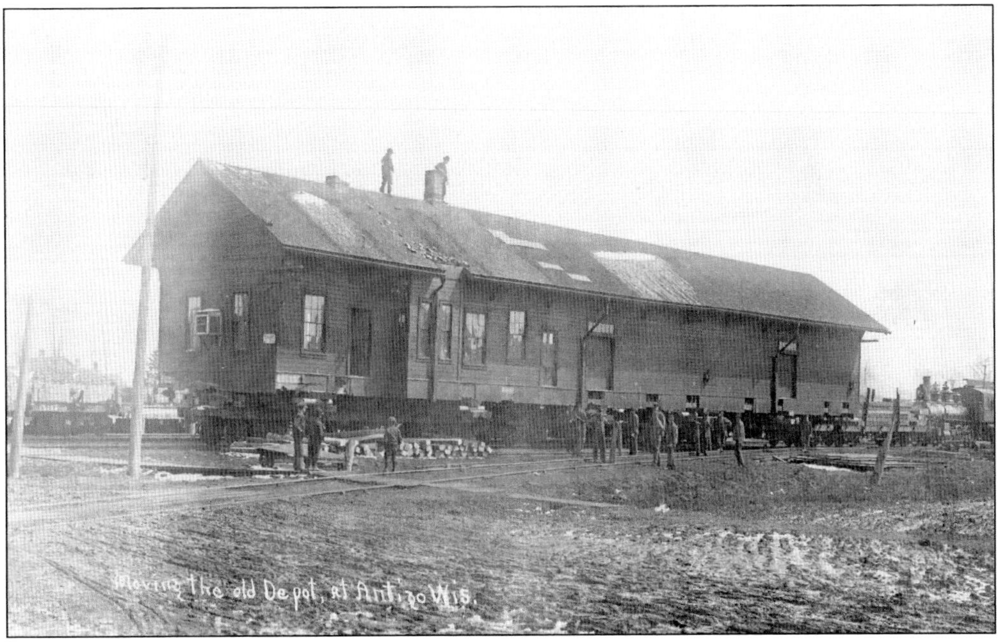

On July 6, 1906, the *Antigo Daily Journal* wrote, "Antigo's need of a new depot was quite evident the Fourth of July. The platform was filled with people, the passengers could hardly get off the train . . . and the express man was filling the air with blue profanity." The original depot was used until 1907 when a new depot was built. This old depot was moved a few blocks and became the carpenter's shop.

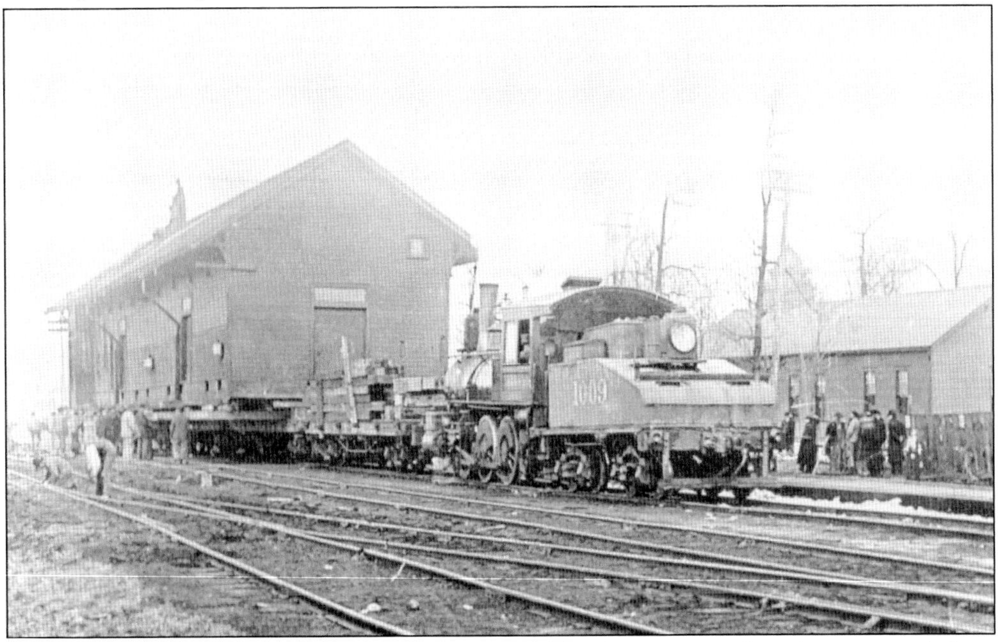

In order to move the depot to its new location, it had to be transferred to the west track from the east track. It was loaded onto flatcars and moved with the engine shown here. When this old depot burned in 1978, it was the last building left on the west side of the tracks. Antigo had become a less important railroad center than it had been for many years.

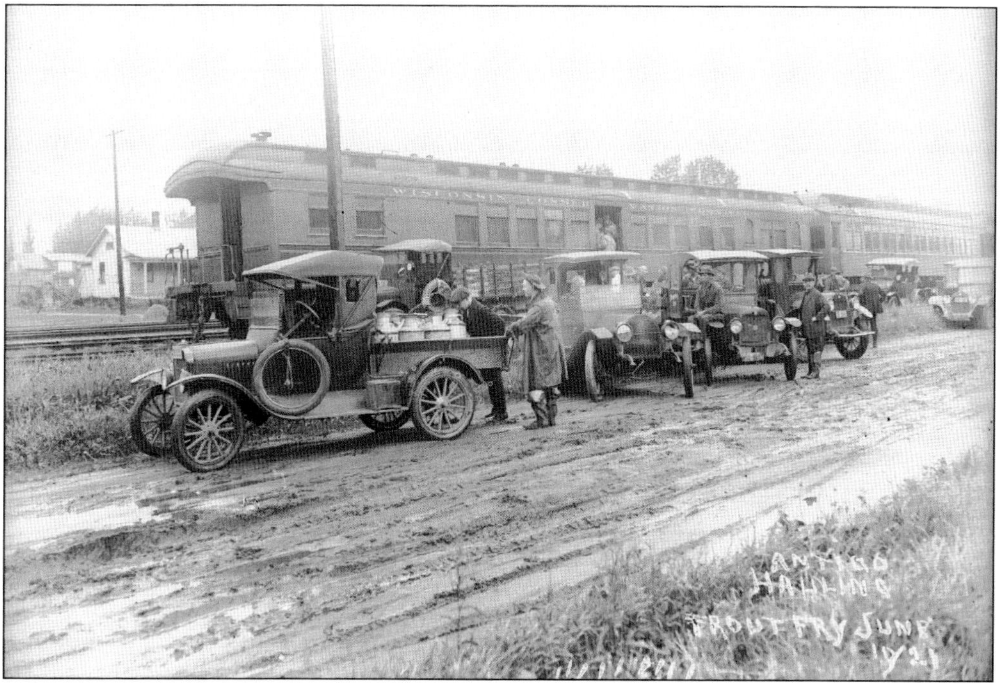

Of all the passengers to come to Antigo, none travelled in greater comfort than the small fish that were raised in hatcheries in southern Wisconsin. They were transported in special cars the held aquaria. Upon arrival in Antigo, they were unloaded, placed in metal cans (possibly milk cans), and taken by truck to stock various lakes in the area. This train car, marked "Wisconsin Conservation Commission," was unloading trout fry in June 1921.

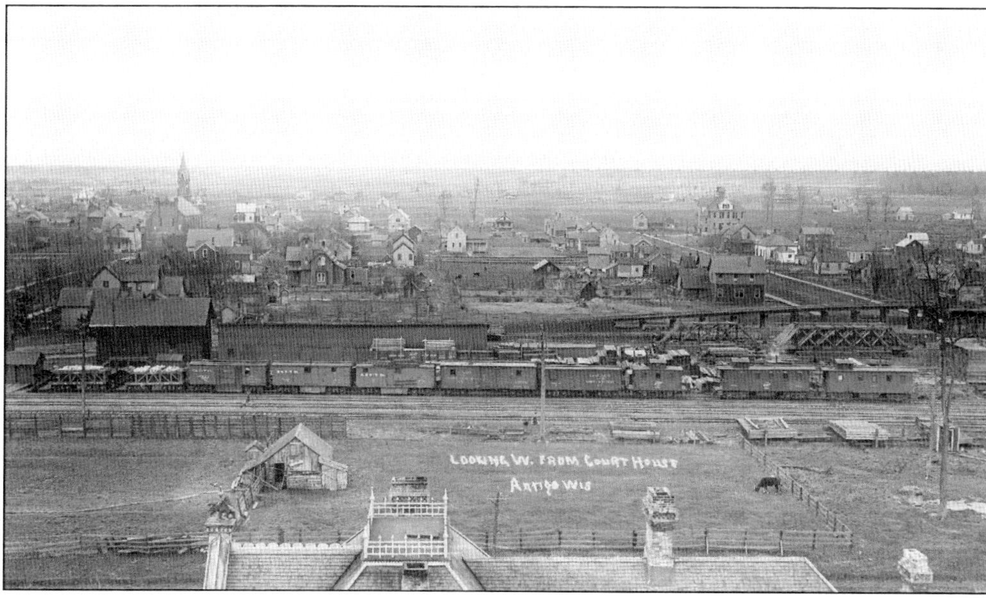

The extent of the Antigo rail yards can only be partially realized in this view from the courthouse roof. In addition to other buildings and workers, there were six building and bridge crews responsible for nearly a thousand culverts and bridges in northern Wisconsin. A large yard stored bridge timber with enough material for a 10-span bridge.

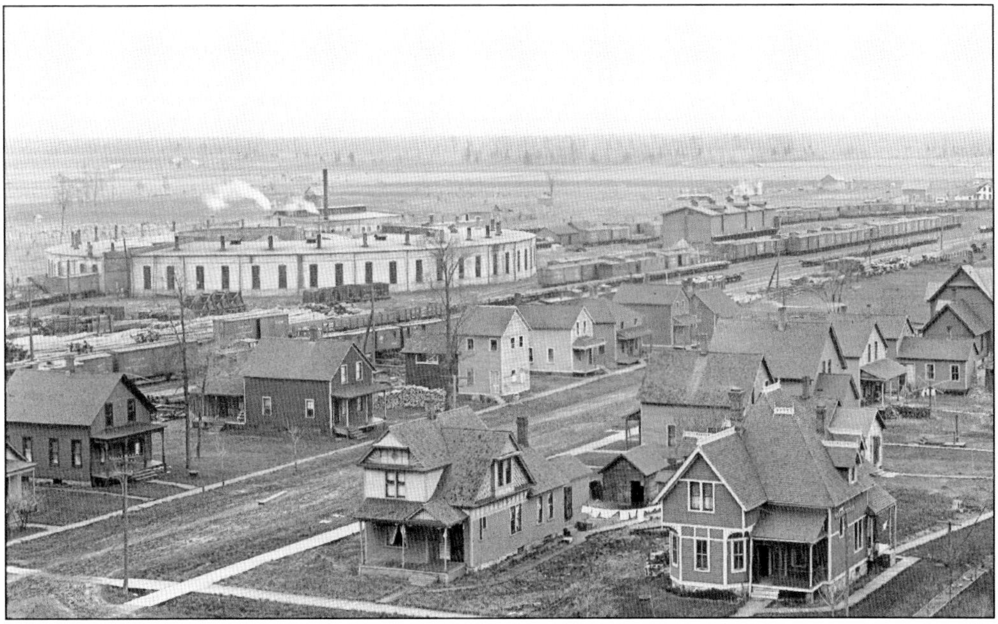

View from the courthouse roof shows some of the Chicago & North Western rail yards. The large roundhouse contained 15 train barns, a 95-foot turntable, machine shop, sand house and tower, masonry cinder pit, and an icehouse. The ice house cooled produce and air-conditioned passenger cars. Buildings associated with the rail yards stretched 10 city blocks. With the advent of diesel, Antigo lost its central role in the Chicago & North Western system.

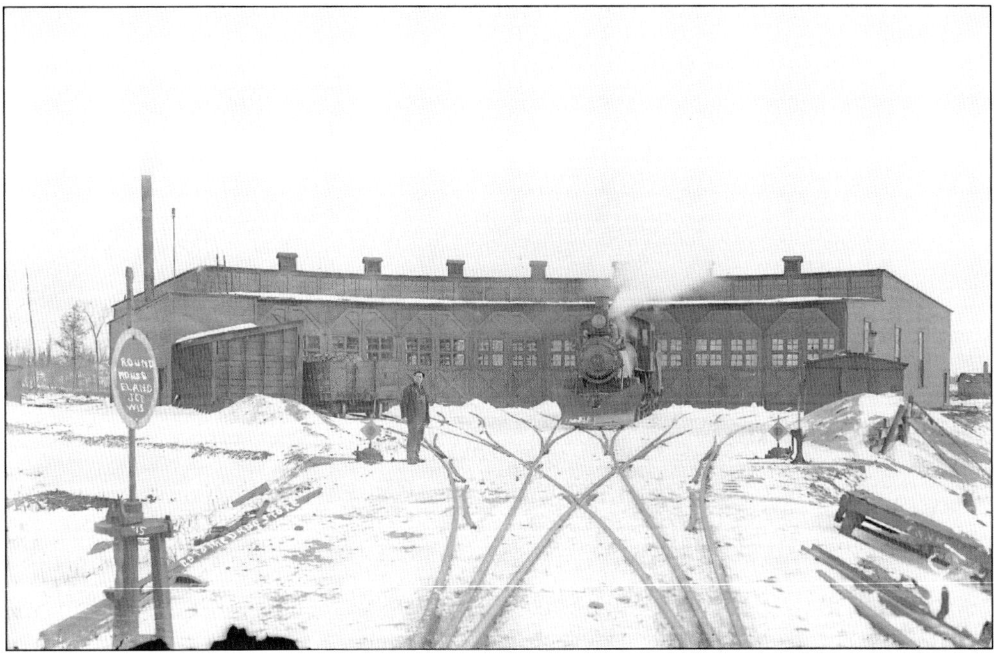

This is a fine example of an eight-barn roundhouse without a turntable. In the 1870s, Eland Junction was part of the Milwaukee, Lakeshore & Western Railroad. When the first MLS&W train pulled into Antigo in 1881, it was greeted by residents with sandwiches and lemonade. Antigo was strong on temperance at the time.

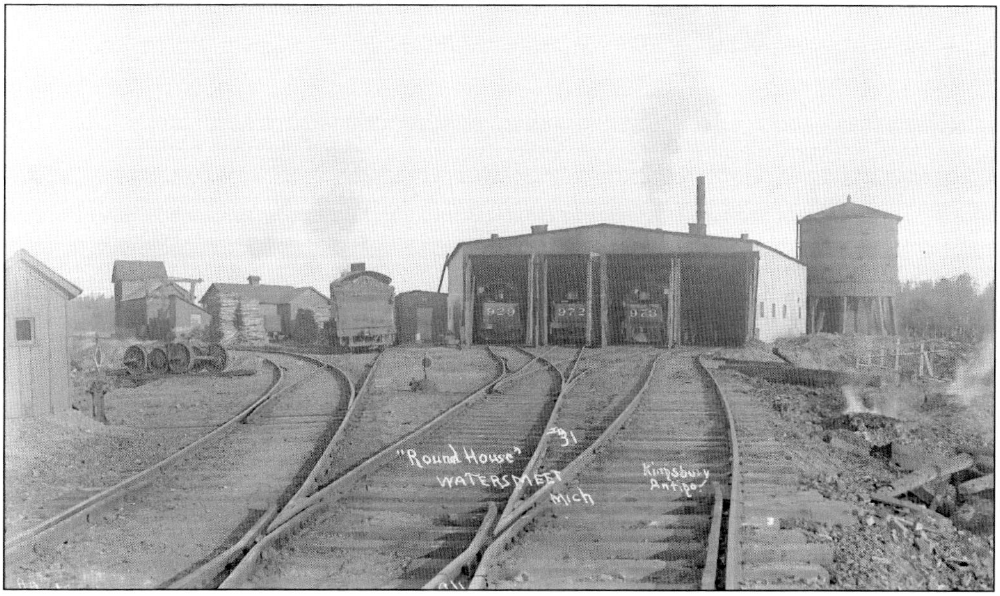

Watersmeet was the end of the line going north from Antigo to Michigan's Upper Peninsula, where it formed a junction with an east-west line. The roundhouse depicted here was built in 1908. All three locomotives inside are former MLS&W engines. Originally a logging community, Watersmeet is now the center of the Cisco Chain of Lakes, which is a series of 15 interconnected lakes and is a popular tourist destination.

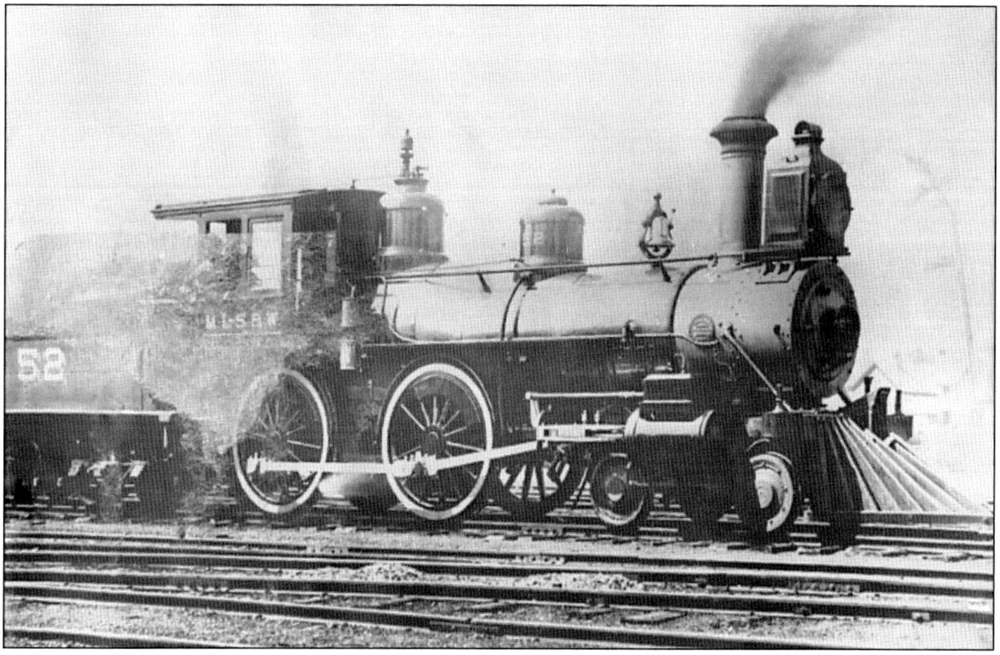

The Milwaukee, Lakeshore & Western Railroad was the line that originally came northward through Antigo to Summit Lake. In 1892, the Milwaukee, Lakeshore & Western Railroad was taken over by the Chicago & North Western Railway. The depot was upgraded, and other rail facilities, including a large roundhouse, were added in Antigo. In 1907, the C&NW made Antigo the division headquarters of their Ashland division.

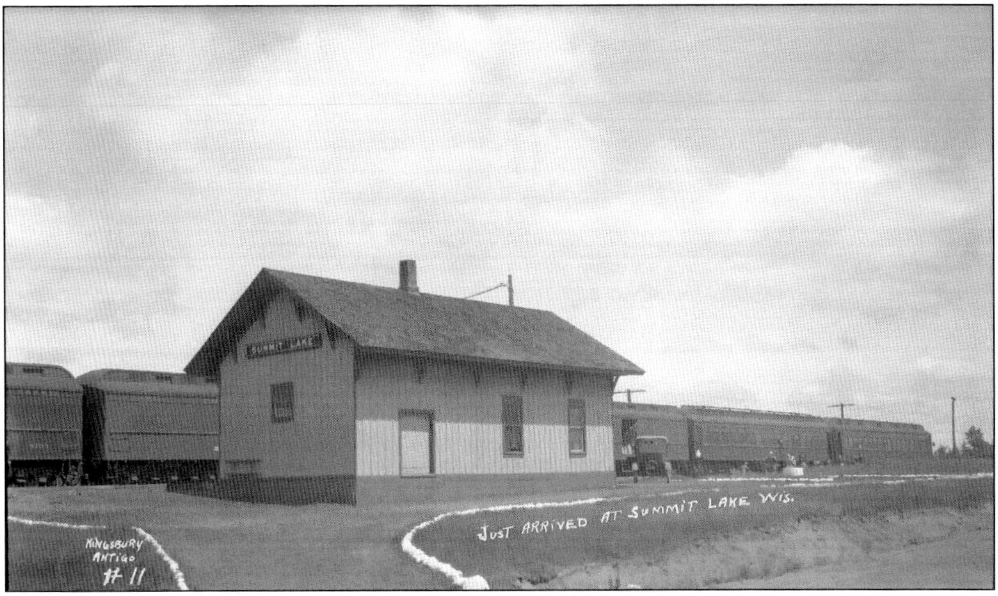

When the Milwaukee, Lake Shore & Western Railroad expanded northward beyond Aniwa, Summit Lake was its destination. It was this expansion that brought the railroad through Langlade County. Many locals still remember Pete Rassmusen, the stationmaster who was used in ads by the Chicago & North Western to promote rail travel.

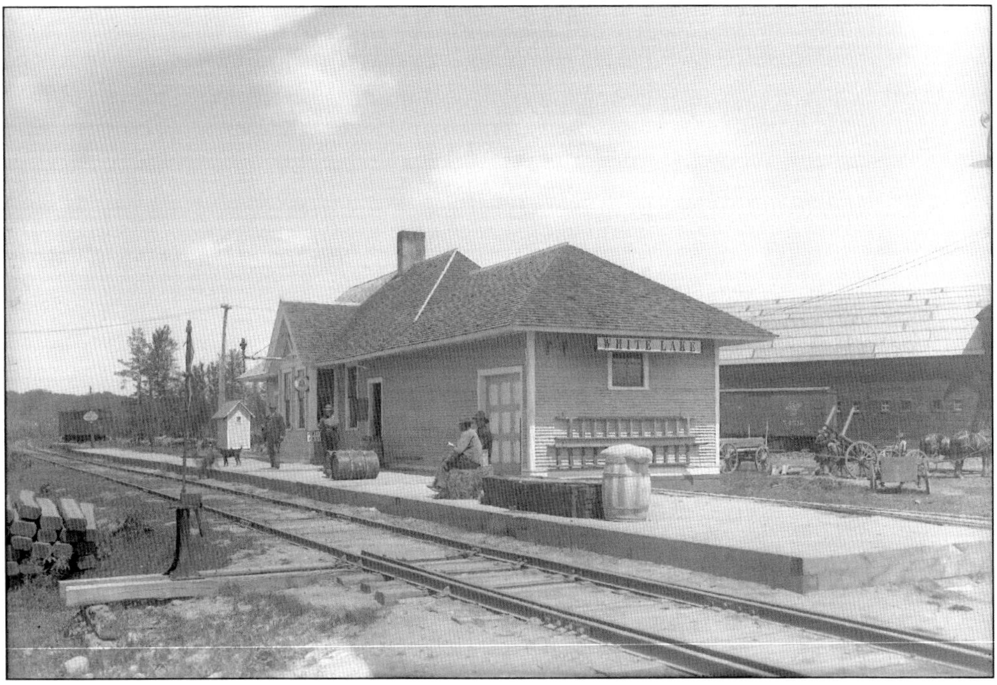

White Lake, in eastern Langlade County, is one of the county's older cities. Like many towns near the Wolf River, its economy was originally based on lumbering. At first, the adjacent town of Van Ostrand was served by the Soo Line, but when expansion required a larger terminal, the Chicago & North Western line came from Antigo, and it built a larger depot. This depot also held the White Lake Post Office. Note the small outhouse on the left.

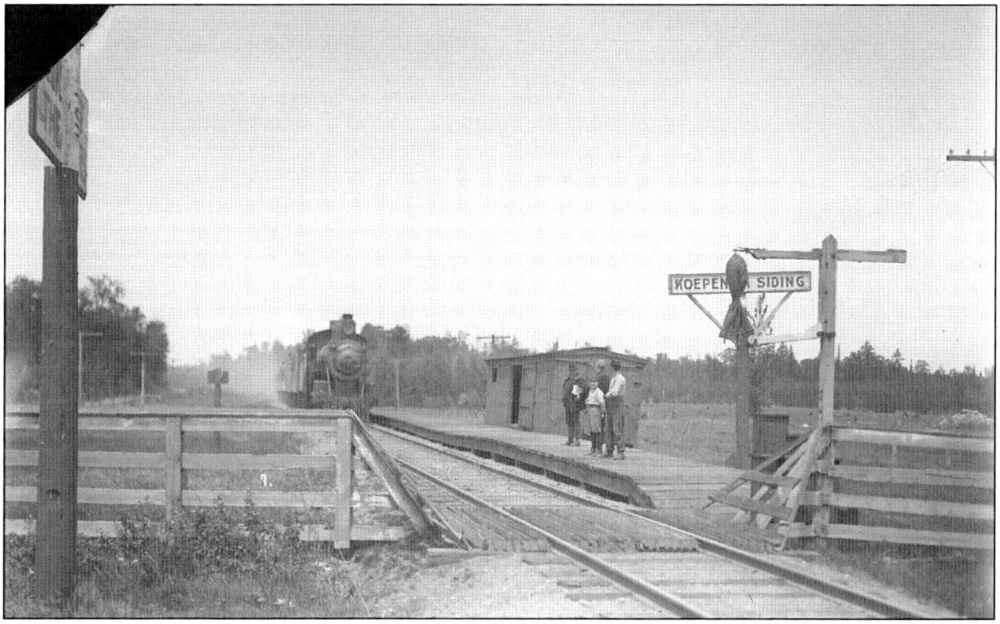

Koepenick was a small settlement north of Antigo in the logging era. It had a rail siding to collect log-filled train cars from the camps and deliver them to sawmills in Antigo and beyond. A cattle guard between the rails and the fences prevented cows from wandering into the depot area. Note that they placed an old box car for use as shelter.

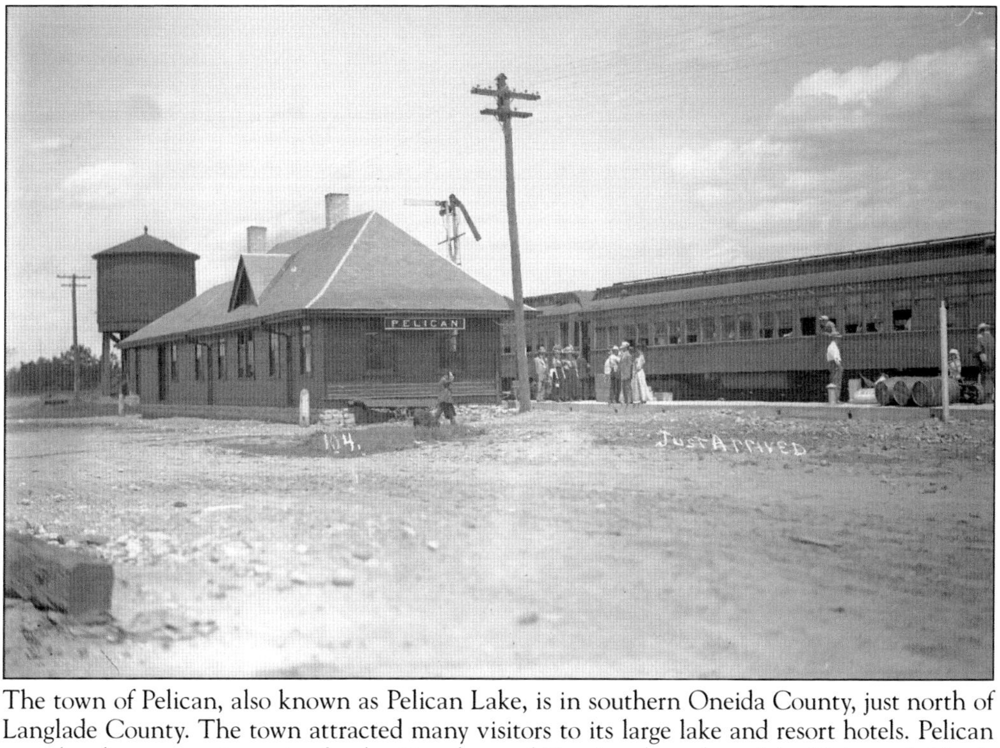

The town of Pelican, also known as Pelican Lake, is in southern Oneida County, just north of Langlade County. The town attracted many visitors to its large lake and resort hotels. Pelican was also the connecting point for the Crandon and Harrison branches of the Chicago & North Western Railway.

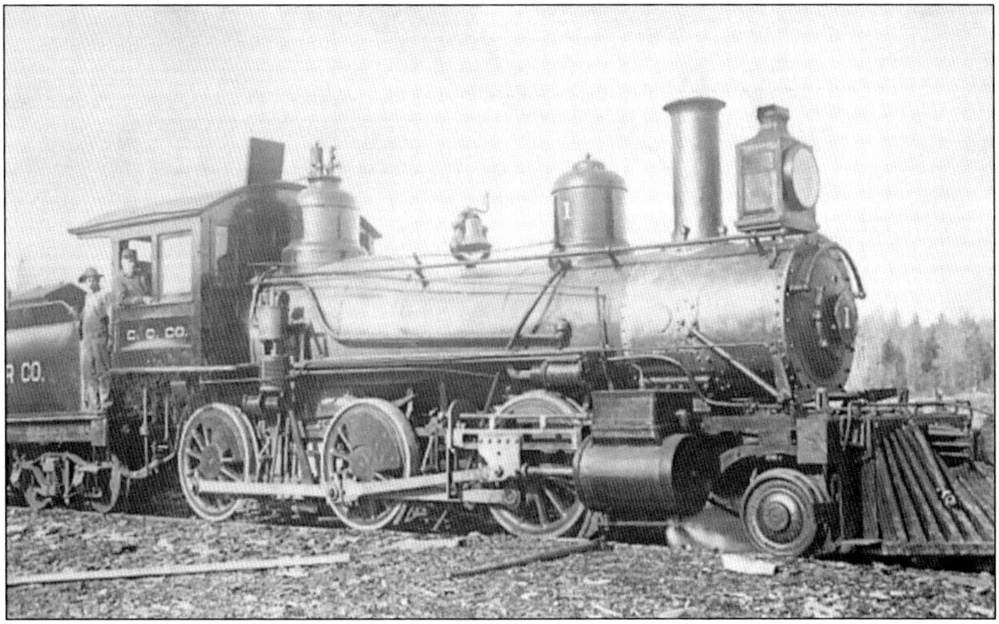

The Crocker Chair Company originated in Sheboygan, Wisconsin, but also had a manufacturing center in Antigo. In the early 20th century, it had extensive land holdings in Langlade County, east of Antigo where it logged. The company had its own locomotives and established rail lines to deliver logs to the sawmill and factory in Antigo. The area it logged is still known as the Crocker Hills, currently a popular area for mountain-bike riding and snowmobiling.

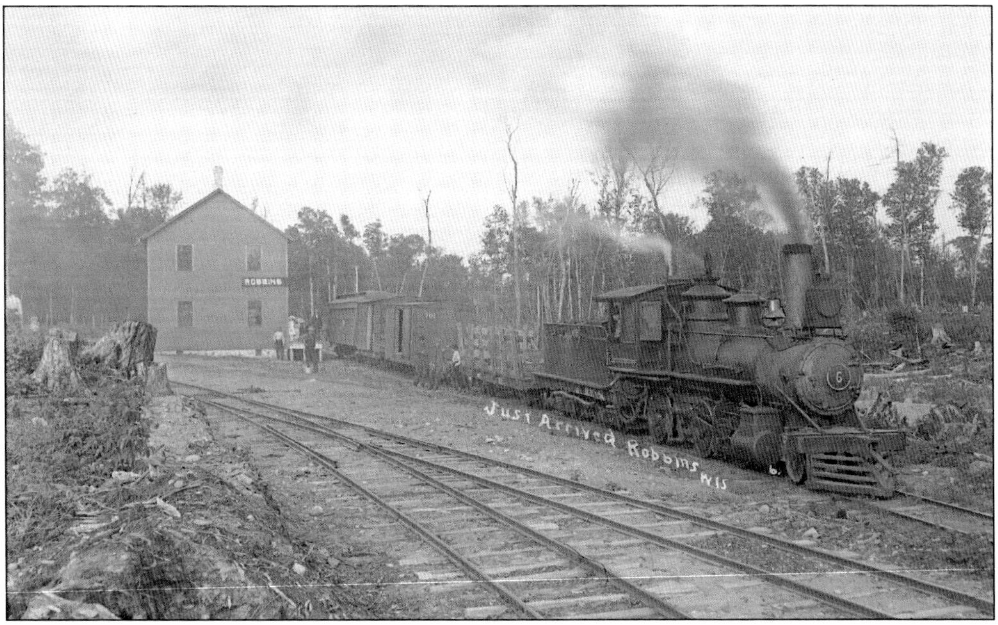

Logging railroads were either standard gauge (four feet, eight and a half inches between rails) or narrow gauge (three feet between rails). Standard gauge was more popular; it could handle bulky loads and was compatible with main-line rolling stock. Narrow gauge, on the other hand, was cheaper to build. The first logging lines used narrow gauge, and they were still in use in 1941. This depot was at Robbins, Wisconsin.

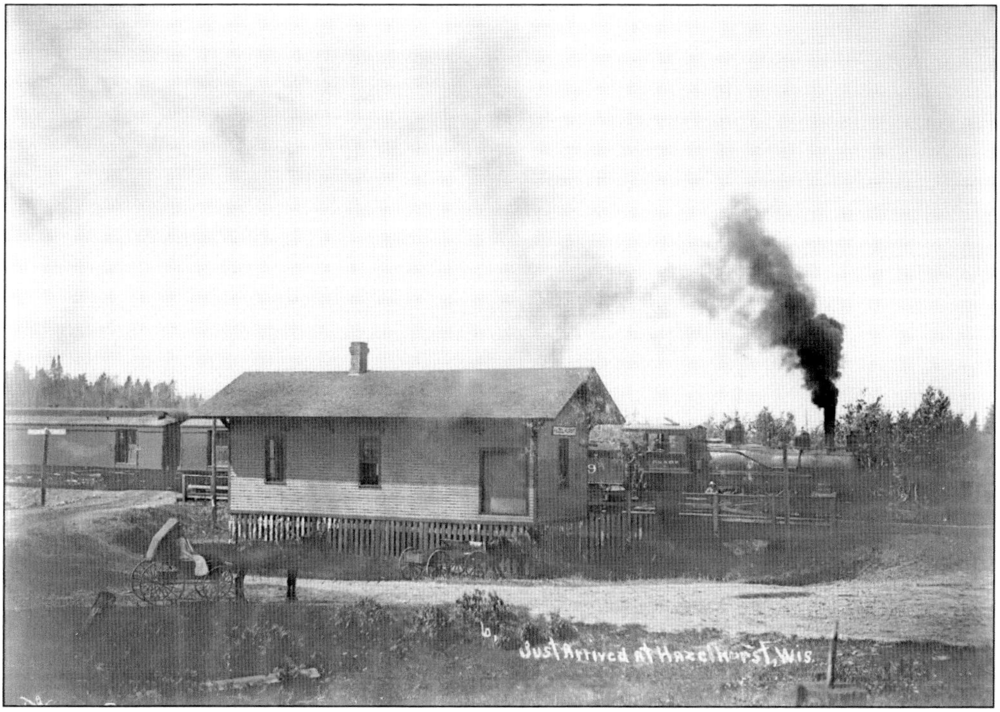

The steam locomotive was noisy and foul smelling, leaving a trail of smoke and cinders in its wake. Yet, retired railroad men remember them with a deep sense of longing. Engineers invented the term *highballing* for moving quickly. The name came about because before telegraph communications, a large red ball was raised on a platform in the depot to indicate the track was clear. The word is still used today. This depot was at Hazelhurst, Wisconsin.

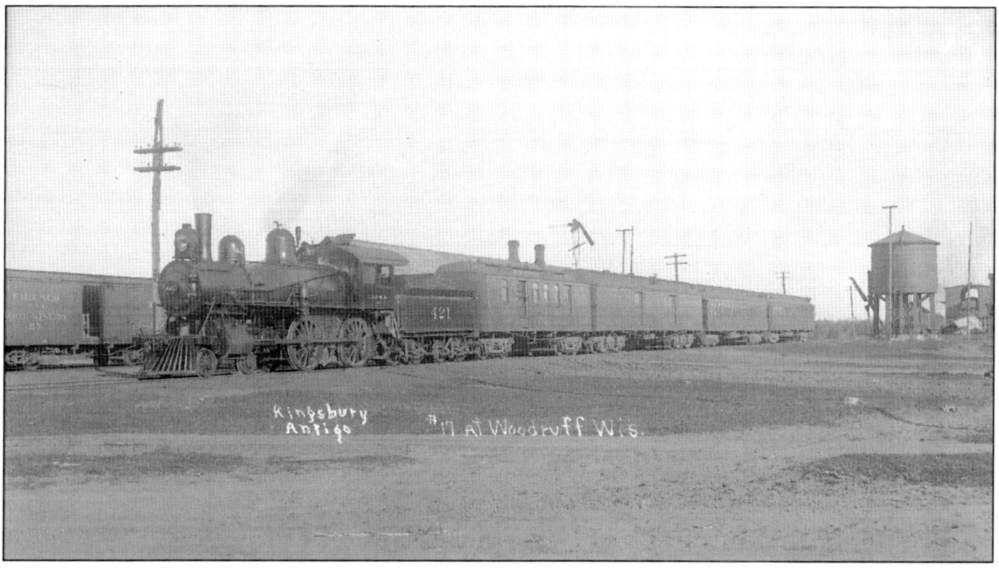

At 38 square miles, Woodruff is part of the Lakeland area, which is considered to have one of the largest concentrations of freshwater bodies in the world. Approximately 95 percent of Woodruff is owned by federal, state, or county interests. Woodruff and adjacent Arbor Vitae are considered the crossroads of the north where Highways 51, 70, and 47 join.

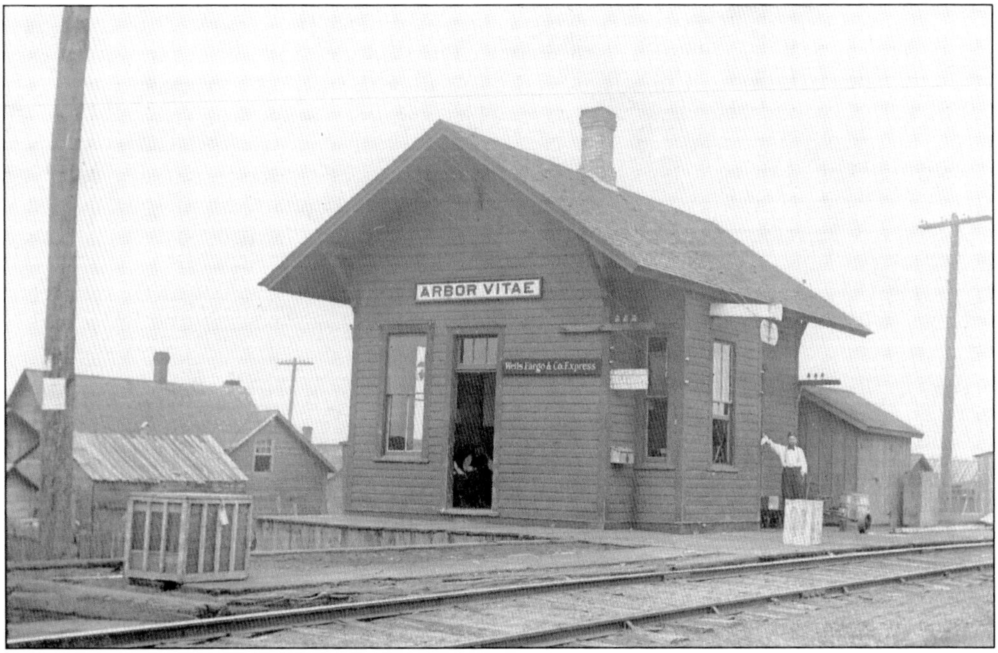

Arbor Vitae, together with adjacent Minocqua and Woodruff, form the center of a thriving tourism area. Even in Kingsbury's day, this was a popular destination for people getting out of the big city each summer. This pretty little depot offered services provided by Western Union Telegraph and Wells Fargo & Co. Express.

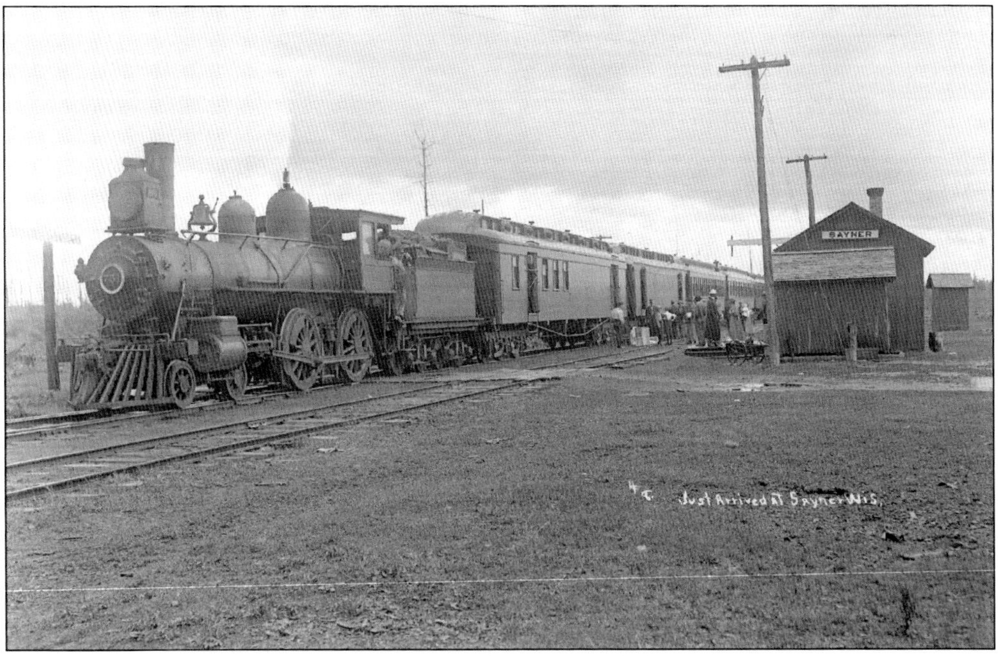

Sayner is part of the town of Plum Lake in Vilas County. It is the home of Camp Highlands, which bills itself as "the oldest private camp west of the Alleghenies." Founded in 1904, it was a boys' camp. Sayner is also credited with being the birthplace of the modern snowmobile, or motor toboggan, in 1924.

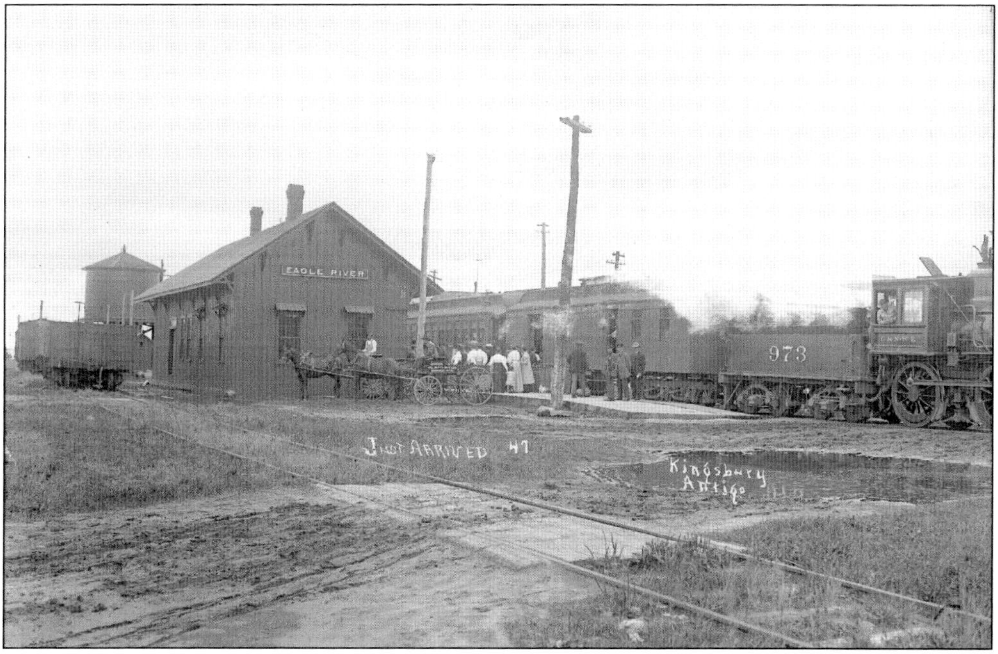

The railroad first arrived in Eagle River in 1883. At that time, it was a logging center. But as early as the 1930s, Eagle River was becoming a tourist destination with its chain of 27 lakes nearby. It was one of the first towns in Wisconsin to attract winter tourism, with its 35-foot ski jump, 90-foot toboggan slide, and a field house for hockey.

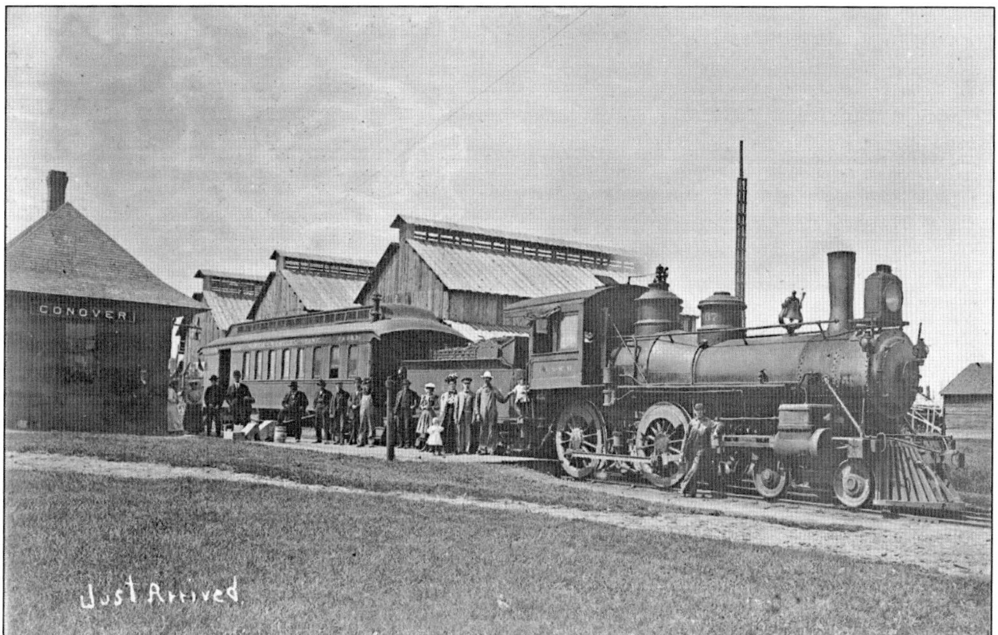

Kingsbury photographed many depots and titled them "Just Arrived." Conover in northern Vilas County is named for Seth Conover, who travelled to the area to hunt and fish. He came by train, even before a depot existed. Railroad men started calling the area Conover's Place. The train here is a one-car local.

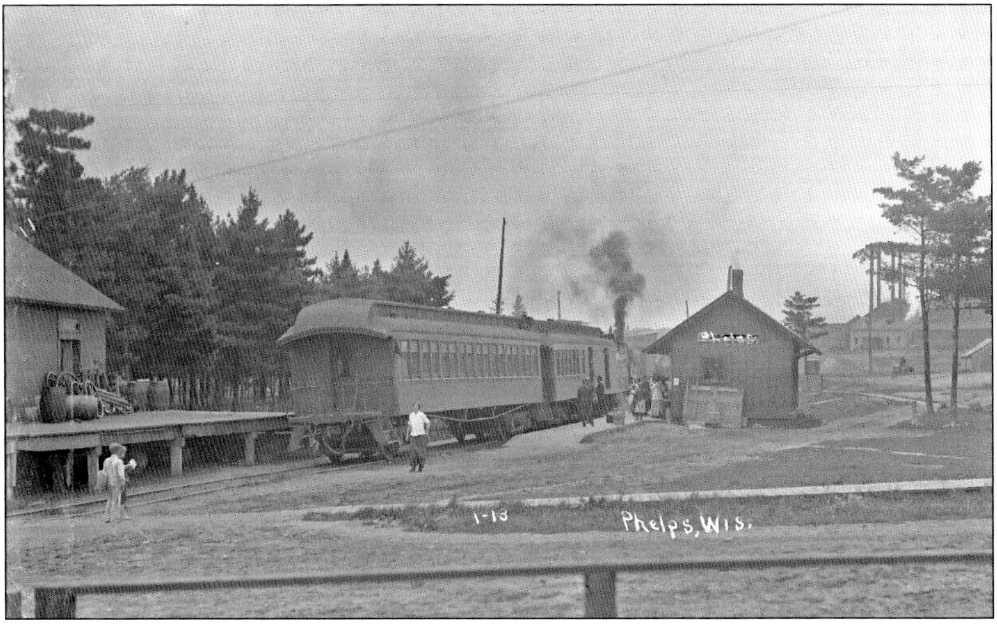

The idea of recreational opportunities in northern Wisconsin developed slowly, but by 1909, the Wisconsin Legislature established a conservation commission to create a system of state forests. Phelps Township in Vilas County is the result of this type of planning. It occupies an area slightly larger than that of Milwaukee, and yet it has a population of only about 1,300. Much of the township is in the Nicolet National Forest.

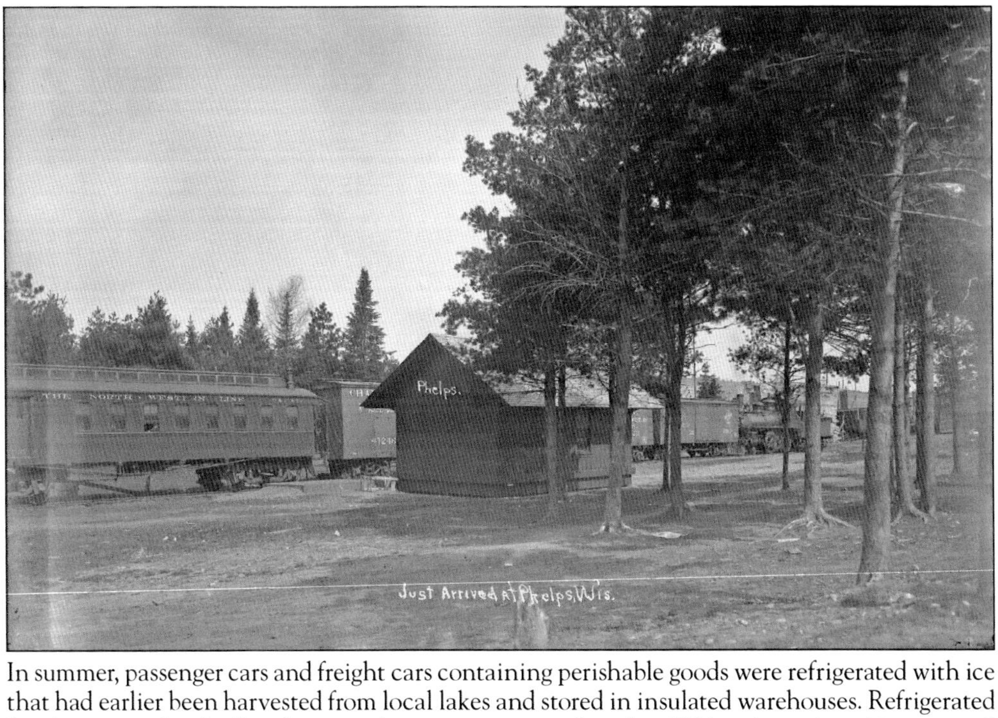

In summer, passenger cars and freight cars containing perishable goods were refrigerated with ice that had earlier been harvested from local lakes and stored in insulated warehouses. Refrigerated freight cars, or "reefers" as they were known, were introduced in 1874 and continued in use until the 1930s, although electrical refrigeration started to replace ice by 1925.

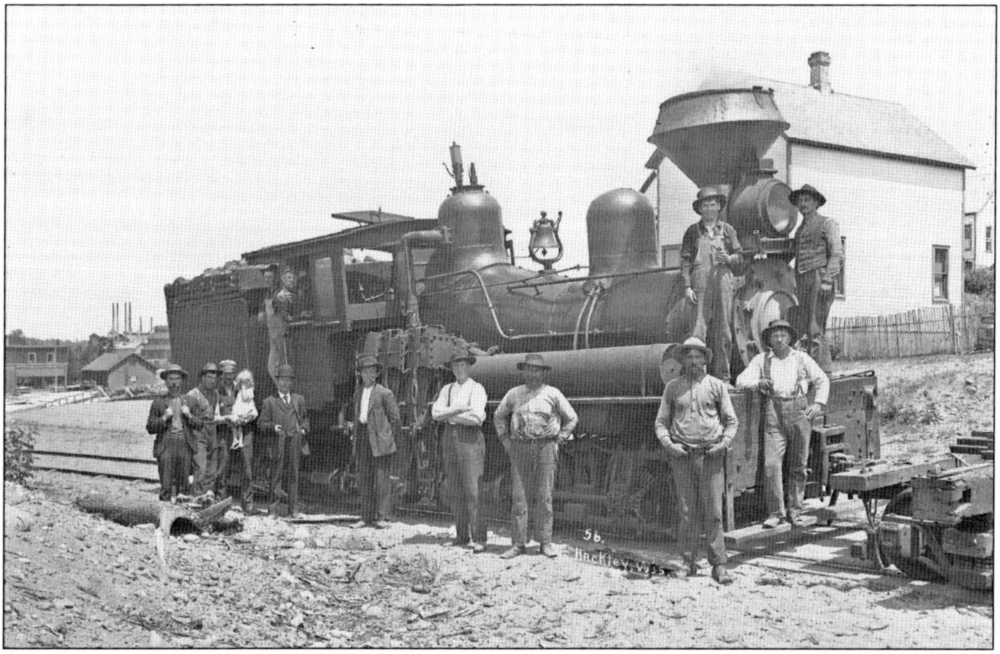

Wisconsin's first logging railroad was built in 1881 and continued operations until 1901. By 1940, the use of logging railroads had largely ceased. These railroads were basically subsidiaries of the mills. Hackley was the site of a large lumber mill. A lumber branch rail line extended to Hackley from Conover. The town of Hackley would later become Phelps.

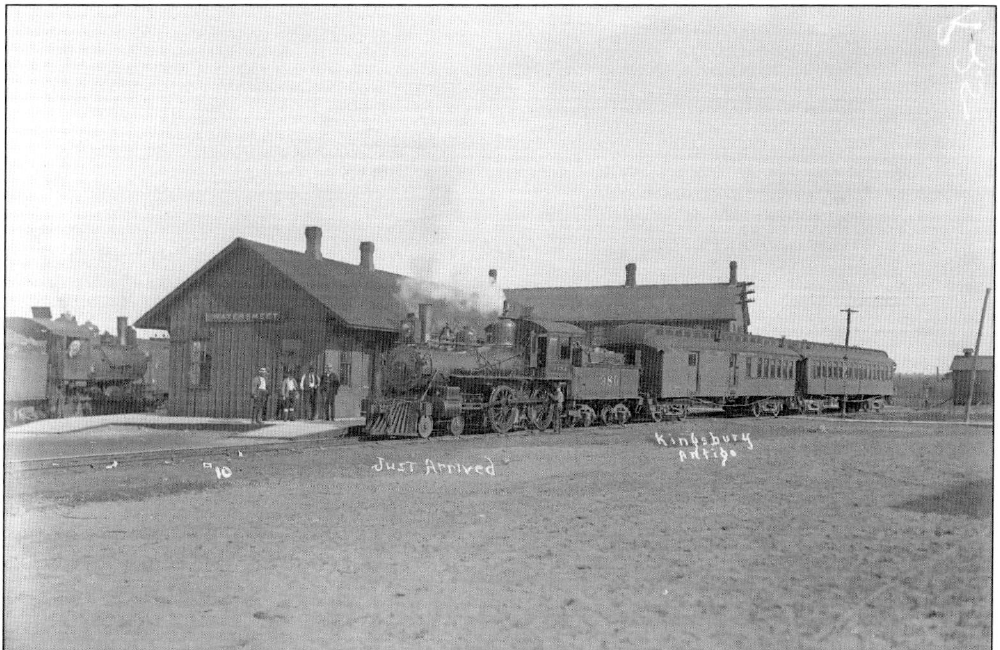

Watersmeet in Michigan's Upper Peninsula is in Gogebic County, the headwaters of the Wisconsin River. The area is the center of a large Indian community, the Lac Vieux Desert Ojibwe. The locomotive was of the Milwaukee, Lake Shore & Western vintage, built in 1887.

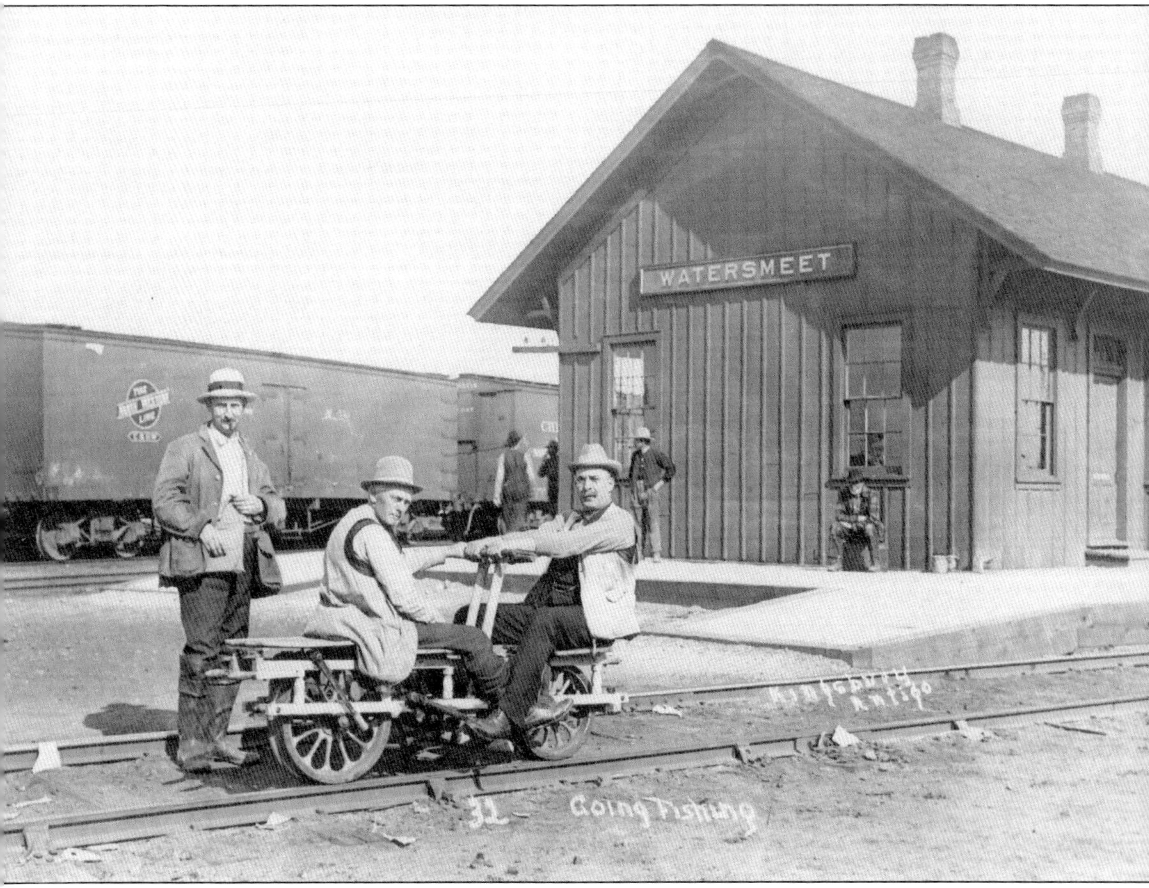

Most interesting in this c. 1920 photograph of three fishermen is the vehicle upon which the men are seated. This is a three-wheel, two-man pump car, sometimes known as a pump trolley, jigger, or velocipede. All rolling movement was attained from the men pumping a mechanism back and forth. It was difficult, physical work. These small railroad cars were used by track bosses or supervisors who wanted to move quickly between locations and for carrying men and supplies to forest areas without nearby roads, among other needs. Some pump cars were one-man bicycle frames with steel track wheels and a small framework connected to a third wheel. Other pump-car models had four wheels and were operated by standing men, while many had a little more flat space for setting down equipment. In 1911, the Fairmont Gas Engine and Railway Motorcar Co. of Fairmont, Minnesota, began selling the first gasoline-powered pump cars, and these motorized trolleys were often called "speeders." Some years later, speeders were given windowed walls, affording protection from weather.

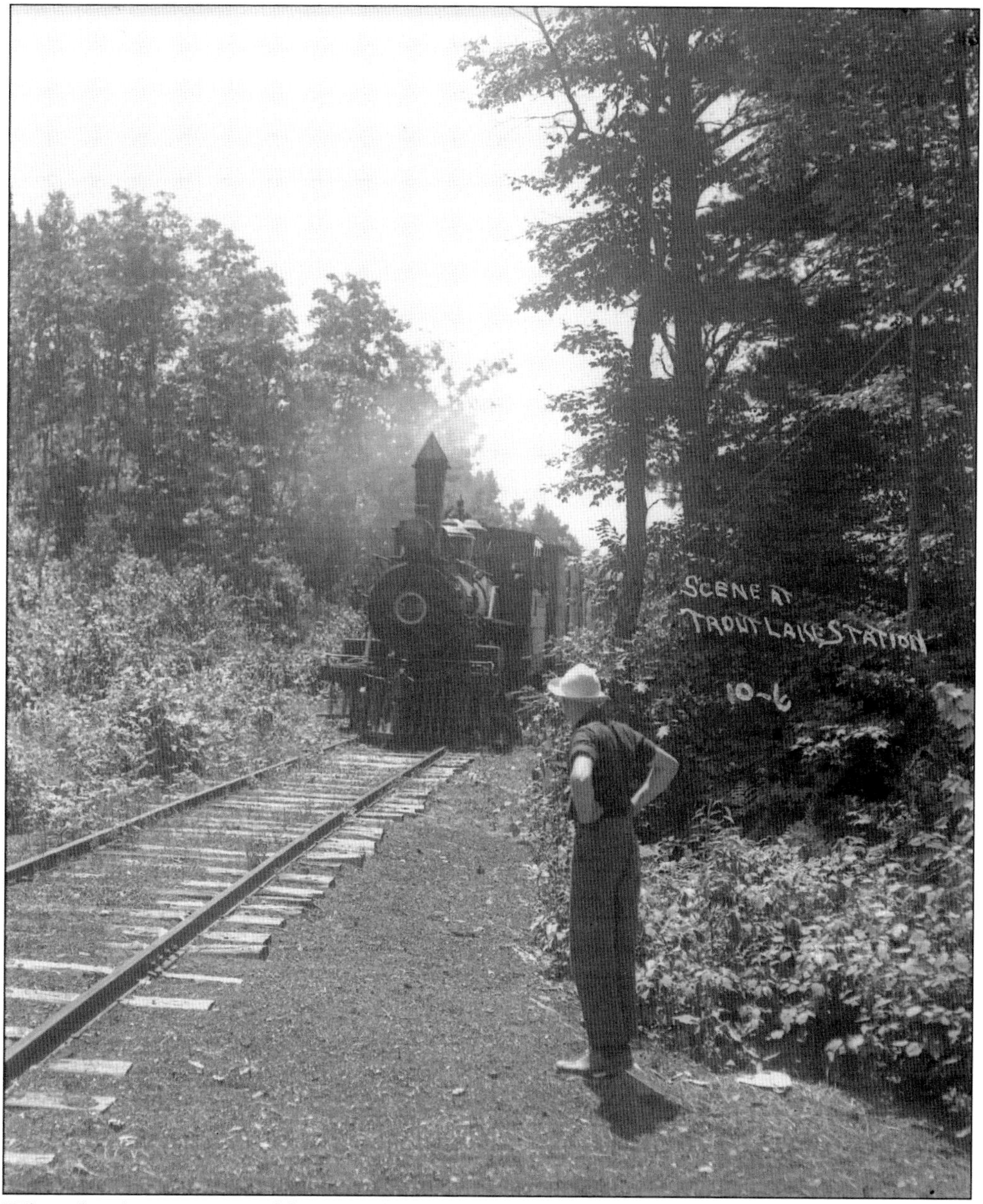

When the glaciers retreated from northern Wisconsin, huge chunks of ice gouged holes and filled them with water, creating kettle lakes. One of the larger and deeper kettle lakes is Trout Lake in Vilas County. It is one of the few Wisconsin lakes to house relic populations of lake trout. In the early 1920s, biologist Edward Birge of the University of Wisconsin-Madison would travel by train to Trout Lake to conduct his research. Birge was a pioneer in the field of limnology, the study of inland waters. Much of his early research was conducted at Lake Mendota on the UW campus, but he sought to expand his studies and chose Trout Lake. In 1925, he and colleague Chancey Juday founded a limnology research station there. Officially known as the Trout Lake Limnological Laboratory of the Wisconsin Geological and Natural History Survey, the research center gained worldwide renown. The UW Center for Limnology still maintains a major research station there.

Consistent with our mission to preserve history on a local level, this book was printed in South Carolina on American-made paper and manufactured entirely in the United States. Products carrying the accredited Forest Stewardship Council (FSC) label are printed on 100 percent FSC-certified paper.